The care of old buildings today
a practical guide

A Grade I Listed Building: The Guildhall, Lavenham

DONALD W. INSALL RIBA AMTPI SPDip

The care of old buildings today
a practical guide

THE ARCHITECTURAL PRESS LTD, LONDON
WHITNEY LIBRARY OF DESIGN, NEW YORK

Pleasing decay': an example of a category observed by John Piper

Architectural Press edition:
ISBN 0 85139 117 6

Whitney Library of Design edition:
ISBN 0-8230-7120-0

© Donald W. Insall
First published 1972
Second impression 1973
Third impression 1975

Filmset and printed in Great Britain
by BAS Printers Ltd, Wallop, Hampshire

Contents

PART III: CASE-HISTORIES IN CONSERVATION

FOREWORD

At no time in our history has there been such an obvious and increasing interest in old buildings. At no time has there been such a need for knowledge in dealing with the problems of decay, repair, maintenance and rehabilitation, or for the continuance of essential crafts and the study of new materials suitable for use in old buildings.

The redundant church, the designation of conservation areas and the routing of roads are problems peculiar to our time and in order to deal justly with our heritage we must bring to bear not only the great technological skills now at our disposal, but imagination, knowledge and sympathy.

Much has been written on the history of architecture but little by comparison on the repair of buildings. In 1957, on the occasion of the 80th birthday of the Society for the Protection of Ancient Buildings, the Architects Journal commissioned Mr Donald Insall to write *The Care of Old Buildings*. The existence of this useful and instructive work has proved of immense value.

The Society is grateful to the Architectural Press for accepting its plea that this work was invaluable and should once again be made available for use by all those concerned with the care and protection of old buildings. It is also deeply grateful to Mr Insall for giving time to the re-writing of his earlier work, bringing to it an added freshness and additional knowledge based on increasing experience of the many-sided problems of conservation and repair, and the very considerable changes in legislation.

Mr Insall's published reports on Lavenham, Thaxted, Blandford and others culminating in his master plan for the City of Chester, commissioned by the Government, are adequate proof of his expertise and familiarity with all the problems pertaining to ancient buildings in the present day.

Grafton

Chairman
The Society for the Protection of Ancient Buildings

Chiswick House: the Palladian Villa after reduction and restoration by the Department of the Environment

PART I : ADMINISTRATION

1. Introductory, the legal background, money

Introducing his subject, the author describes the need for a 'preservation plan' for each building, which will take into account the relative urgency of each repair, the money available, and the best use of craftsmen's time. He then discusses legislation which particularly affects preservation work. The last part of this first section deals with the all-important question of how to find the money, with Local Authority Improvement Grants, and with Historic Buildings Grants.

1.1   The owner and his architect

Every architect must have experienced the problem of giving the best possible advice, not only on the needs of a building, but to a great variety of owners, with widely different standards of repair and depths of pocket.

With old buildings, the problem is even more acute than with new ones. For the building has already, as it were, its own standards and needs, which may or may not match those of its present guardian. It is the architect's task to help in solving the needs of both. What is needed above all in intelligent maintenance is a definite policy. This policy must take into account both the general state of the building, and also the special needs of its present owner.

The architect, like many professional men, may here find that he can be much more helpful than his client had expected. The owner will naturally tend to see the problem in terms of a draught to be stopped, or damp plaster to be waterproofed—or, on the other hand, a crack of earthquake significance. His architect should from experience be equipped to take the wider view and to give him a balanced picture, taking account of the whole state of the building. In fact, the most valuable service of all he can render is first to give him a clear idea of the *relative* importance of every attention a building requires.

Perhaps the next most useful service will be to help with financial problems. Money for repairs and maintenance is nearly always hard to come by, especially for the owners of old buildings. Balanced attention to repairs by their relative urgencies will enable the most to be done with a small budget. Further, there are now various systems of grants and assistance for building owners, aimed at making the situation of people living in old houses less impossible than it might otherwise have been. Local Authority Improvement Grants and Historic Building Grants will be discussed later in this survey. A building owner often needs advice on these points; and it is the architect's job to help him with them.

1.2   The preservation plan

The first step in preparing the 'preservation plan' is to strike a balance between the increasing cost of disrepair and depreciation and that of carefully phased repair works. Neglect to such points as roof gutters must inevitably accumulate a high unseen toll. Any form of 'galloping' decay such as dry rot, the collapse of beam bearings, or of the joints of a structural frame, is obviously going to accumulate rapidly like compound interest, and just cannot be ignored. On the other hand, the repair of relatively spectacular damage due to expended structural movements, or of the gradual weathering of eroded wall facings, is often less urgent than an owner might have feared, and can perhaps be timed to cheer his bank manager.

Another important aspect of economic property maintenance is the fluctuating cost and availability of suitable labour and of specialist trades. When the demand for building labour is great, not only are prices forced up, but more seriously, the quality of the job may suffer. When despite the rising spiral of inflation, building costs stand at abnormally favourable rates, it is undoubtedly worth while to take advantage of them in catching up on maintenance work, of which at other times contractors may be shy.

The architect's next task is to assist his client in finding the best possible contractor. He must decide whether it is more economic and efficient to carry out a job by inviting in an army of operatives for a month, or by maintaining a constant small staff over the years. If the owner is himself a capable organiser, really interested in his estate, a good two- or three-man repair team can accomplish wonders without invoking heavy 'on-costs' to carry temporarily idle staff elsewhere. For example, a repetitive job in one trade, requiring little heavy plant and administration, may well be more cheaply undertaken over a period. A typical case is that of an estate with several miles of iron railings. Here a contractor's overheads might considerably reduce the work possible on a limited budget. Whether or not an outside contractor is employed, the programme will further be influenced by the need in some trades for good weather and long daylight hours. Work must be found for skilled men like masons during frost, when fingers are thumbs, and when expensive external scaffolding is likely to be unusable for much of the time. The question of disturbance is important too; and there is always the likelihood of repeated damage to furniture and personal effects which have to moved around by contractors. If a house is opened to the public during the summer months, loss of revenue might be thought a consideration, but thanks to the undying devotion of the British public to a 'hole in the road', the problem is less serious than might have been expected. For institutions like schools, universities, theatres and similar organisations, however, the disruption of daily life will necessitate the shortest, sharpest possible burst of work during vacations, even at increased cost in terms of building.

A variant of the problem occurs when a ceiling figure for expenditure has been clearly defined and agreed, eg by trustees. It may then be best to undertake the phasing of work not only by priorities in terms of structural urgency, but also in order of predictability with regard to cost. Unmeasurable outlays are thus dealt with first, before cutting into the rest of a limited cake—appetite being, as it were, tempered by table-manners.

When specialist labour has to be engaged—as when bells are being recast, stained-glass re-leaded, or steeplejacking work done—it is obviously economic to take the fullest possible advantage of skilled trades while they are available. An owner will then be well advised to bring forward certain elements of maintenance work to save extra future costs. Accessibility is also a factor; roof carpentry is much more likely to be repaired thoroughly when tiles and leadwork have been stripped than later on. When a spire is scaffolded, it would be foolish not to overhaul the weathercock; but less dramatic examples are surprisingly easy to forget until it is too late.

Sometimes a roof protects specially precious decorations, such as gilded and painted plasterwork ceilings, or irreplaceable artistic treasures such as valuable wall-paintings. Then normal structural priorities are overridden, and repairs and renewals must be carried out not only when materials are worn right out, but before the first disastrous leak can start. Even if such repairs are not urgent, it is the architect's duty to give some idea of when to expect them.

1.3 Buildings in corporate and public ownership

If private clients are still in a majority among the owners of buildings, more and more properties are also being taken over by corporate bodies, who tend to require special services. In the case of family trusts, as for instance where the finances of an estate are governed by the Settled Land Act (1925), it may be necessary to obtain High Court permission for expenditure, when the architect may be called as an 'expert witness'. Church properties are a special case, and their administrative arrangements will be described later. In this connection the provisions of the *Inspection of Churches Measure* have given a new turn to Church advisory work. Lastly, more and more buildings are passing into the hands of Public Authorities, whether of local councils or the centralised Government departments. Public bodies will usually prefer, for the sake of maintaining procedure, to arrange for their own departments to carry out formal legal steps such as inviting tenders and placing contracts. It is then the duty of the nominated architect to advise and co-ordinate these specialist departments.

Where public bodies are concerned, it is specially necessary for the professional man to indicate the limits of his own survey, recommending detailed tests of items such as services where these seem called for. A committee of laymen may be quite unaware of the claims of ageing wires and pipes, lightning-conductors and the like; and it is the architect's concern to see that proper tests are not forgotten.

No organisation or individual should ever acquire property without a proper examination and report by an independent, qualified observer. Specialist bodies such as the National Trust will usually also have committees of experts in such matters as the architectural and historic aspects of old buildings. Such committees require only the straight facts, ably presented. The layman, or a specialist in a non-architectural subject, may on the other hand need information which at first seems incredibly obvious, but which he has never had to think about before. Once the defects and their remedies have been pointed out, he will often be perfectly capable of doing everything else needed. When a property is acquired by a public organisation, its future lease to a suitable tenant is frequently arranged at the same time. In this case, both the landlord and tenant may simultaneously require works to be carried out under their own separate responsibilities. By virtue of his professional position, the architect may conveniently be retained by both parties to supervise the whole of the work, in which case entirely separate but parallel contracts can economically be run through the same contractor.

Building or repair work undertaken for trustees, or for a property-owning Company of any kind, is usually subject to approval by their permanent architect or surveyor. Contract costs should then also include generous contingencies allowances, so as to permit any reasonable variations found necessary without additional legal work. The surveyor's fees are often payable by the tenant as a condition of the lease, or of any licence to carry out alteration work; and the architect must ensure that appropriate conditions and arrangements are made to indemnify his client.

1.4 Preservation and the public

At least three different types of authority are concerned with representing and protecting the public interest in relation to old buildings; and as each of these may affect the architect and his work in some way, it may next be of value to rehearse what the various bodies concerned can do, and how they do it. The authorities mainly involved are the Central Government, the Local Authorities and the various private property-owning and advisory bodies. Their interest is very diverse and often conflicting. Apart from the ways in which financial provision can be made, the architect is caught up in the perpetual tug-of-war between the Local Authorities, whose concern is the maintenance of public health, protection against dangerous structures and the finding of extra space for new buildings —all of which leads them to wish for old buildings to be pulled down—and the Central Government as executor under the Town and Country Planning Act, together with the various preservation societies, whose concern it is to keep them up. It is important for the architect to have at his finger-tips a knowledge of the powers given to the Local Authorities to pull down, to make safe and to make healthy, and of the ways in which planning legislation enables an old building to be protected, and by which preservation and amenity societies can advise and represent the public interest. He must also inform himself about the particular legal requirements of special organisations, such as the Church, and of procedure with regard to alterations and repairs to buildings in communal ownership.

1.5 Listing buildings of architectural and historic interest

In 1944 (under Sections 42 and 43 of the Town and Country Planning Act) and again in 1971 (by Section 54 of the new Act) the Nation required the then Minister of Town and Country Planning to compile lists of all buildings in this country considered to be of architectural or historic interest.

This work was obviously of quite primary importance in arriving at any national assessment of the preservation problem. And until this first listing was completed in 1968, it was difficult to achieve any balanced general picture, or to relate the merits of any particular building either to changing local land use, or to the conflicting aims of other historic buildings elsewhere.

Listing is a continuous process. The responsibility for the job rests with the Secretary of State for the Environment, whose team of investigators is now engaged in revising the original lists, which will need to be constantly reviewed and extended. Priority in this work is being given to known historic areas; to towns and cities vulnerable to redevelopment; and to areas where the lists are particularly old or likely to be out-of-date.

The principles of selection for these lists were originally drawn up on the advice of an expert committee of architects, antiquaries and historians, and these are still broadly followed. In choosing buildings, special attention is paid to:

(a) Good examples of a particular architectural style or piece of planning, or good illustrations of social or economic history (eg industrial buildings, railway stations, schools, almshouses, mills, market halls, vernacular buildings).

(b) Technological innovation (eg cast-iron prefabrication, or the early use of concrete).

(c) Association with well known characters and events.

(d) Group value. An individual building of little architectural interest may blend together into an important group (eg squares, terraces).

Early in 1970, these criteria were modified. It was decided to give a higher priority to buildings of group value, and to include good examples of planned layout (such as Bedford Park and Bourneville), as well as more examples of Victorian architecture.

In practice, any building dating before 1700 is now listed automatically. Most buildings of 1700–1840 are listed, although selection is necessary. Between 1840 and 1914 only those of definite quality and character are listed, and these would normally include important works by principal architects of the day. A start is now being made on selecting buildings dating from 1914 to 1939.

It is important to note that buildings are listed on their merits and irrespective of present condition, although where structure is in poor repair a note to this effect may sometimes be included in the description.

At present, there are two grades of building which are listed in this way for statutory protection:

GRADE I Buildings of such importance that only the greatest necessity would justify their demolition.

GRADE II* Buildings of exceptional quality which are not quite eligible for Grade I.

GRADE II Buildings of considerable historic or architectural importance which have a good claim to survival.

A third grade which was known sometimes as the Supplementary List has now been discontinued. This comprised mostly buildings of group interest. Although these were not regarded as having a sufficient degree of architectural or historic interest to deserve statutory protection, they nevertheless were important enough to be drawn to the attention of Local Authorities and others, so that the case for preserving them could be fully considered. This grade has now been abolished, and the buildings included in it are either being moved up to Grade II or informally notified to Local Planning Authorities.

An owner or occupier is served with a notice when his property is first listed, notifying him of the effect of listing, and requiring notice of intended demolition or alterations. The provisions of listing are thereafter transferred with the property in every change of hands.

When listing was completed for the first time in 1968, there were in England and Wales 4351 buildings listed as Grade I, and 111 300 as Grade II, making a total of over 115 000 on the statutory list. A further 136 752 were earlier included in the old Grade III or Supplementary List. The current up-grading of many of these, combined with the new emphasis on protecting visually attractive groups and the new inclusion of more modern buildings, will mean that by the time the full revision is completed in 1985, the statutory lists will contain an estimated 250 000 buildings.

But there are still shortcomings. Since the lists were first compiled, many buildings of all grades have been lost, and not all the lists have yet been amended to take this into account. And as yet, surprisingly little has been done in collating and analysing the lists on a country-wide and comparative basis.

All buildings included in the statutory lists now enjoy

A Grade II Listed Building: Belchamp Walter Hall, Suffolk. This charming house has since been further improved by the removal of later wings from its right-hand flank

immediate protection under the Town and Country Planning Act 1968, from demolition and alteration. The vast majority are no doubt cared for adequately by their owners; and only a small proportion are likely at any one time to be at risk. The provisions of the Civic Amenities Act and the Town and Country Planning Act 1968 have greatly helped to reduce the number of listed buildings demolished. In 1965, buildings on the statutory List were being swept away at the rate of 400 or 500 each year. In 1971, the figure had dropped below the 200 mark. Yet the figures are less encouraging if the old Grade III buildings are taken into account, and many have been demolished or substantially altered without consent.

Under Section II of the Civic Amenities Act 1967, Local Authorities and the Department of the Environment must allow free public inspection of the statutory lists, copies of which are available at the National Monuments Record.[1] Records of listed buildings are also now being published in booklet form for each Local Authority. Each booklet lists the Statutorily protected buildings in the area and gives a brief description of their significant architectural features.

A listed building is distinct from an Ancient Monument which has been scheduled, the arrangements for the protection of which are explained in Section 1.16.

1.6 Legal protection for listed buildings

The Town and Country Planning Act 1968 (Section v) substantially amends and strengthens the statutory provision for protecting historic buildings and conservation areas, and imposes new restrictions on demolition and other works. Listed Building Consent must be obtained from the Local Planning Authority for demolition, alter-

[1] 23 Savile Row, London, W.1.

A Grade II Building: Old Thetford Mill, Halstead, Essex

ation or extension of any listed building 'in any manner which would affect its character'. This consent is thus necessary even in the case of a minor alteration, such as, for example, the removal of glazing bars from Georgian windows.

Authority to *demolish* depends on the issue of Listed Building Consent which in this case is further subject to prior notification to the following six bodies (Section 40 (4) and Circular 61/68: para 8):

Ancient Monuments Society
Council for British Archaeology
Georgian Group
Society for the Protection of Ancient Buildings
Victorian Society
Royal Commission on Historical Monuments (England)
Royal Commission on Ancient Monuments in Wales and Monmouthshire

One month must also be given to allow the Royal Com-

mission the opportunity of recording the building. If this is owned by the Local Planning Authority, then the application for Listed Building Consent must be sent for decision to the Secretary of State.

Local Planning Authorities are required by Regulation 4 of the Act to *advertise* any application for Listed Building Consent which would involve either demolition or alteration of Grade I or Grade II* buildings (but not those which affect only the interior of ordinary Grade II buildings). The advertisement should indicate the nature of the works proposed and the place where the relevant documents can be inspected during the following 21 days. Site notices relating to the proposed works must also be displayed for a minimum period of 7 days. In determining the application, the Local Planning Authority must take account of any objections and representations they may receive.

Where the Local Planning Authority intends to *grant* Listed Building Consent to allow a building to be demolished or altered, it must first notify the Secretary of State, who may call in the application for his own decision. In this event, the applicant or the Local Planning Authority may ask for a formal hearing by an Inspector from the Department.

If Listed Building Consent is *refused*, the applicant on appeal may claim that the building is not of special architectural or historic interest. Local Authorities have the power to make orders revoking or modifying Listed Building Consent but these must be confirmed by the Secretary of State, and compensation may be payable.

If the owner's application for Listed Building Consent is refused, he may claim that the land 'has become incapable of reasonably beneficial use', and he may serve on the Authority a Listed Building Purchase Notice requiring it to purchase his interest in the land. In considering such a notice, no account is taken of any prospective new developments unless a valid planning consent exists. Relatively few Purchase Notices are served, and fewer confirmed. This is usually due to the reluctance of Local Authorities to acquire a dilapidated building which needs money spent upon it.

The *penalties* for unauthorised demolition or for the extension or alteration of a listed building 'in any manner which would affect its character' are severe. A person found guilty is liable on summary conviction to a fine of up to £250 or a 3-months term of imprisonment or both; or on conviction on indictment, to a term of imprisonment of up to 12 months, or to a fine which takes into account 'any financial benefit' likely to accrue from the offence or both. It may, however, be a defence to prove that the works were urgently necessary in the interests of health and safety.

The Department of the Environment has issued a useful guide (Circular 61/68) indicating in general terms how the Secretary of State hopes Local Authorities will use their powers under the 1968 Act. This lists a set of criteria which gives broad guidance to Local Planning Authorities in dealing with applications for Listed Building Consent. They are asked to consider:

(a) The importance of the building, both intrinsically and relative to other special buildings in the area. A building may be important because few of its type exist, or it may be valuable because of its contribution to the townscape.

(b) The building's architectural merit and historical interest, including the light it may throw on the character, skill or technology of a past age.

(c) Its condition, the cost of repairing and maintaining it, in relation to its importance; and whether any grant is available. (In estimating cost, account should be taken of the value of the building once it has been repaired, and to any saving in not having to provide alternative accommodation in a new building. It should also be borne in mind that the effect of defects 'can be easily exaggerated.')

(d) The importance of any alternative uses of the site, particularly if some public development might enhance the environment, including other listed buildings in the area. In a rundown area, limited redevelopment might for example bring new life to other buildings.

But Local Authorities are reminded (para 4) that the list of historic buildings has been constantly reduced by demolition, especially since 1945, and that the 'presumption should be in favour of preservation'.

1.7 Repair and maintenance of listed property

Repairs Notice A Local Authority can now prevent an owner from destroying a listed building by deliberate

Loss by demolition: the Duke of Norfolk's House, Gloucester

The house before demolition

neglect. If the Authority considers that he is not taking reasonable steps to preserve such a building, it may serve on him a Repairs Notice specifying the works 'reasonably necessary' for the proper preservation of the building and explaining that if the necessary works are not carried out, the Authority or the Secretary of State may, after two months, make a Compulsory Purchase Order. This may relate not only to the building, but to any adjoining land required to preserve it and its amenities. Further, in the event that the building has meanwhile itself been illegally demolished, this will still not prevent compulsory purchase of the property.

If it can be shown that a listed building has been deliberately allowed to decay in an attempt to justify its demolition, the compulsory purchase may, with the approval of the Secretary of State, be subject to 'minimum compensation'. This means that the Local Authority may acquire the building at a price which does not take account of the redevelopment value of the site. Appeal lies to the Magistrates' Court, but the onus of proof is on the owner.

Listed Building Enforcement Notice Where it appears to a Local Authority that an owner of a listed building has demolished or altered part of it in contravention of the Act, they may serve on him a Listed Building Enforcement Notice requiring him to take steps to restore the building 'to its former state'. This Notice takes effect after 28 days, and during that time the owner may appeal to the Secretary of State on any of eight grounds specified in Schedule 5 of the Act. The enforcement notice is of no effect pending the result of an appeal against it by an owner.

If a Listed Building Enforcement Notice is not complied with, then the owner is liable on summary conviction to a fine of up to £400, or on conviction on indictment to a higher fine. If after conviction the Notice is still not complied with, the owner of the building is guilty of a further offence and liable on summary conviction to a fine of up to £50 for each day he fails to do the work, or on indictment to an unlimited fine.

If the work is still not done after a Listed Building Enforcement Notice has been served, the Local Authority may enter and make the necessary repairs, and recover the cost from the owner.

1.8 Building Preservation Notices

To protect threatened buildings which are of special interest, but which have not yet been listed, Local Authorities have been given power to serve emergency Building Preservation Notices under section 48 of the Act. These come into effect immediately and remain in force for a period of 6 months. They ensure that the building is protected as if it were in fact listed. This gives time for the Secretary of State to list the building, so that Listed Building Consent must be obtained before demolition can take place. A claim for compensation may arise out of a Building Preservation Notice, if this expires without the building being listed, or where the owner has suffered loss through countermand of contract works.

1.9 Demolition and Closing Orders

The major part of the law concerned with the demolition or closure of old buildings is conveniently encompassed within Sections 16–29 of the 1957 Housing Act and Sections 65–69 of the 1969 Housing Act. The legal requirements are fortunately quite straightforward and comprehensible; and a working knowledge of this Act will thus equip the Architect to advise the unhappy owner who may have crossed its path.

More often than not, the first shot in the battle is discharged by the Local Authority, as represented by its Medical Officer of Health, or Public Health Inspector. If a building comes under the consideration of this Officer as to whether or not it may be regarded as fit for human habitation, he may test it by applying certain standards to defined aspects of the planning and construction.

These are listed in the Act as follows:

(*a*) Repairs
(*b*) Stability
(*c*) Freedom from damp
(*d*) Natural lighting
(*e*) Ventilation
(*f*) Water supply
(*g*) Drainage and sanitary conveniences
(*h*) Facilities for storage, preparation and cooking of food and for the disposal of waste water

These headings are deliberately general; and it is left to the Local Authority to decide what items shall be included under each heading, and the standards to be set in each case. In practice this usually results in reference to the Building Regulations as something of a touch-stone; but since in different places, standards of relaxation vary, so different standards will still prevail.

If the building under consideration does not reach the required standard in any one or more of the aspects mentioned, the Local Authority may first demand of the owner that they be remedied within a certain stated period. Often, of course (and one hopes with an architect's advice), the work is carried out at this stage; the Local Authority is then satisfied, and there the matter ends. However, if the owner refuses or otherwise neglects to conform to their requirements, there are then four courses of action open to the Authority:

(*a*) It may itself do the work and charge the owner for it.

(*b*) It may issue a Closing Order, prohibiting the use of the building for all but limited purposes (for example, as a warehouse) for an indefinite period. The Closing Order may be withdrawn when the Local Authority is satisfied that the building has been brought up to a standard sufficient for human habitation.

(*c*) If it does not consider that the building can be put right for a reasonable sum, it may issue a Demolition Order.

(*d*) It may compulsorily purchase the property.

An important modification to (*c*) is that if the building is of architectural or historic interest and appears on the Statutory List, or should do so in the opinion of the Secretary of State, then a Closing Order must be made instead of (or in substitution for) a Demolition Order.

If the owner is now stirred to action by his circumstances, conscience, or architect, or in official parlance is 'aggrieved' by the Local Authority's action, he may appeal against—

(*a*) a demand for recovery of expenses,

(*b*) an order made with respect to any such expenses, or

(*c*) the serving of any notice demanding repairs. The appeal must be made to the County Court in whose jurisdiction the property lies, within 21 days.

The Judge has the right to confirm, quash or alter any notice as he thinks fit. The Local Authority can also demand his opinion on whether he considers the state of the building in such as to warrant repair or renovation. If the Judge considers that it is not, the Local Authority is empowered to purchase the property compulsorily, at the value of the cleared site. If a Demolition or Closing Order is issued, the Local Authority must reimburse the inhabitants displaced by it, to the extent of paying for the cost of moving their belongings. In the case of a shop, they must also pay a sum as compensation for damage to the business and for loss of goodwill, as agreed either privately or if necessary in a Court of Law. A building must be vacated within 28 days of a Demolition Order becoming operative; and the Local Authority may itself demolish the building, if the owner has not done this within six weeks from the date of vacation. A useful proviso of the Act, of particular concern to architects, is that after the serving of a Demolition Order, the Local Authority can agree to hold it in abeyance for a certain specified time, if the owner then brings forward suggestions for repair. Furthermore, at the end of that time it may remove the Order altogether if it is satisfied that the work is about to start, is under way, or has been satisfactorily completed. On the other hand, if it is not satisfied, the original Order can be enforced. Whether or not a Local Authority holds such an order in abeyance is left very much to its discretion.

Where an area is so planned as to be 'injurious to the health' of the people living or working in it, or if the houses generally are all below bye-law standard, and are not worth repairing and renovating, the whole area can be designated as a Clearance Area. Demolition Orders are then served individually on each property, and the whole matter is referred to the Department of the Environment. In these circumstances, any appeal goes to the Minister, whose decision is final.

1.10 General Improvement Areas

Part II of the Housing Act 1969 allows Local Authorities to concentrate, in a way not possible before, on improving and upgrading whole areas to be called General Improvement Areas. The Act sets no upper or lower limits on the size of the area to be improved: but the expectation is that such areas will contain between 300 and 500 houses. So, for the first time, it is possible for a Local Authority to inject money into urban areas on a much wider scale than before. It can now pump funds into rundown areas,

A Conservation Area in Thaxted, Essex: Town Street, looking towards the Guildhall

stimulate renewal in small islands of buildings or deal with large groups of older houses. The Act should help give new life to many older areas where basic amenities are lacking, where repair and improvement are needed, but where many houses are still structurally sound and quite capable of complete renovation. Already by the end of 1971, over 200 such General Improvement Areas had been declared by Local Authorities in England and Wales. Before deciding to declare an area as a General Improvement Area it is essential that the Local Authority should have considered a report upon it by its Planning Department or an outside Consultant or some other qualified body (Section 28). The Report should deal with:

(a) The planning future of the area.
(b) Its physical potential.
(c) The attitude of the people in the area.
  It should also contain data (Para 17) as to:
  (i) The number of buildings in the area, classified by age, fitness, standard amenities, need of repair, tenure etc.
  (ii) The roads and their traffic functions.
  (iii) Car ownership and parking provisions.
  (iv) Situation of the area relative to town centre, shops, schools and other local amenities.

The Act has increased the amounts payable to Local Authorities towards the expenditure incurred in carrying out works in General Improvement Areas. The Secretary of State, subject to Treasury approval, has power to make a contribution towards certain loan charges incurred by Local Authorities.

1.11 Conservation Areas

The Civic Amenities Act of 1967 made important changes in the law relating to old buildings.

Conservation is a more positive doctrine than building preservation alone. It starts from the realisation that the case for keeping an isolated building of outstanding beauty may be lessened if the character of the surrounding area is destroyed. Perhaps no single building may itself rank as a fine work of architecture, intrinsically deserving preservation, but seen together as a group, a number of them may combine in a way which simply demands conservation. It is this concern with protecting the texture of the townscape that is the essence of urban conservation. The Act itself has four parts, the first of which asks Local Planning Authorities in England, Scotland and Wales, after consultation with the Local Authority, to designate Conservation Areas 'the character or appearance of which it is desirable to preserve or enhance'. Thus the Act makes provision for the first time for the protection of areas, as distinct from individual buildings of architectural or historic interest.

Once a conservation area has been designated, the Secretary of State must be notified, and if this is later varied or cancelled, the fact must be published in the *London Gazette* and at least one local newspaper. Where a development is proposed which, in the opinion of the Authority, would affect the character or appearance of a Conservation Area, the Local Planning Authority must publish notice of the application in a local newspaper, allowing 21 days for representations to be made.

Conservation Areas designated under Section 1 of the Act had by the end of 1971 included 1723 groups of buildings, town centres, many villages and parts of cities throughout the country. But careful individual survey and analysis are needed, if these areas are in fact to be 'enhanced' as the Act provides. It is pointless to designate if there is no real intention to enhance.

Circular 53/67 explains the policy of the Department of the Environment under the Act. Paragraph 14 stresses that the Government and Local Authorities have a special responsibility to protect buildings of architectural or historic interest, and must set an example to other owners. The Circular stresses that most listed buildings are

A monument re-used: a doorway transposed as the central feature of a new public garden in a crowded area of the City of London

The disused doorway before removal

19

capable of beneficial use in the present day, and that 'given skill and understanding, new development can usually be made to blend happily with the old'. It reminds Authorities that 'the destruction of listed building is very seldom necessary for the sake of improvement; more often it is the result of neglect, or of failure to appreciate good architecture'.

A separate Memorandum on Conservation Areas is added as an Appendix to Circular 53. Special attention is drawn to the need for action. Designation will only be a preliminary to action, and the Local Planning Authority is urged to adopt a positive scheme of action for each area and to consider it in the context of an overall plan. This may include measures aimed at reducing traffic congestion and the provision of offstreet parking and pedestrian ways. The plan should also provide for 'the diversion elsewhere of harmful pressures for redevelopment within the Conservation Area'. The Memorandum in a separate Section deals with the problem of controlling development with Conservation Areas. New buildings should not be designed as a separate entity but as part of the larger whole. Planning Authorities are advised by using article 5(2) of the General Development Order 1963 to insist upon detailed plans and drawings of the proposed development, rather than giving merely outline planning permission.

The Memorandum reminds Local Authorities that they can help to raise the environmental quality of an area by paying grants for repairs, or by setting an example in restoring particular buildings themselves, in this way encouraging others to follow suit. They are encouraged to enhance the character of Conservation Areas by using well-designed street furniture and removing unwanted direction signs, unsightly advertisements and other clutter, and by planting trees and encouraging face-lift schemes of the kind pioneered by the Civic Trust. They are also urged to enlist public support for their conservation policies and to collaborate with local civic societies.

General advice on development near to buildings of architectural and historic interest was given in Circular 51/63, which urged Local Planning Authorities to give maximum publicity to applications which might adversely affect listed buildings. 'Development near such buildings should be carefully considered in light of the effect which it might have on the building or on the scene of which the building forms a part'.

Circular 61/68 suggests that Local Planning Authorities might establish Conservation Area Advisory Committees to consider applications affecting the character or appearance of the Area. It suggests that nominations to serve on such committees may be sought from the Royal Institute of British Architects, the Royal Town Planning Institute, other national bodies, or local archaeological, historical and civic and amenity societies (para 21). In considering applications 'special regard should be paid to such matters as bulk, height, materials, colour, vertical and horizontal emphasis and grain of design' and it may be necessary to relax planning standards (use zoning, density, plot ratio, daylighting and other controls) in the interest of Conservation. This last suggestion is particularly welcome. The Circular calls for similar care in considering planning applications for new development in Conservation Areas.

The impetus that the Civic Amenities Act has given to protecting the delicate fabric of our best urban townscape is enormous, but the problem still remains formidable. Nearly 1750 Conservation Areas had been designated by late 1971. Many are traditional town-centre shopping streets. Often the upper storeys lie empty—not because old houses of themselves have become uninhabitable, but because the environment has killed them. Heavy traffic has made the flats above such High Street shops into noisy and unpleasant places to live, and with this trend the city's spirit has slowly disappeared. In addition there is the problem of back-street industry that creeps in and sometimes chokes the character of the area. More recently the prospect of large out-of-town shopping centres has posed a new threat, for once the commercial life-blood is drained away from a town centre, then the job of conservation can often become virtually insoluble.

Already there are signs that the Government is beginning to take action to tackle some of these problems. In June 1971, the Secretary of State for the Environment announced plans to divert long-distance and particularly heavy goods vehicles from a large number of towns and villages. In the new programme the Government has given especially sympathetic consideration to the traffic relief of historic towns, and individual improvements are planned in over 80 towns listed by the Council for British Archaeology as being of special historic interest. Another welcome decision is to permit no increases in the size and weight of heavy lorries. The Secretary of State has pledged to give Local Planning Authorities power to control demolition of unlisted buildings in Conservation Areas. But only by individual analysis and positive planning can the environmental quality of conservation areas be actively improved.

1.12 The Preservation Policy Group

Shaken by traffic, gutted by central re-development, threatened with decay and changing commercial use, the historic towns of this country are still rapidly losing their unique character. To find ways of stopping erosion, the Government commissioned in 1966 four pilot studies on the historic towns of Bath, Chester, Chichester and York. A Preservation Policy Group was set up at the same time to co-ordinate and consider the reports, to review experience elsewhere and abroad, and to recommend on legal, financial and administrative arrangements for preservation. The report of the Group brought convincing evidence of progress: 'We do not think' said the Group, 'It would be an exaggeration to say there has been a revolution over the past five years in the way old buildings are regarded, and in the importance now attached by public opinion to preservation and conservation'.

The Policy Group formed the opinion that Public Authorities' powers of control were, with one or two exceptions, adequate for the time being. But it was less happy about finance. If the new legislation was now reasonably adequate, Government funds were not. It was not the lack of powers that discouraged many Local Authorities from promoting conservation schemes, but lack of money and sometimes lack of will.

The main proposal put forward by the Group was that Local Authorities should be able to initiate conservation programmes, in the knowledge that Exchequer grants would be forthcoming to cover half the approved net annual deficit. The Group pointed out that a grant of this kind was available for development of central areas and it would certainly help conservation schemes.

The report recommended possible legislation for guarantees to building societies granting mortgages for historic buildings (as suggested in the report on Chester). More effective action was proposed in instances of deliberate neglect, and it seems certain that future legislation will further tighten these provisions.

Bath, Chester, Chichester and York were urged to carry out immediate pilot conservation schemes. These were seen as a new and comprehensive category of town scheme, on the analogy of General Improvement Areas under the Housing Acts. To meet half the cost of any net annual loss incurred by Local Authorities, a gradually increased budget of up to £1½ million in 1973–4 was envisaged. The Government has reserved judgment for the time being on the Group's financial recommendations until the detailed results of the town schemes have been studied.

It seems logical that there must be national help to preserve the character and beauty of Britain's finest cathedral cities and market towns, and it follows that if the Government is sincere in its wish to safeguard this part of our national heritage, money and energy must be allocated on a much more appropriate scale than it has been in the past.

1.13 Grants and loans

Unfortunately, finance is nearly always a serious problem in preservation work, and it is therefore important for the architect to have full knowledge of the various ways in which money can be found. Grants are available in certain circumstances both from central government funds and from Local Authorities. They are almost always made at the discretion of the body giving them, and listing does not for example give any automatic entitlement to a grant. There is another source of funds in the many different private trusts, but these are so numerous that their activities are described separately in a later section.

Exchequer Grants The Secretary of State for the Environment has the power to make grants for the maintenance and repair of buildings of 'outstanding' architectural or historic interest. As comparatively few buildings qualify for this distinction, the scope for these grants is limited. Listing does not necessarily qualify a building for an Historic Buildings Grant, but is plainly on the credit

Wotton House, Buckinghamshire: a house saved by grant aid to a private purchaser from the Historic Buildings Council

side when an application is being considered.

The Historic Buildings Councils The Secretary of State is advised on the making of grants by the Historic Buildings Council for England, and similar Councils in Wales and Scotland, all appointed in Autumn 1953. Their function is to keep the Secretary of State informed about the general state of preservation of buildings of outstanding historic or architectural interest, and to advise him on the making of grants towards the repair or maintenance of such buildings or their contents or adjoining land, or towards the acquisition of buildings under Section 50 of the Town and Country Planning Act 1968 and Section 71 of the Town and Country Planning Act 1962, by Local Authorities and by the National Trust. The Councils further advise the Secretary of State regarding the acquisition of properties and of the contents of Ancient Monuments and National Trust buildings 'by purchase, lease or otherwise, or their acceptance as a gift', and on possible uses for particular buildings whose future may be in doubt. The Government announced in 1953 that it was prepared initially to provide funds of £250 000 per annum. The figure was raised to £450 000 in 1964 and to £1 000 000 in 1971.

Since the Historic Buildings Council was formed in 1953, grants totalling more than £7m have been made on its recommendation. Between 1953 and 1970, 6222 applications were received in England. Grants were awarded in 1601 cases. Of these, 1486 were towards structural repairs, 104 towards repair of mural paintings and chattels and 9 towards annual maintenance costs. 12 properties were approved for requisition by the Secretary of State, and 5 grants were made to enable purchases to be made by public bodies. No separate system of listing buildings has been set up for grant purposes, principles of selection being allowed to emerge empirically from the applications received. Only buildings of 'outstanding' interest are eligible, but in practice a building of only general character with particular outstanding features might still be considered for a grant.

Application for a grant should be submitted by letter to the Secretary of the Historic Buildings Council for England, and may be made either by a private owner, or by a public body or Local Authority unable to carry out works from its own resources.[1] The name, neighbourhood and a description of the building should be given, together with a photograph and brief details of the proposed repairs towards which the grant is required. Work carried out before application does not qualify for a retrospective grant. At the next meeting of the Council,

[1] 25 Savile Row, London, W1X 2BT.

preliminary consideration is first given as to whether the building is in fact of sufficiently 'outstanding' historic or architectural interest to qualify for aid. If insufficient information is available, a visit may be made to the building, either by one of the members of the Council, or by an expert on historic monuments. If it is decided that a building is sufficiently outstanding, the Council then considers such questions as the necessity and suitability of the proposed works and whether the estimated cost is reasonable. Confirmation of the necessity for repairs is obtained by the Council from an architect of the Department of the Environment, and it is of assistance to the Council in considering a case if a detailed report has been obtained by the owner from an architect with special experience of the preservation of historic buildings.

In order that the limited finances available may be fairly distributed to the greatest public advantage, the owner is usually asked to state to the Chairman in confidence the maximum contribution towards the cost of the work which he can make from his own resources, and in most cases to give brief details of his financial resources.

Recommendations are then made by the Council to the Secretary of State who will decide whether or not assistance is to be given. If an award is made, the conditions of a grant will generally include the submission and approval of a detailed specification, and the inspection and approval of the works at intervals by the Department's specialist architects. An undertaking to provide some degree of public access to grant-aided houses is also usually required. In special circumstances instead of the single award, a Maintenance Grant may be made over a period of years. The State is, however, chary of undertaking maintenance responsibilities, and such a grant is unlikely to be made to a property thought capable of attracting another purchaser, who can himself afford to meet the maintenance costs and who may be reassured by the possibility that in a future emergency, a repair grant might still then be available. Equally, a maintenance grant is unlikely to be made when there is any prospect of a building's purchase for use as a school or other institution. An important exception has however been made in the case of certain properties offered by their owners to the National Trust, in circumstances where the endowment would otherwise be too

The King's Bed at Knole, Sevenoaks: 'chattels' eligible for a grant

small to prevent their loss to the nation.

Items such as pictures and furnishings are also eligible for grant as 'chattels', provided they are ordinarily kept in a house of historic or architectural interest. Such grants are normally made only when the value of a house would otherwise be greatly diminished by their loss. Thus a series of family portraits related to the history and ownership of a house, or a collection formed by its founder as part of its basic furnishings, would be more likely to attract a grant than a recently purchased masterpiece. The maintenance and repair of libraries and archives is eligible for assistance as well as furniture. When a grant is made for the repair of chattels, the owner is asked to give an undertaking not to dispose of any item without giving the Secretary of State, through the Council, at least three months notice. If he thereafter decides to sell without the agreement of the Council, an appropriate refund may then be required.

Under section 4 of the Civic Amenities Act 1967, the Historic Buildings Council has the power to recommend the Secretary of State to make loans under the Historic Buildings and Ancient Monuments Act 1953 for the maintenance of historic buildings. In practice, owners of historic buildings have mostly preferred instead to apply for an HBC Grant in the normal way.

The Historic Buildings Council has pointed out that the subdivision into lots of any large estate which includes an historic house is unhappily often so contrived that the principal lot containing the house is of sufficient size to interest only a demolition contractor. The division into many plots of a large site presents an almost insoluble problem. The imposition of excessively awkward conditions of sale or bequest have also sealed the doom of many an otherwise attractive property.

Local Authority Grants (*Improvement Grants*) Local Authorities have a wider scope for making grants for old buildings.[1] They may make grants for any building of architectural or historic interest, whether it is listed or not. There is an obvious need for funds for renovating older property. Of the 17 million dwellings in Great Britain, over 4 million are more than 80 years old, and there are still 2 million homes without bathrooms or indoor sanitation, which have today become essential. Others, particularly of Victorian date, were intended for large families with a whole staff of servants, and are now much too big to be managed as a single unit. If all these properties were to decline into slums, a tremendous number of new houses would be needed; and the cost of a large proportion of these would have to be found from the local pocket, to be borne by the ratepayer and taxpayer.

The Housing Act of 1969 has made available further financial aid to Councils to encourage owners of old houses to improve them. Grants may be made for the subdivision of old houses into flats. The basic principle of all grants

[1] Enquiries should be addressed to the appropriate Local Authority.

under the Act is that the owner will match the value of the grant with at least the same amount of his own or borrowed money. In no case can an owner obtain a grant of more than 50% of the cost of the work (including professional fees).

There are three types of grant:

1. *Discretionary Improvement Grants* are payable at the discretion of the Local Authority. The amount of the improvement is fixed by the authority approving the application, within a maximum limit[2] of £1000 for each house improved. When a house of three or more storeys is converted into flats, the upper limit[1] of the grant is £1200 for each flat. Higher grants are available if the building is listed as of architectural or historic interest.

To ensure a minimum standard in qualifying for aid, Discretionary Improvement Grants are made subject to 12 requirements, with which as far as possible every converted property must comply. After improvement, it must:

(i) be in a good state of repair, and substantially free from damp;

(ii) have each room properly lighted and ventilated;

(iii) have an adequate supply of wholesome water laid on inside the building;

(iv) be provided with efficient and adequate means of supplying hot water for domestic purposes;

(v) have an internal or otherwise readily accessible water closet;

(vi) have a fixed bath (or shower) preferably in a separate room;

(vii) be provided with a sink or sinks and with suitable arrangements for the disposal of waste water.

(viii) have a proper drainage system;

(ix) be provided in each room with adequate points for gas or electric lighting (where reasonably available);

(x) be provided with adequate facilities for heating;

(xi) have satisfactory facilities for storing, preparing and cooking food;

(xii) have proper provision for the storage of fuel (where required).

It is recognised that there are exceptions, and that not always will all 12 points apply—for example, where

[2] 1971.

24

public services such as gas and electricity are not available. In these cases the Local Authority use their powers of waiver. 'Improvement' includes any alteration or enlargement and such repairs and replacements as are incidental to some other improvement, or needed in the opinion of the Local Authority for the purposes of making the other improvement fully effective. The conversion of a building not previously used as a dwelling is equally eligible for aid.

Normal work of repair and maintenance is on the other hand excluded from financial assistance. This is taken to include redecoration, joinery repairs (unless, for example, a window is at the same time enlarged to provide adequate daylight), and the renewal of services such as electric wiring. Only work of this type which is actually consequent upon the improvements or conversion—such as the redecoration of a bedroom which has been divided off to form a new bathroom—can be included in the eligible expenses. The replacement of out-of-date structural equipment such as an obsolete grate by a modern slow-combustion stove would also be eligible, but not, of course, the installation of movable 'tenant's fittings' such as a new refrigerator, which some optimistic applicants have sought to include. Subject to waiver by the Local Authority, the converted and improved property must have a reasonable prospect of at least 30 years of further life.

There is no restriction on the maximum expenditure, but the amount of the Grant may be up to 50% of the cost of the work (or in practice, what the Local Authority thinks the cost should have been) with a maximum (except in special cases, with the concurrence of the Minister) of £1000 per dwelling. In calculating the amount of Grant, professional fees are eligible for inclusion. In practice, some Authorities, for no particular reason, seem to exclude the cost of travelling and expenses. Payment may be made either on completion, or by instalments during the work. No enquiry is made into the financial position of the applicant: the grant is made in effect to the property, in the interests of the community. It is sometimes possible for an Authority to lend an owner part of his own share of the cost, at reasonable rates of interest. Before an elaborate scheme is prepared, the owner may make

Domestic improvements aided by an Improvement Grant: a mews house on the Grosvenor Estate, London

preliminary enquiries in outline from his Local Authority to find out whether his property is likely to qualify for Grant. If the response is encouraging, he will then obtain professional advice. Although the Act only requires one estimate and particulars, including a specification together with drawings before and after conversion, some Authorities require competitive tenders to be submitted. The specification must divide the works under separate headings for improvements and repairs. Since the application must first be considered by the Building Inspector, then be passed to the next meeting of his Health Committee for subsequent recommendations to the Council, the process is not always a rapid one. Increases in cost due to the lapse of time between the estimate and execution of the works are not admissible, nor are any contingencies allowances, beyond the very barest provisional sums for items of built-in equipment. Alterations in a scheme involve such complex referrings-back that they are better avoided at all costs. Applications must normally be made before any work is carried out, and cannot be granted retrospectively unless the Authority is satisfied of very good reasons. Many grants have been fortified by ignorance of this provision.

Care should be taken to ensure that any Building Society or other mortgage is kept fully informed of any proposed scheme of improvement under Grant Aid.

It should be stressed that for better or for worse, these Discretionary Grants are permissive, but not obligatory. The Authority must itself contribute a proportion of the Grant, in the knowledge of a saving in housing costs. Not all Authorities are willing to make Improvement Grants; and despite the obvious advantages to the Nation, the Local Authority, the owner and the tenant alike, there are still those who for one reason or another feel themselves justified in withholding the application of the scheme within their areas. If an Authority is bent upon this course, there is little that can be done—except perhaps to flee the area, before the increase in rates in which its short-sighted policy must inevitably result. 49 out of every 50 housing authorities in England and Wales are now in fact giving discretionary grants, and receiving the advantage of Central Government funds in this valuable contribution to the housing problem.

2. *Standard Improvement Grants*, on the other hand, are obtainable by owners as of right. A Local Authority has a duty to pay a grant to a suitably qualified applicant. These grants are for the provision of standard amenities which a building may lack; and to qualify for a grant, the house must have been in existence before October 1961. The standard amenities must be for the exclusive use of the applicant; and the Local Authority must be satisfied that once improved, the dwelling will be in a good state of repair, having regard to its age, character and locality and will in all other respects be fit for human habitation and likely to remain fit for at least 15 years. There is no longer any statutory restriction on conditions about re-sale, once a property has been improved with grant aid.

The amount allowed for each item is clearly specified in Schedule 1 of the Act:

Fixed bath or shower	£30
Hot and cold water supply at fixed bath or shower	£45
Wash-hand basin	£10
Hot and cold water supply at wash-hand basin	£20
Sink	£15
Hot and cold water supply at sink	£30
Water closet	£50

The fixed bath or shower must be in a bathroom, except where this is impracticable, in which case it may be in any part of the dwelling except a bedroom. The water closet must be accessible from within the building, or where this is not practicable, readily accessible from the dwelling.

Extra money can be granted, up to a maximum[1] of £450, for other works which may be necessary. These include half the cost of bringing a piped water supply into a building for the first time; half the cost of building a new bathroom, if the only practicable way of providing one is by converting an outbuilding attached to the dwelling; and half the cost of installing a septic tank where the connection of a water closet to a main drain is not possible.

3. *Special Grants* are available for the improvement of houses in multiple occupation, where there is no immediate prospect of conversion into flats. The grant is half the cost of the works, subject to a maximum related to the amounts specified in the schedule for Standard Grants.

1.14 New uses for old buildings

A problem at the root of most difficulties in the saving of old buildings is the question of their use. So many properties owe much of their architectural and historic interest to their design in more opulent times, for uses which no longer occur. Often it is impossible to preserve the original

[1] 1971.

A kitchen eminently eligible for grant-aided improvement

use of the building, which depends for its survival on sympathetic conversion and reconditioning.[1]

Listed buildings require the greatest skill and care to avoid damaging them. On this subject, the Department of the Environment in Circular 61/68 urges Local Planning Authorities to seek professional advice on alterations and suggests that, where no historic buildings department exists within an Authority, consultants with special knowledge of repair and restoration work may be asked to assist. When considering applications for restoration and conversion of historic buildings, Local Authorities may relax the Building Regulations (Circular 53/67).

To assist the Secretary of State in finding new uses for historic buildings, and in collecting information about organisations interested in this type of property, an Historic Buildings Bureau[2] has been set up. Owners who wish to buy or sell historic buildings may register them with the Bureau, which distributes 1000 copies of its quarterly lists of properties (containing usually 60 or so buildings). The Bureau's advisory service, principally for Local Authorities, offers professional advice on possible alternative uses for buildings.

The Bureau will only take listed buildings into its books and they must first have been in the hands of an estate agent for at least two months.[3] No charge is made for its services.

Much positive work in rescuing and adapting worthwhile buildings for modern use has been done by local historic building trusts. A survey of their work has been made by the Civic Trust[4] which recommended the establishment of a National Building Conservation Fund to help local trusts in their work.

Nearly all trusts are registered as charities, and many are constituted as companies limited by guarantee. Their assets accrue in various ways. Funds may be raised from subscriptions, donations, covenants, grants, gifts and loans. In some cases the Historic Buildings Council, a Local Authority or the Pilgrim Trust has contributed to an appeal fund. In the case of county sponsored trusts, funds may be raised from local councils in the area.

Some preservation trusts retain ownership of the buildings they restore, notably Housing Associations who let them to tenants under the terms of their rules. Others operate a revolving fund, buying up old property, restoring it and selling it under a Conservation Agreement.

The assets of trusts vary considerably, but a Civic Trust concluded that a newly formed trust needed a working capital of between £20 000 and £25 000 to restore two buildings each year on a revolving fund basis.

---

[1] See *New Life for old Buildings*, HMSO 1971, also *Architectural Review*,'New uses for old buildings' May 1972.

[2] Enquiries should be addressed to the Director, Historic Buildings Bureau, 2 Marsham Street, sw1.

[3] The Society for the Protection of Ancient Buildings also issues lists of threatened properties to its members, see p. 35.

[4] *Financing the Preservation of Old Buildings*, Civic Trust, 1971.

New use for an old building: Monmouth 'New Market' gutted by fire, and reconstructed behind its remaining facade as the Nelson Museum, Local History Museum, Government Offices and Post Office

1.15 The Acquisition of Buildings by the Nation

The National Land Fund was set up by Hugh Dalton in the Finance Act 1946 with a capital of £50 000 000. The Fund performs the function of reimbursing the Inland Revenue for real properties (historic houses, amenity lands, and since 1953 also chattels) accepted by the State in lieu of estate duties, and also provides moneys to reimburse the Secretary of State for the Environment and the Secretaries of State for Scotland and Wales in respect of purchases under the 1953 Historic Buildings and Ancient Monuments Act. The Fund's capital was reduced to £10 000 000 in 1957. Recent acceptances include Chartwell (chattels only) and Sissinghurst Castle, Kent.

Purchase by the Nation under the 1953 Act is undertaken only when no other means can be found to preserve a threatened building of the very first importance. In these circumstances Heveningham Hall was acquired by the Secretary of State for the Environment in 1970.

The recipient of an historic building which has been accepted in lieu of estate duty, such as the National Trust, is like any other owner, free to seek assistance towards the repair of the building under the terms of the 1953 Act. The accounts of the National Land Fund, published annually, reflect in the acceptances of property in lieu of estate duty the crippling effects that duty has on both great and small estates. The number of visitors shown over Britain's historic homes has shown a phenomenal increase in recent years from an estimated 2 or 3 millions in the late fifties to almost 28 millions in 1971. Our historic towns and buildings draw both tourists and money to Britain and are an asset of the highest potential, deserving strong national investment.

1.16 The protection of scheduled Ancient Monuments

The Ancient Monuments Branch of the Department of the Environment[1] administers for the Nation a large number of ruined or unoccupied buildings—mainly Abbeys and Castles—together with a few roofed buildings (eg Audley End, and the Tower of London). The Ancient Monuments Acts 1913–53 define the term 'Ancient Monument' so widely as to allow the inclusion of almost every building or structure of historic interest, provided it is not in-

[1] Department of the Environment, Sanctuary Buildings, Great Smith Street, London, SW1P 3DD.

Heveningham Hall, Suffolk: purchased for the Nation in 1970 by the Secretary of State for the Environment, under the terms of the Historic Buildings and Ancient Monuments Act, 1953

Bourne Park, Kent: a house which passed through the hands of the Historic Buildings Bureau

Rievaulx Abbey, Yorkshire: a Scheduled Ancient Monument under the guardianship of the Department of the Environment

habited. Ecclesiastical buildings still in use are, however, excluded.

One of the principal provisions of the Acts is concerned with the Scheduling of monuments of national importance. The Ancient Monuments Board advises the Secretary of State on monuments suitable for Scheduling and he is bound to follow their recommendations. The Board also offers advice on individual cases and policy matters.

After a monument has been scheduled, the owner or occupier must give three months notice to the Department of the Environment of any proposed alterations. There are penalties for failure to give notice and for damaging scheduled monuments.

If a monument is threatened, the Local Authority may issue a Preservation Notice placing the monument under the protection of the Secretary of State for six months. The owner must then obtain written permission before carrying out any works.

There are countless unscheduled monuments all over the country without legal protection, but Local Planning Authorities are asked to consult the Department of the Environment about development which may affect them. The work on Ancient Monuments is controlled by a headquarters secretariat which is responsible for the administration of the service. The Chief Inspector of Ancient Monuments is the Department's principal adviser on all archaeological and historical matters. His office is in London and he is assisted by a staff of Inspectors and Assistant Inspectors, who are professional archaeologists. They work in close touch with architects on technical problems, and make regular joint visits to sites to discuss what work should be done.

A separate Architects' Branch, under the direction of a superintending architect, employs a direct labour staff numbering approximately 1000 in England, Scotland and Wales. The work-force includes foremen, masons, carpenters, joiners and other craftsmen, who are highly specialised in their own fields, and many of whom have spent their working life-time in the service of the Department. Their sympathetic and careful treatment of buildings and structures are of the highest standard. The work ranges from the removal of vegetation to complicated structural problems. Reconstruction is very rarely undertaken; but if it is done, a precise survey and photographic record is first made, stones and timbers being numbered and rebuilt to correspond exactly to the original. The Department's architects keep local control and supervision of projects, and they are helped by Superintendents based in each area.

Architects and their staff are also called upon to give advice on monuments not in the Department's care. In some cases work may be undertaken for private owners at cost.

2. Organisations which can help

In this Country public interest in conserving old buildings is so many-sided, and is maintained by so many different organisations, that no account would be complete which did not attempt to give a concerted picture of them. In this section, the author lists many interested organisations and explains what they do. He divides them, so far as is practicable, according to their chief functions, which are the providing of technical information (or archaeological data), the rousing of public opinion, and the finding of money. The second part of the section summarises the present position concerning ecclesiastical property.

Public bodies whose concern is with the care and preservation of old buildings fall from the architect's standpoint into three clearly defined classes. Firstly, there are the official advisory bodies, maintained to advise on technical problems, and to whom reference may be made in time of difficulty or where a second opinion is needed. Then there are the private societies, equally qualified and able to give specific technical advice, but which may also champion the cause of individual buildings, and are active in maintaining a lively public opinion and awareness of old buildings from the public point of view. Thirdly, there are the charitable bodies, whose funds enable financial assistance to be given, or who in some cases are actually property-owners and can themselves take over and administer old buildings and help to preserve them.

2.1 Official organisations

A number of official bodies can advise on the technical problems involved in conservation and repair work:
The Building Research Station[1] has a special advisory service on a wide range of problems affecting old as well as new buildings. Advice is available by telephone or letter, by consultation or site visit, or as a result of laboratory study. Where a problem has to be examined by technical observers and advice is given, a charge is made

[1] Bucknalls Lane, Garston, Watford, Herts, WD2 7JR.

Shandy Hall, Coxwold, Yorkshire, which was saved as a museum of Sterneana by a local trust formed for the purpose

for the service. The BRS publishes useful leaflets on such technical problems as the cleaning of external surfaces of buildings, water-repellents for masonry and colourless preservative treatments for stone.

The Council for Small Industries in Rural Areas[1] (formerly the Rural Industries Bureau) was founded in 1921 and is an advisory service set up by the Government to assist small firms in rural areas of England and Wales.[2] The services are grouped under three headings: finance, business or technical advice, and general problems such as power supplies, apprenticeship schemes, the recruitment of labour etc.

The Council runs or arranges courses in furniture restoration, wrought ironwork and thatching; and technical advice is available on these subjects, and in electrical specification and clay product technology. A register has been compiled of all known and recommended specialist craftsmen in rural areas, and information is available upon request.

The Forest Products Research Laboratory[3] will examine infected timber samples and give a firm diagnosis of fungus types in cases of doubt. A fee may be chargeable in certain circumstances. The FPRL publishes a number of very useful bulletins on technical problems affecting wood.

Institute of Geological Sciences and Geological Museum[4] advises on the geological aspects of building and decorative stones. From a comprehensive collection of 18 000 samples, the Institute can determine the rock type used in any particular building and can advise on matching of stones for repair. No charge is made for this service.

The Royal Commission on Historical Monuments (*England*)[5] is a Government agency employing some 40 specialists in its work of recording monuments county by county. The term 'monument' covers all the structural works of man

from earliest time to 1850. The recording includes noting, planning and photographing all the significant monuments. The following Inventories have so far been published: Buckinghamshire (2 vols); Cambridge City; Cambridgeshire (West); Dorset (3 vols); Essex (4 vols); Herefordshire (3 vols); Hertfordshire; Huntingdonshire; London (5 vols); Middlesex; Oxford City; Westmorland; York (Roman). Additionally, the Commission has produced a number of Occasional Publications comprising monographs on special subjects.

Further Inventories are in hand for Dorset, Wiltshire, Cambridgeshire, York City, Salisbury City and Stamford, and for the earthworks of the Cotswolds.

Thatcher at work: the Council for Small Industries in Rural Areas exists to co-ordinate and encourage local craftsmen and to maintain traditional crafts

[1] 35 Camp Road, Wimbledon Common, London, SW19 4UW.
[2] In Scotland, The Small Industries Council for Rural Areas in Scotland, 27 Walker St., Edinburgh 3.
[3] Princes Risborough, Aylesbury, Bucks.
[4] Exhibition Road, London, SW7 2DE.
[5] Fielden House, 10 Great College Street, Westminster, SW1P 3RX.

Montacute House, Somerset: saved by the Society for the Protection of Ancient Buildings

All the detailed records which are the basis of the Inventories and Occasional Publications are held by the Commission.

At one time there was some measure of overlapping with the work of the Victoria County Histories of England, but present policy is for the VCH to leave the preparation of objective accounts of surviving monuments to the Commission.

The Commission is also responsible for the National Monuments Record, which incorporates the archives of the former National Buildings Record. The NMR comprises a collection of exclusively illustrative records of structures of all ages. It includes approximately a million photographs, arranged typographically by counties and alphabetically by names, which are available for study by the public. Reprints may be obtained at very reasonable rates. The Commission, with the NMR, is therefore responsible for the national archive of records of buildings of all kinds in England. There are separate Commissions for Scotland and Wales with responsibilities and collections similar to those of the English Commission.

The Council for Places of Worship[1] is the central organisation for all matters relating to the construction, care and use of places of worship belonging to the Church of England. Formerly known as the Council for the Care of Churches, it has been in existence since 1923 and one of its primary functions is to co-ordinate the work of the forty-two Diocesan Advisory Committees (DACs) for the Care of Churches.[2]

Both the Council and the DACs are concerned with the contents of churches and their curtilages as well as the fabric of churches themselves.

The Council for Places of Worship has a statutory duty to advise on churches which are being considered as possible candidates for redundancy under the Pastoral Measure, 1968 (this is discussed later), as well as the duty, which it shares with the DACs, of advising diocesan Chancellors when requested on applications for faculties.

The Council for Places of Worship has a widely based membership of fifteen, and its Chairman is appointed by the Archbishops of Canterbury and York; it has an executive committee, with a preponderance of specialist membership, which meets monthly to deal with a heavy burden of case-work. In addition to this, the Council's staff is always willing to advise on specific problems. A Conservation Committee, working through a number of sub-Committees, gives specialist advice on conservation problems and also advises the Pilgrim Trust and other grant-giving bodies on applications for grant-aid relating to the conservation of historic church furnishings and fittings. The range of these is very wide and includes organs, painted and carved woodwork, stained glass, monuments, wallpaintings and the like. There is also a New Churches Committee which meets on an ad-hoc basis to co-ordinate research and information on the building of new churches

An annual conference is held for members of DACs; and the Council's staff organises a triennial conference for architects and, from time to time, conferences for architects engaged in the inspection of churches under the Inspection of Churches Measure, 1955. The Council maintains close liaison with the relevant Government Departments, the national museums and amenity societies, and with all those who are concerned with the conservation and care of buildings and problems of construction and maintenance. A full index of artists and craftsmen is maintained, and may be consulted on request; the Council has a fine library devoted to the several branches of ecclesiology, and an extensive collection of visual and documentary material built up over the years.

The Cathedrals Advisory Committee shares the Council's offices and staff, but it is virtually independent and its dealings are confidential between the Committee and the Deans (or Provosts) and Chapters, and cathedral architects concerned. The Committee meets monthly and, in addition to making available information to Chapters and cathedral architects, maintains a watching brief on legislation which may affect cathedrals and parish churches.

Museums and Libraries The Print Room of the British Museum, professional and private organisations such as the Society of Antiquaries, the RIBA and the Soane Museum, and local museums and libraries up and down

[1] 83 London Wall, London, EC2M 5NA.
[2] Addresses of DAC Secretaries may be found in the Church of England Yearbook, the diocesan handbook of the Diocese concerned, or in DAC Newsletters published three times a year by the Council for Places of Worship.

the country, all have extremely valuable collections of information, often unpublished, including early prints and photographs, original drawings and manuscript notes of varying authenticity, accumulated over a long period. Many of the known archives are listed at the NMR but many more can be located by patient searching. The local archivist, whether professional or amateur, will always be found glad to suggest likely sources of information. Care must be taken to establish the authority of references, especially where romantic imaginations have been at work, involving 'observers' such as the Bristol poet Chatterton's entirely fictitious but convincing 'Rowley'.

2.2 Private organisations and societies

Whereas the official organisations are mostly precluded from sponsoring individual causes, the larger private organisations and societies often exist for the double purpose of giving technical advice, and some also champion individual 'cases' in which their aid may be sought:

The Society for the Protection of Ancient Buildings[1], pioneer of all the private bodies and pre-eminent in giving technical advice, was founded in 1877 by William Morris. The Society relies for its work on the subscriptions of its members. Courses of public lectures are given annually in London, and the Society has pioneered the idea of annual short courses for architects in the care of old buildings.

The Society's greatest concern is to ensure the continuance of informed technical knowledge in traditional methods of construction and repair. The Lethaby Scholarship, and more recently also the Banister Fletcher Scholarship, enable selected applicants to receive six months' specialised training and experience of this type of work, and offer one of the best means of practical study available.

The Society is particularly well qualified to give skilled advice on technical matters, and its Technical Panel meets fortnightly to deal with conservation and repair problems. Arrangements can also be made for a visit and report by one of the Society's architects. From its initial foundation, the SPAB has been concerned that repairs and restoration should be no more expensive and elaborate than a building needs, and it is a champion of the cause of 'daily care and

[1] 55–59 Great Ormond Street, London, WC1N 3JA.

Church at Winterbourne Tomson, Dorset: saved by the Society for the Protection of Ancient Buildings

conservative repair'.

The Society for the Protection of Ancient Buildings has also set up a Section that keeps a detailed index of threatened properties, and this is circulated regularly by the Society to its members. The list provides possible purchasers with information and by this means buildings often find a new owner and sometimes a new use. The SPAB's lists are broadly based and include unlisted buildings. As a result of this excellent facility, very many threatened buildings have already been saved.

The Ancient Monuments Society[2] was founded in 1924 for the study and conservation of ancient monuments, historic buildings and fine old craftsmanship. It is one of six bodies which must be notified of all applications to demolish or alter listed buildings. It is the only national society to examine all cases referred to it, regardless of the age or period of a building. The Society at present deals with about seven hundred cases each year and, in each case, appoints an architect or surveyor to examine the threatened building and to report back on its condition and merit. A letter may subsequently be sent to the local authority expressing the Society's views. In particularly

[2] Alexander Street, London, W2 5NT.

Mawley Hall, Cleobury Mortimer, Salop: saved by a Georgian Group campaign

important cases, representations are made at public inquiries. The Society also makes small financial grants to assist projects of special interest. The Society publishes an annual volume of Transactions, which have gained a high reputation for the scholarly character of its pages, mostly available as re-prints.

Council for British Archaeology[1] provides liaison at national level between archaeological societies and the Government bodies concerned with the preservation of ancient monuments and historic buildings, including those of the industrial revolution. The Council promoted research on these subjects and on early urban development, through its conferences and publications. The CBA encourages co-operation between amateur and professional archaeologists and serves as a national information centre on all aspects of British archaeology. It is among the bodies notified of planning proposals affecting listed buildings and itself makes representations about national preservation policy. The Council has produced a list of towns in Britain, the historic quality of which particularly requires careful treatment in any planning or re-develop-

[1] 8 St Andrews Place, Regents Park, London, NW1 4LB.

ment proposals, and other useful papers on historic towns and the planning process.

The Georgian Group[2] was founded in 1937. The Group deals with problems affecting buildings erected since 1714, and performs a similar function to the SPAB. The aims of the Georgian Group include the creation of interest in Georgian architecture, the giving of advice as to the preservation, repair and use today of Georgian buildings, and their protection from destruction and disfigurement. The Group also aims to ensure that when an area is re-planned, Georgian buildings are not wantonly destroyed, and that new buildings 'harmonise, though they may contrast', with the old.

The Victorian Society[3] founded in 1958, has sought to

[2] 2 Chester Street, London, SW1X 7BD.   [3] 29 Exhibition Road, London, SW7 2AS.

Mawley Hall interior, showing a remarkable serpentine handrail

St. Pancras Station, London, saved by the Victorian Society

convert unfavourable public opinion towards Victorian and Edwardian design (covering the period 1830–1914). Arousing interest and discrimination in the arts of the period is as much the Society's purpose as saving buildings and works of art. A primary task of the Society is to ensure that all major Victorian and Edwardian buildings receive protection under the Town and Country Planning Acts: lists of such buildings are in course of preparation. The Society gives evidence for the protection of important buildings at public inquiries and offers specialist advice on architectural and design problems.

The Society has formed regional groups in Liverpool, Manchester and Birmingham and organises study tours, visits, conferences and exhibitions at national and regional levels.

A *Joint Conference* now co-ordinates the activities of the Society for the Protection of Ancient Buildings, the Georgian Group, Victorian Society and the Civic Trust. This is active in securing concerted legal and administrative action in the joint interest of all its member Societies, and in cases affecting major groups of buildings of varying dates.

The Council for the Protection of Rural England[1] was founded in 1926 to organise concerted action to secure the improvement, protection and preservation of the countryside and its towns and villages; to act as information and advisory centre and to arouse and educate public opinion on matters affecting rural amenities and usage.

It has 53 constituent bodies but does most of its work through its 40 county branches. It maintains close contact with the Departments of Government and Local Planning Authorities and endeavours to ensure that not an acre is lost unnecessarily. A separate council for Wales was founded in 1928.

The Association for Studies in the Conservation of Historic Buildings[2] aims to keep members informed of current practice in the conservation of historic buildings and monuments; to provide a forum for meetings and discussions; and to give close study to training methods in the techniques and philosophy of building conservation.

[1] 4 Hobart Place, London, SW1W 0HY.
[2] Institute of Archaeology, 31–34 Gordon Square, London, WC1H 0PY.

Chesterton Windmill, Warwickshire: designed by Inigo Jones and saved by the Windmill and Watermill Section of the Society for the Protection of Ancient Buildings

and many 'consumer' organisations whose buildings require the attention of architects with special experience and qualifications in this field. Its main pre-occupations are in seeing that all architectural education provides an appreciation of old buildings and their care, and that adequate training is thereafter made available for those whishing to specialise. The Conference maintains a List of architects with experience of this work or requiring assistance.

The Institute of Advanced Architectural Studies[2] a Department of the University of York, is primarily concerned with the technicalities of preservation and the professional and legal issues involved. It has regularly included in its annual programme, short residential courses on the protection and repair of historic buildings for architects, surveyors, clerks of work and builders, and has commenced a one-year post-graduate course of conservation studies leading to a diploma. The Institute does not undertake the championing of individual cases, but it can sometimes advise on the appointment of a professional consultant.

Societies interested in particular building types
The National Association of Almshouses[3] is a private organisation founded in 1951 to assist the Trustees of Almshouses, to encourage the improvement of old premises, and to foster the foundation of new almshouse trusts. The Association gives grants for the repair and improvement of almshouses, and advises how funds may be raised for their restoration and maintenance.

The Windmill and Watermill Section of the SPAB concentrates on the promotion of public interest, the support of individual cases and on the giving of technical advice regarding any problem in connection with the preservation of windmills and watermills.

Civic, amenity and local societies
The Civic Trust[4] is an independent body, founded in 1957, with foyr associated Trusts in Scotland, Wales, the North-West and North-East. Each is supported by voluntary contributions from industry and commerce and governed

Visits are arranged to buildings under repair and other works relevant to conservation. Membership is limited and by invitation.
The Conference on Training Architects in Conservation[1] is one of the most widely representative organisations, and has representatives from bodies including all the principal Government Departments, the major amenity Societies

[1] 19 West Eaton Place, London, SW1X 8LT.

[2] University of York, The King's Manor, York, YO1 2EP.
[3] Billingbear Lodge, Wokingham, Berkshire.
[4] 17 Carlton House Terrace, London, SW1Y 5AW.

Magdalen Street, Norwich: a pioneer street improvement scheme by the Civic Trust, before and after

The New Victoria Cinema, London; will there soon be a Jazz Age or Cinema Conservation Society?

and new buildings in historic areas. Data on these awards form a valuable source of information for local authorities and others. Conferences, projects, reports and films have been sponsored and focus attention on major issues in town planning and architecture. These have included proposals for re-development and improvements in historic towns, and publications have included a number of useful booklets on conservation.

The Trust has pioneered many street improvement schemes designed to brighten and tidy up drab streets, and now publishes detailed guidance on the way in which such schemes can be sponsored locally. Through its President, and in close co-operation with the Government, the Trust was closely associated in the drafting of the Civic Amenities Act, and has been strongly concerned in the subsequent programme of designating and enhancing Conservation Areas.

In the field of public conscience, the *local County, Civic, Archaeological and Preservation Societies* are of the greatest value, as is the local Press, in bringing publicity to bear where it is needed. Being generally composed of non-technical people with a sprinkling of aesthetic, historical and artistic specialists, these societies often need careful and tactful guidance in maintaining a balanced opinion. As with all organisations of any kind, the success and energy of these bodies will depend upon one individual—the secretary—through whom a group of individuals either becomes an articulate unit or does not. But by the power of personal ties and friendships, local societies can achieve very much while the larger and more distinct organisation would still be knocking at the door. A comprehensive directory of these local societies has been compiled by the Civic Trust.

The preservation societies would be the first to lament their own necessity, but they do constitute a most valuable organ of the public conscience.

Societies Administering Trust Funds

Private Trusts There are said to be in England and Wales over 100 000 registered charities, varying widely in their resources and in the scope of their activities, and some of whom are interested in old buildings. Some operate unobtrusively in order to husband limited resources.

by a Board of Trustees. Each Civic Trust has a director who in turn can call upon the aid of technical staff.

Over 800 civic and amenity societies throughout Britain are registered with the Trust. There is no individual membership. No charge is made for registration and the societies receive the Trust's newsletter and may borrow exhibitions, films, slides and publications from the Trust's library. The Trust endeavours to support and advise these societies in their local work and offers them guidance, but is not able to take up local cases and does not normally appear at Local Inquiries.

The Civic Trust has a Scheme of Awards annually for good development of all kinds, including restoration work

The best known of all the private organisations are, of course, the National Trust and the Pilgrim Trust, which are described by way of example. But very many smaller trusts are glad to assist local preservation projects, if only the contact can be made before it is too late.

If external sources fail, a Private Appeal Fund may be set up, as for example for Croft Castle, which was then handed over to the National Trust. Here, the necessary endowment to enable the Trust to accept the property was raised by private and public subscription and by a private loan. The Castle has meanwhile been formally taken over by the Trust, and the fund remains active in securing for the Castle suitable furnishings, works of art and other permanent exhibits.

The Charity Commissioners[1] give advice to trustees, including advice on transactions in charity property, and they maintain a Central Register of Charities which is indexed by name, locality and objects and which can be inspected by the public. Many local authorities keep a duplicate index of local charities. The Commissioners themselves do not administer charities, nor can they recommend charities which might be approached for help.

The National Trust[2] is a private body founded in 1895, whose privileged position and responsibilities have been acknowledged by several Acts of Parliament—notably the National Trust Acts of 1907, 1937, 1939 and 1970. It is not a Government Department but depends for its existence on the voluntary support of the public.

The Trust is a property-owning body, whose aims are the permanent preservation for the Nation's benefit and enjoyment of land of special natural interest or beauty, and of buildings of national, architectural or artistic importance, or of furniture pictures and chattels, and of gardens.

The Trust works closely with such bodies as the CPRE, the SPAB and the Georgian Group. From an earlier pre-occupation with protecting unspoilt natural scenery, the National Trust has become more and more concerned with the preservation of important historic buildings, particularly of country houses. A further impetus has been given to this side of the Trust's activities in recent years by the gradual transfer to public ownership of so many of the larger estates in danger of being broken up by death duties.

The Trust is not State subsidised, and property can only be accepted if it is sufficiently well-endowed to form a self-contained financial unit.

Each case is considered on its merits, and arrangements can often be made for the previous owners and their families to remain as tenants of a house. Under the National Trust Act of 1939, property 'settled' under the Settled Land Act of 1925 can also be accepted, the lease being revested in the statutory owner or tenant for life. Conditions can be made that an endowment must be devoted by the Trust entirely to the maintenance of the particular property, and that the tenant must admit the public, and may not use the property other than as a dwelling, nor sublet without consent.

Properties given to the National Trust and the requisite maintenance funds are also, subject to reasonable limits, immediately exempt from estate duty. The principle of economic self-sufficiency applied to all estates has helped to give a genuine and unforced quality which is such a happy characteristic of the National Trust's steadily growing list of properties.

Pilgrim Trust[3] In 1930, Mr Edward Harkness, a private citizen of the USA, decided to make a gift of £2 000 000 to this country. To administer this fund, a trust was established with wide and generous terms of reference. Although until the 1939 war about half of the income was devoted to social welfare work, mainly amongst the unemployed, the new organisation, which was named the Pilgrim Trust, has always devoted a large part of its resources to the preservation of the national heritage of architecture and history, and to the promotion of art and learning: and these objects are now its main pre-occupation. By 1950 so many grants were being made towards the repair of parish churches in England that it was decided to suspend these from the scope of the Trust's assistance, and to urge the establishment of the obviously needed separate Trust for this purpose. Generous assistance has since been given towards the work

[1] 14 Ryder Street, St James, London, SW1Y 6AH.
[2] 42 Queen Anne's Gate, London SW1H 9AS.

[3] Millbank House, 2 Great Peter Street, London, SW1P 3LX.

of the Historic Churches Preservation Trust. Individual grants are still however made to cathedrals, and to parish churches in Scotland and in Northern Ireland, and towards the repair of Church 'treasures' such as fine books and furniture, monuments, wall paintings and ancient glass. Grant assistance is available only for objects recognised as charitable in the United Kingdom. Applicants are expected to have contributed considerable personal effort before seeking charitable aid. The Trust is allowed to invest without restriction, and under wise management its capital has been greatly increased. As a charitable institution the Trust is exempt from income tax. Grants are made from income, and currently average about £360 000 in each year.

The Mutual Households Association Ltd[1] One of the most interesting schemes, which has received a great deal of attention over the 15 years since its inception, is the Mutual Households Association. This Association has two aims—to save large country mansions from demolition and decay, and to create in them apartments for independent retired and semi-retired people.

The problem of preserving large country houses of historic or architectural value urgently needs solution if many are able to survive the unprecedented destruction of recent years. The mounting cost of repairs makes it increasingly difficult for the individual owner to maintain a country mansion, but given 30 or 40 people willing to share the running costs, many of these houses can be adapted to provide a very high standard of comfort and amenity.

MHA works energetically and with expert knowledge of what can be achieved. The cost of repairing, restoring and converting these large old houses is under-written by grants from the Historic Buildings Council, from County Councils, from legacies and from those who wish to take up residence in any particular house. In this way the large country mansion lives again for the purpose for which it was built.

MHA now administers ten houses and some fine examples are Aynhoe Park near Banbury, Danny at Hurstpierpoint and Albury Park near Guildford. All the Association's houses are open to the public every Wednesday and

Thursday afternoon from May to September, although the private apartments are not available for viewing.

MHA, is a registered charity for the preservation of buildings, and welcomes supporting members who appreciate its aims.

Incorporated Church Building Society[2] founded in 1818, administers charitable funds from which grants may be made towards the construction, re-seating, repair or enlargement of both ancient and modern Anglican Churches in England and Wales.

The Society is interested in all churches and not only those of special architectural or historic interest; so that it is useful to know that any sacred building, even of remarkable ugliness architecturally, is eligible for consideration: in this respect the Society is unique.

The Society's resources are limited, and grants cannot be large; but every effort is made to assist each worthy claim

Pythouse, Tisbury, Wiltshire: purchased and converted by the Mutual Households Association

in some measure. Application should be made to the Secretary by an incumbent before any work is commenced, enclosing architects' drawings and detailed specifications, as well as any available photographs, postcards etc. The submission of a Report alone is not sufficient, and will entail delays. Each case is studied by a Committee of Honorary Consulting Architects who meet monthly; and grants are conditional upon their expenditure under proper architectural supervision, and upon a contribution being sent annually to the Society. This financial support provides the means from which the grants can be made. The Society publishes various useful booklets and

[1] 41 Kingsway, London, WC2B 6UB.

[2] 7 Queen Anne's Gate, London, SW1H 9BX.

Blanchland, Northumberland: the Pilgrim Trust gave grants towards the repair and improvement of this remote moorland village by the Trustees of the Lord Crewe Charity

pamphlets about the requirements of new and old churches.

Friends of Friendless Churches[1] is a body founded in 1957 to secure the preservation of churches and chapels in the United Kingdom, when these are of architectural or historic interest and irrespective of pastoral considerations. Its aim is to secure the preservation of churches

[1] 12 Edwardes Square, London, W8 6HE.

St. Bartholomew's Church, Basildon where the chancel is taller than the nave. Many chancels are under separate ownership

St. Mary's Chapel, Tal-y-Llyn, adopted by the Friends of Friendless Churches

and chapels of architectural or historic interest which fall outside the scope of other organisations. It is particularly concerned to prevent the demolition of such churches and chapels, and is prepared to oppose petitions for faculties or pastoral or redundancy schemes having such an end in view, and if necessary itself to apply for a Faculty for repair. The body normally itself undertakes the whole cost of repair, but occasionally makes grants where the ecclesiastical authorities are willing to undertake the work. It is financed mainly by the contributions of its members, but sometimes also opens an appeal for which public support is invited. Local correspondents give the Society early information about threats to churches of architectural interest.

It is impossible to mention all the professional, craft and learned societies whose interest includes old buildings, but the Society for the Protection of Ancient Buildings will gladly supply information on request. Names and addresses of local, civic and amenity Societies may be obtained at any time from the Civic Trust.

2.3 Church properties and their administration

The listing of Church property The list of buildings of special architectural or historic importance also covers Church properties. Church of England properties are classified in grades showing their relative importance:

GRADE A Cathedrals and churches of absolutely outstanding importance.

GRADE B Buildings of very great architectural importance.

GRADE C Churches of less importance but worth preserving. It was estimated in 1971 that approximately 2000 churches were listed as Grade A and 5172 as Grade B; with 2981 not yet allocated between these two grades. This means that as many as 11 000 church buildings in the country are listed as being of outstanding architectural merit.

The grading of Church of England properties is quite separate from that of secular buildings, and the gradings used in no way correspond with the Grade I or Grade II classification for lay buildings. But church buildings of other denominations such as Roman Catholic churches, non-conformist chapels, meeting-houses and rectories are on the other hand classified on a Grade I and Grade II basis.

As the law stands today, all church buildings, of whatever denomination at the present time 'being used for ecclesiastical purposes' have been repeatedly excluded from the provisions of the various Town and Country Planning Acts concerned with the protection of historic buildings. This exclusion, which has been the subject of increasing criticism, can be traced to the Ancient Monuments Act of 1913. When the Bill left the House of Commons its protective provisions extended to ecclesiastical as well as secular buildings; but in the House of Lords these provisions were excluded, after the Archbishop of Canterbury had argued that it was best left to ecclesiastical authorities themselves to safeguard their own buildings. Against this, it is often argued today that the first interest of the church must be in the cure of souls and not the care of stones, and that in a changing climate of public opinion, it is now time the nation took a greater share of responsibility in looking after ancient churches.

Church buildings Today alterations or additions to a church or its contents are subject to the authorisation of a Faculty, in effect a licence issued by the Consistory Court of the diocese. This system is of great antiquity, and a Diocesan Chancellor sits as judge of the Consistory Court and as legal representative of the Bishop. The majority of cases are settled by the Chancellor in chambers, but in cases of contention or special difficulty, a hearing takes place in open court. The authority of a Faculty is required for all major repairs, for constructional alterations and additions, for the addition or removal of furnishings, stained glass, ornaments, memorials and other fittings, and for the sale of goods belonging to the church. A Faculty also has to be obtained for a new heating or lighting installation, for repair work to bells or organs and for the provision of general services. For the erection of a gravestone in a churchyard, the incumbent's consent is normally sufficient within limits laid down by the Chancellor, and regulations relevant to this will generally be found in the diocesan handbook concerned; but again in cases of special difficulty a Faculty must be obtained. Similarly by custom, the incumbent may on his own authority carry out day-to-day repairs and replacements to the buildings (eg repair of gutters and downpipes, fallen tiles etc).

Repairs or re-decorations which do not involve a substantial alteration in the appearance of the building may be carried out on the authority of an Archdeacon's Certificate. Fees are payable by the Parish for Faculties and Archdeacon's certificates, as set out in the diocesan handbook obtainable from the Registrar.

The procedure for applying for a Faculty is as follows. Application is made by the Parochial Church Council, which will have formally recorded the resolution approving the work proposed. In cases of difficulty, an informal application 'in principle', lodged through the Diocesan Registrar as with an ordinary application, may be a useful preliminary step. The address of the Diocesan Registrar may also be found by reference to the Church of England Yearbook or the relevant diocesan handbook. The responsibility for authorising, or refusing to authorise, the proposed work then falls upon the Consistory Court. If the application is refused, it is open to the petitioners to appeal to the Provincial Court (ie of Canterbury or York) and ultimately, from the Provincial Court to the Judicial Committee of the Privy Council. Such instances are rare. The Diocesan Advisory Committees were set up as the result of a widely felt need to provide Diocesan Chancellors with specialist advice on the artistic, architectural and archaeological aspects of work proposed to church fabrics or their contents. Membership of the DACs is varied, and generally includes antiquaries and specialists of various kinds who are well qualified to advise on matters concerned with churches. The Archdeacons of the diocese are automatically members of the DACs. Membership of the Committees is published from time to time in the newsletters of the Council for Places of Worship. Meetings are usually held monthly, and the DAC will send a visiting sub-Committee to consider an application with the petitioners on the site.

It is strongly emphasised that the system works most satisfactorily when there is early consultation between the parish and the DAC. To advise parishes, and to help them in this way, is a primary function of these Committees. A second function is to advise the Chancellor when proposals have reached the stage of a formal application for a faculty, and when the Chancellor seeks their advice. In addition, the DACs must approve the granting of an Archdeacon's Certificate. A further duty laid upon DACs, under the Inspection of Churches Measure 1955, is the approval of an architect before he can undertake inspection work in any church in the diocese—the purpose being to ensure that architects with no experience in caring for historic buildings are not placed in charge of parish churches of major importance.

Quinquennial inspections The preservation of churches has been placed on an entirely new basis by the Inspection of Churches Measure, 1955. This requires that every church should be inspected by an architect once every five years. It does not, of course, require that his advice should be taken, but this insistence on inspection is already a beginning.

The Places of Worship Commission and the Ecclesiastical Architects' and Surveyors' Association have set up a working party with representatives of the RIBA and client bodies to look into all relevant aspects of the inspection and repair of churches; and their findings have been published by the RIBA in an excellent handbook, *Church Inspection and Repair*.[1] This sets out a method of appoint-

[1] Obtainable from RIBA, 66 Portland Place, London, W1N 4AD.

ing architects, together with guidance on their remuneration and a letter of engagement, and makes useful recommendations about the form of report expected and its distribution.

The following is the latest version of the check-list now recommended in quinquennial church inspections, (noting that if a lay rector has responsibility for the maintenance of the chancel, he may have his own special requirements). On his first visit the architect should examine and report under each of these headings, noting materials, construction and current condition: on subsequent occasions he may refer only to items where changes have occurred and where repairs are needed:

Structural condition General report on structural stability, including notes on settlements, etc.

Walls and Masonry Type and condition of the stone or brickwork, condition of pointing, external rendering or plastering, location and diagnosis of cracks and other defects.

Tower, if any Walls, floors, roof, roof access, parapets and spire (if any); vanes; bells, their number, sizes and condition of fittings; bell frame and stability of the latter related to tower, clock, clock weights, etc.

Roofs and gutters Description and condition of coverings on all pitched and flat roofs, including as far as practicable, fixings and linings; the condition of metal or other box and parapet gutters; internal valleys, roof valleys and flashings; the effectiveness of heat-loss insulation and adequacy of ventilation in the roof spaces; the state of timbers and trusses below pitched and flat roofs; the safety of plaster ceilings; evidence of presence of fungal rot and insect attack.

Rainwater disposal system and drainage Condition of eaves, gutters, rainwater pipes, gulleys, dry areas and provision for surface-water drainage and outfall; deleterious vegetation; adequacy of the sub-soil drainage.

Internal decoration Internal plastering and finishes; reference to any revealed, or possibly concealed mural paintings.

Floors and galleries Stagings, suspended and solid floors; pavings in stone, tile, and composition; heating and ventilating ducts and gratings.

Glazing and ventilation Leakages, draught sources, condi-

Redundant churches can suffer rapid loss of character when their fittings are re-used elsewhere. St. George Great Yarmouth in 1959 and 1971

tion of ferramenta and wire guards (if any); efficiency of ventilation; notes on stained glass, especially ancient stained glass, and ancient clear glass.

Fittings Monuments; fittings and furniture of interest or value of whatever period.

Boundary walls, paths and gates General condition of churchyard and trees, etc, in so far as this affects public safety and the church building.

Useful general clauses are suggested in *Church Inspection and Repair*, concerning items likely to be common to all quinquennial reports, such as the scope of the Report, with a note on estimates of cost and instructions to put work in hand, services such as electrical installations, heating apparatus and lightning conductors, and useful notes on maintenance and insurances. The architect should refer in detail to this excellent publication.

Redundant churches The problems of churches are in some ways more complex than those of other historic buildings. With congregations falling and maintenance costs rising, the burden of administering the outstanding architectural legacy of the churches becomes increasingly difficult to meet. Inevitably some churches will have to be declared redundant; but if these are to be limited to a reasonable number, then adequate funds must be made available on a fairly wide scale; and money will probably have to come from outside sources. The loss of many parish churches, with their irreplaceable historic and architectural associations, could be tragic. So often they represent all that is best in our national and historic achievement, and their continued survival is of the first importance, even when only as works of art.

A variety of factors may result in a particular church becoming redundant, insofar as its pastoral function in the life of the Church is concerned. These factors are not limited to any one denomination; but because of the high proportion of architecturally or historically important churches belonging to the Church of England, that body has recently evolved a complex system for dealing with the problem. The Pastoral Measure 1968 follows, with regard to redundant churches, the recommendations made by a Commission under the chairmanship of Lord Bridges which, reporting in 1960, sought to ensure that no worthwhile building is lost. Anyone who is familiar with the problems of adaptation and re-use of buildings generally will know the difficulties that are involved; the Pastoral Measure has been in operation only since 1969 and it is too early to say with confidence how successful its provisions are proving to be—but it can claim to be comprehensive, and with safeguards built into the system which are probably superior to those relating to secular buildings. There is no universally accepted forecast of the number of churches likely to be declared redundant, this was suggested as 790 by the Bridges Commission.

The procedure is first for the Diocesan Pastoral Committee to consult the Council for Places of Worship, receiving from it a fairly detailed report setting out the architectural qualities and historic interest of the building concerned. Reference is also made to 'other churches in the area', as a choice—and often an invidious one—may well have to be made between one building and another (for example in underpopulated rural areas). Having finally decided upon a recommendation that a particular church should be declared redundant, the Pastoral Committee sends the papers relating to the proposal to the Bishop, who may forward them (with or without comment) to the Church Commissioners. The Pastoral Measure defines (section 3) those interested parties, including the local Planning Committee, who have to be consulted before this stage is reached. If the Church Commissioners finally agree to seal a declaration of redundancy, advice is sought on the future of the building from the Advisory Board for Redundant Churches, a national body, set up under the Measure, with a distinguished membership. If the church is of architectural or historic importance, or contains fine furnishings integral to it, the Advisory Board may well recommend vesting the church in the Redundant Churches Fund. This Fund is another new body established by the Pastoral Measure, provided with an income from Government and Church sources, and enabled to act as a holding body for churches which are of such interest that they ought to be preserved 'in the interests of the Nation and the Church of England'. The Bridges Commission tentatively suggested that the Fund might be asked to accept responsibility, ultimately, for between 300 and 400 churches. If this is to come about, it will clearly be desirable to increase the present income of the Fund (£500 000 during the first quinquennium) but there is no reason to expect that this will not be possible. Architects specialising in conservation work will be required to supervise over the years a great deal of repair work on churches which in recent years have been 'run down' and have had very little money to spend on repair work.

Those churches not vested in the Redundant Churches Fund fall into two categories: either (a) they will be demolished, although the Advisory Board may in the first place withhold a demolition certificate, or (b) they may be adapted to one of a wide variety of alternative uses. The Church Commissioners have the right to declare a particular use as being unsuitable, and the Advisory Board is required to approve or withhold approval of the proposed adaptation. Every diocese which is actively pursuing this problem has appointed a Redundant Churches Uses Committee, whose task it is to seek out suitable alternative uses. Possibilities already projected or carried out include their use as a Guildhall, library, school, music rooms, domestic use, agricultural purposes, record offices and a restaurant. A great deal of work has been done recently in converting other historic buildings such as mills, barns and the like, even of a comparatively minor order, to new domestic and community purposes, and it is to be hoped that, where the quality of a church does not merit preservation by the Fund and it is too worthwhile to consider demolition, similarly imaginative schemes will be put forward and successfully carried out. Enquiries relating to redundant churches, and especially their adaptation, should be addressed in the first place either to the Secretary of the Diocesan Redundant Churches

Uses Committee (see Diocesan handbook) or the Secretary of the Redundant Churches Committee of the Church Commissioners.

Financial aid for churches

A Commission was appointed by the Church Assembly in June 1951 to consider 'problems concerned with the repair of churches, and with proposals for securing their regular inspection.'

Four recommendations were made by the Commission. Firstly, a sum of £4 000 000 was considered likely to be needed within the ensuing ten years to supplement the efforts of the parishes in putting church buildings into good repair: after this, an annual maintenance expenditure of £750 000 was estimated to be necessary. It was therefore suggested that a Historic Churches Preservation Trust, and local County Trusts associated with it, should be set up with the aim of raising funds. The Commission also recommended a quinquennial inspection by a qualified Architect, together with a system of Repair Grants for works to be carried out under suitable supervision.

Apart from the Trust and its affiliated bodies, funds are also available for church repair work from Diocesan funds, and from many other Trusts and private bodies enumerated above.

To provide financial aid the *Historic Churches Preservation Trust*[1] was established in 1952. Its main aim was to help parishes carry out essential repairs to their churches by raising money by public appeal. Since its inception the parent Trust and its affiliated County Trusts have received in cash and promises approximately £2 000 000. From these funds grants have been given to some 2500 churches in every part of the country. The Trust, however, is a voluntary body and is entirely dependent on public support. No aid from any official source is available.

In addition to its financial assistance, the Trust attaches great importance to the execution of repairs in the most appropriate possible manner. In this respect it has the assistance of eminent architects skilled in the techniques needed in handling ancient buildings.

Applications for assistance must state the name of the church and its dedication together with the diocese,

[1] Fulham Palace, Bishop's Avenue, London, SW6 6EA.

archdeaconry and civil county, and must give a brief history of the fabric before stating the repairs thought necessary. An indication of the population of the parish is also required. The anticipated cost of repairs, including supervision and contingencies, and the name of the architect must be stated, as must the availability of other funds raised and promised, whether from donations of the patron or parishioners, the Diocesan Board of Finance or any other source. Recent photographs (at least one interior and one exterior view, and preferably additional details of the required repairs) and an architect's report and specification must in every case be included with the application.

The overriding criterion as to whether a church building is eligible for grant aid from the Trust is always its historical and architectural merit.

The normal Faculty procedure is applicable for work carried out with the help of grants, which are payable on completion of the works in question. Professional fees and expenses are allowable, and a reasonable contingencies allowance may be included in the application. Where the extent of work cannot reasonably be envisaged until scaffolding and stripping work have been carried out and proper access obtained, a separate grant may first be made for this preliminary work, if it is quite beyond the means of the parish.

Since the County Trusts are autonomous, applications for grants may likewise be made to these bodies. The Trust is solely concerned with assisting repairs to parochial churches, and is not associated with the major appeals which are made from time to time.

It is interesting to note that although Anglican claims inevitably overshadow all others, all historic churches, including those of Roman Catholic and Free Church tradition, are eligible for consideration if funds are available.

Parsonage houses Special provisions have been made for the maintenance of parsonage houses. In law, the incumbent becomes the *owner* of a parsonage house for the duration of his incumbency. The Ecclesiastical Dilapidations Measures required each diocese to set up a Dilapidations Board, whose duty it is to ensure that parsonage houses are maintained in good repair. For this purpose a

Free churches: a Friends' Meeting House at Long Sutton, Somerset

Diocesan Surveyor is appointed to survey each property every five years, reporting what repairs are needed and how much these will cost. The Dilapidations Board then makes an order stipulating the work to be done, which becomes the responsibility of the incumbent. When the Diocesan Surveyor makes his inspection, he also gives an estimate of the money likely to be required for repairs during the next five years, and the amount for which the building should be insured against fire. In recent years the Diocesan Authorities and the Church Commissioners have been able to make arrangements so that, with the help of the parishes, no incumbent is called upon to bear personally the cost of maintaining his parsonage house.

Under a new measure which is expected to come into operation in 1974, the entire responsibility for keeping parsonage houses in good repair will pass to a new diocesan board, to be known as the *Parsonages Board*, and replacing the present Dilapidations Board. There will continue to be five-yearly inspections of parsonage houses by the Diocesan Surveyor. An incumbent may only dispose of a parsonage house or provide a new one

The problem of church extension at St Peter, Thundersley, Essex. The roof-pitch and materials of the original have

been maintained, but without falsification of style. (Civic Trust Award: Donald W. Insall and Associates)

with the specific consent of the Bishop, the Dilapidations Board and the Church Commissioners. The patron and the parochial church council must also be consulted. The consent of the Board and the patron must further be obtained to any alteration or addition to the building. In other respects an incumbent is in the same position as any other owner, and must satisfy all the usual Local Authority and Planning regulations.

In his capacity of owner, an incumbent may employ any outside architect, who must however be approved by the Dilapidations Board. If an application is made for an Historic Buildings Grant or Local Authority Improvement Grant, this will similarly be lodged in the name of the incumbent, who becomes the 'employer' under the contract and is responsible for the relevant fees.

The Diocesan Surveyor has not necessarily any connection with actual churches, the quinquennial inspection of

which is a separate responsibility.

Free Church properties

Information regarding the ownership of churches belonging to the various nonconformist organisations can be obtained from the General Secretary of the Free Church Federal Council[1] or from the appropriate denominational headquarters.

Generally, the property of the nonconformist churches is administered either directly by the denominational headquarters as managing trustees, or else legally held by this body as custodian trustee and actually managed by the local body. The Baptists and Congregationalists encourage the incorporation of property in the local regional or County Union, and the Methodist church generally prefers the system of local personal trustees. In each case,

[1] 27 Tavistock Square, London, WC1.

Before and after: a church re-ordered and tidied at Belchamp Otten, Suffolk

it is the local church meeting or its appointed representatives who will appoint the architect, and to whom he will be responsible.

There is in general among the free churches no set system of inspections nor of 'Faculty' procedure; and as the manse is usually held by the body corporate, for lease to its Minister, the incumbent has no responsibilities like those of the Anglican parsonage house.

3. Job Organisation

In this third section, the author outlines methods of Survey and report, and comments on the drafting of specifications. He then discusses the problem of how to choose a contractor (and sub-contractors) for repair work, how to go about getting realistic estimates, and the handling of the job by the architect.

3.1 Survey and report

When an architect is asked to report on an old building, how should he set about the job, and what should he look for?

The first point to establish is the reason for which advice is being sought, and what purpose the Report is to serve. The Client may be an owner or potential purchaser who wishes to know the structural condition of the property, and whether it is suitable for conversion to new uses. A Report may on the other hand be needed as legal evidence, possibly in the form of a Dilapidations Survey describing the condition of the property at a given date. Or the owner may be interested in the architectural history and development of his building, its restoration and improvement—possibly with Grant assistance, if this can be obtained. In either case, the specific purpose of the Report must be borne in mind from the beginning.

A full and detailed Survey cannot possibly be done in a hurry; and if possible a visit is best made at a time when the clock and train times can be forgotten, and a maximum of attention given to the job. For survey visits, either some extremely old clothing or preferably an all-enveloping boiler suit will be found useful. There should be little need of any instruments to detect trouble of any kind, except two eyes, sometimes a nose, and a knife and a strong torch. Spare torch-batteries are a 'must' and are easy to forget. Plenty of paper and a ball-pen will be needed, or a pocket tape-recorder is useful. For most purposes a measuring rod, old screwdriver and a hammer should then complete the outfit.

The inspection A painstaking and exhaustive circuit of the building will then be made on one's own, every detail being noted down for reference. In order to make sure

Distortion of timber framing: an ancient window twisted almost out of recognition at Lower Bridge Street, Chester

that nothing is missed, it is wise to follow a definite plan of coverage. The architect may for example examine the exterior first, then the interior, starting from the roof-space, thereafter exploring clockwise every room and space on each successive floor, and finally examining the foundations, drains and services. Everything should be noted down directly it is seen: it is easier at this stage to group one's observations, as they occur. Later, after the whole picture has been studied, they can be edited into a related sequence.

Cracks can give valuable clues to the direction of structural movement

A fractured hood-mould will quickly admit weather

A neglected hopperhead, between square lead downpipes, attracts vegetation and causes overflowing. The interior could here immediately be suspect and liable to dry rot

A pier disrupted by rusting iron cramps

Window-head sags under load: frequently this is a result of replacing mullioned windows with sashes at an earlier date

Outside, the architect will first note the general structural design, the materials and present condition of the building and its elements, including the date and sequence of its construction, and any signs of past alterations and extensions which might give a clue to its history. If there are structural movements, it is important to decide what settlement is alive, and what is now expended. Leaning walls, dipping lines of eaves or brickwork courses, and signs of past and present movement must all be carefully noted with regard for their cause, significance and possibility of future remedy. A vigilant watch will be kept for all signs of damp, like mossy patches, efflorescence and other staining. The path of rainwater, from roofs into gutters, downpipes and drains will be imaginatively pictured under the worst possible conditions. Damp-proof courses, dry areas, and every defence against the weather require close inspection. Relative rates of decay should be looked into, with special attention to points like damage by iron fixings built into stonework, the effects of differential movements between materials of varying shrinkages and dates, and the condition and weathering of joints and ledges, which might cause accelerated damage to the structure and fabric.

Passing to the interior, the roof-spaces will first be inspected, their construction and materials, alterations and movements being noted and checked in detail. The constructional form of the roof, beyond reach of everyday alterations, will often reveal a great deal about the architectural history of a house. The rafters may for example be of heavy, squarish scantlings of oak, laid flat and pegged together in pairs at their apex. A projecting wing may then have been constructed against it at a later date, with obviously newer valleys laid against the old rafters. The youngest additions may in turn have ridge-boards and newer lighter timbers in deal, of deeper and narrower scantlings. Purlins and struts may be found to have been added or internal gutters roofed over, and sometimes braces and even whole trusses have been cut away or removed. A great chimney stack may have been taken away, leaving tell-tale soot marks where there were once flues, and trimmed openings in the ceilings—the whole perhaps giving clues to the cause of a leaning gable above.

A heavy chandelier pulling dangerously loose at its support from the plaster ceiling

Door frame dropping at its hinge side with opening mitre joints, produces a tapering gap above the door. The top rail of the door has already been cut to adapt it, but the movement has continued

Lead gutter with a half-hearted coating of pitch or asphalt: this not only fails to exclude the weather, but conceals the whereabouts of defects in the leadwork

At the eaves, a mediaeval timber frame may be revealed behind a later red-brick Georgian facing. Perhaps the existence of hearths in what is now a roof-space will show a building to have been reduced in height. The ventilation, dryness and cleanliness of the roof space should all be noted, together with the cause of every defect.

Passing to the floor below, each room in turn will then be inspected, and its ceiling, wall and floor finishes, joinery, windows, fireplaces, fittings, services and decorations, and any special features all carefully noted, with comments on their condition and repair.

The architect should be prepared to lift linoleum and boarding at frequent intervals, particularly in areas near external rainwater pipes, under internal roof gutters and at all similar danger points. The adequacy of subfloor ventilation will be checked, the size, material and condition of members noted, and timbers such as wallplates tapped and probed with a penknife. 'Dead' sounding timbers are always suspect, and a sharp watch will be kept for the tell-tale piles of bore-dust and for the clean, bright exit holes which denote active beetle attack. Surprisingly often the direction of floor boards proves to be misleading, an original and worn floor having been 'cased' with later boarding in a crosswise direction. In this event before any holes or inspection traps are cut, it will be wise to check whether the older boarding underneath

Piles of bore-dust indicate that beetle activity in the flooring remains alive

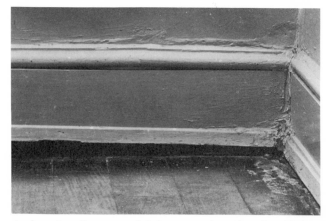

A dropping floor revealed by a crack under the skirting. This suggests trouble from rotting timbers, especially at their bearings on the walls

Worn and beetle-eaten floorboarding. Where necessary, patches should always renew a complete board at a time

could with advantage be opened up and carefully repaired. But in all too many cases, defective and beetle-infested boarding will prove to have been simply encased with new wood without any attempt at eradicating the pest; and frequently both old and new wood will now be infested. Inspection holes must be large enough to insert one's head and a torch, so as to reveal as much as possible of the surrounding structure. The condition of timbers and the bearing of heavy beams near fireplaces may call for special notice and remark, especially if damage has been caused to chimneys and flues, for example by slow-combustion stoves or oil-fired heaters.

If for any reason part of the structure is inaccessible, this fact should be carefully noted: and it may be helpful to collect together a list of enquiries and requests for keys, for a final sally with the building owner.

At ground level, the architect will note the nature of the subsoil and foundations (if any), the damp-proof courses, (again, if any) site cover and subfloor ventilation, and the existence of any special features like sealed or open wells. The presence of cellars should always be suspected, whether or not they are known to the owners; and an open eye must be kept for rising damp, such as may have

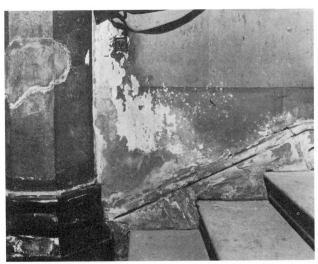

Rising damp, drawn upwards is here damaging decorative finishes

Heating pipes run through a basement with characteristic moulded openings

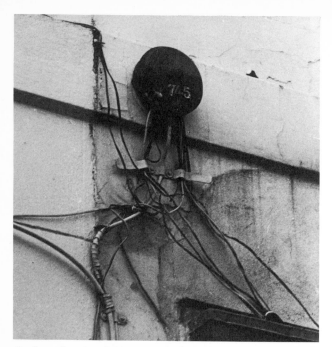

Surface electric wiring: a typical tangle

Plumbers' joy: more 'spaghetti' on a building

been caused by any normal water-table of the surrounding ground, or by natural underground water movements.

Cellars are indeed almost invariably under-ventilated as well as damp, and this is in innumerable cases due simply to the thoughtless blocking of ventilators, sometimes by flower-beds and sometimes simply for added winter warmth.

The condition of manholes gives a good indication of the state of the drains. The sewage disposal or collection arrangements will need at least inspection if not testing, and so will details like lightning conductors, provisions for fire-fighting, water supply and tanks, and the general state of electrical installations. If a full electrical report is needed, this can be supplied by the authorities at reasonable charges, varying with the amount of work involved.

When an occupant has lived in a building for very many years, or particularly if there is perhaps an elderly and trusted maintenance hand, it will be invaluable for him to accompany the architect on his inspection, when a whole mine of half-forgotten details and memories may be uncovered.[1]

During the whole of a visit, a weather eye will meanwhile be kept open for old pictures and plans of the house, often framed and almost forgotten, and quite irreplaceable as archives.

Lastly after finding one's spectacles, discarding used batteries and shaking off the cobwebs, the only remaining duties are to thank the hostess, note the telephone number and the names of people met, and to write promising or enclosing the Report.

The Report The subsequent sifting and winnowing of all the information garnered is best undertaken while fresh in the memory, and preferably on the way home.

The purpose of the Report must once again be clearly studied, with regard for its scope, emphasis and presentation. If it is to be read to a Committee, it must either be succinct and short, or else must gather the main facts into a short final summary. If it is required to arm a prospective

[1] At the same time, beware of the owner who has lived with a crack for thirty years before the heady stimulation of the architect's visit inspires him to notice it! Some tenants catalogues of complaints reach a crescendo of justified relish during an inspection; all are worth hearing, but comments about the Landlord, while often justified, equally often deserve a pinch of salt. The architect or surveyor will certainly wish to spend some of his visit 'on his own with the building', and to avoid offence, this can usually be explained at the outset.

owner, any long and lugubrious catalogue of local points of decay should in fairness to the building be lightened by a proper appreciation of the offsetting virtues and advantages. A purely historical description is best set out in chronological sequence. No general rules can be made, except to consider the needs of the recipient, and how these may best be met.

It is at this point most important to distinguish between the requirements of a Report and a Specification. The Report must aim at giving to the lay owner the clearest possible picture of the building its history and condition, and the nature and relative urgency of any repairs. A Specification is a document prepared so as to obtain competitive tenders, and to place a legal contract. If properly detailed advice and full supervision are likely to be needed in carrying out the recommended repairs, now is the time to say so. Nothing is so heartbreaking as to see repairs badly executed even after careful outline recommendations have been made; and there is no substitute for thorough supervision.

A Report will usually advance from the general to the particular. From an historical survey or appreciation of a building's setting and landscaping, it will move on to describe its materials and construction, before particularising about individual joys and faults. There may be a detailed description of the exterior and a floor-by-floor account of the interior, described under whatever headings seem most appropriate. Lastly will follow details of fittings and services, and possibly of furnishings.

The description of the fabric and the architect's comments about its condition may either be woven together with the description, or should preferably follow separately, after the facts, as a matter of opinion. It is particularly important to group any matters of conjecture, or needing further exploration. If possible and prudent, at least a general idea of cost should always be given; and if detailed figures are required, estimates may be obtained and set down in tabulated form; listing their sources and date, and noting any limitations. If the Report is likely to be required in any application for grant aid, the expenditure can be particularised in some such form as (a) the urgent and essential, (b) the necessary but less urgent, and (c) the 'desirable'—a dreamboat category, often the first sacrifice

to cold truth. At all events, it is important to stress the relative urgencies of all work recommended, so that easy and attractive items do not steal the golden egg, at the expense of unseen but more vital ones.

Recommendations should be as definite and specific as possible—particularly in describing any works which an owner may undertake to do for himself. So, for example, in commending the removal of ivy from a wall, one must remember to explain that the plant should first be killed and left to shrink, and only later stripped, when it is dead. It is again important that where for lack of access not every part of a building could be fully, inspected, this

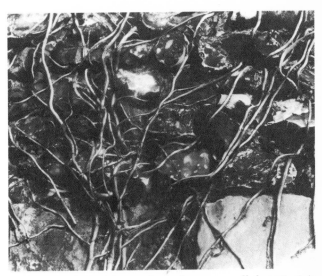

Ivy roots seek out joints and can destroy a wall, but Virginia creeper is less destructive

should be clearly stated in the subsequent report. Above all there is always the possibility of hidden local dry-rot, which might later spread to involve the whole of a building. Whereas it may be an architect's duty to examine everything reasonably accessible for inspection, it is simply not practicable to dismantle a building entirely for the purpose. The architect will thus clearly state the limits of his responsibility and of his inspection. It is total folly to suggest that a building 'is free from dry-rot' when what is meant is merely that 'no evidence of dry-rot was seen' and it is helpful to draw attention to any points which should nevertheless be watched. Any formal disclaimer should form part of the main body of a Report, or must be noted as an enclosure.

Before a full historical report can be made, research may be necessary into archives and old maps. The Map-Room at the British Museum, whose staff are always glad to advise by prior appointment, may offer valuable data on the growth and history of the buildings. Further useful sources of information include histories and guides, such as the proceedings of local archaeological societies, the Surveys of the Royal Commission on Historical Monuments and the Victoria County Histories. By reading these after visiting and not before, there is a much greater opportunity of producing a useful and original survey.

The Council for Places of Worship has a collection of past Reports and Specifications for Church repairs dating back to 1917, and the Society for the Protection of Ancient Buildings has records dating back to 1878.

The presentation of the Report is worth care. A standard size and format such as A4 is desirable. A heavy grade of paper should be used, to withstand handling, and pages are best stitched together—brass fasteners and clips tend to catch up other papers and are a nuisance. If detailed sub-reports are needed on engineering services, or on specialist trades such as past eradication or leadwork repair, these can also be included.

A Report should wherever possible be illustrated; and any drawings should be bound up together with it and noted as an enclosure, to avoid separation or loss. Dyeline prints, being liable to fade, may not be satisfactory: 'true-to-scales' are more durable and presentable. Photographs may well be attached within the main body of the Report, but must be properly washed and suitably mounted with tissue or colourless latex—never with animal glues. Excellent photographs can often be obtained at very reasonable charges from the National Monuments Record. To a recipient who has not seen the building, the illustrations will bring a report to life and give essential flesh to its otherwise dry bones.

When a Report is intended for consideration by a Committee, several copies will be welcomed, and these may be needed in advance, for distribution; in any case, the organising Secretary will appreciate advance notice, so as to be able to arrange for its inclusion in the Agenda. Any valuable Report, or one which may have legal consequences, should always be posted by recorded delivery.

3.2   Specifications for repair work

The next main document to be prepared is the Specification, defining and describing the exact nature of the job to be done, the materials used and the legal responsibilities of all concerned, as a part of the Contract.

The preliminaries of a repair specification should thus first make particularly clear the responsibilities of the employer and contractor concerning insurance and the protection of the structure and personnel, and all arrangements made for the mutual convenience of contractors and occupiers. Typical clauses are suggested in the appendix to this section. On the other hand it is all too easy, by providing in the preliminary clauses for every possible contingency from treasure trove to the disposal of uncovered human remains, to convey a vastly inflated idea of the complexity of the job. In a working specification, it is necessary to be realistic and crystal-clear about all reasonably likely day-to-day hazards. In repair work, the specification is generally intended mostly for the guidance of the site foreman; and it should for this reason repeat any instructions already contained within the Form of Contract which the foreman will need to know.

In proceeding to the detailed instructions, it is important to give full information, but without repetition and confusion. If fair competition is intended, it is difficult to be too exact in stating the requirements: but confusing demands and stipulations can only result in inflated estimates.

Whereas in new work and for taking-off Bills of Quantities, a grouping of works under trades is preferred, there is no doubt that in old buildings, the most convenient way is to set out the works on a room-by-room basis. The inter-relation and extent of works can then be readily grasped 'at a glance' on the site. If a pricing column is added throughout the specification, individual costs can also be entered against each item, which is generally in practice the most useful arrangement.

Everything should as far as possible be specified in its

natural building order: thus protection and shoring are first described in detail, followed by demolition and removal, and then new work. With each item, materials, construction and finishes should be noted, together with their relationship with the existing. Disposal instructions and credits for fittings, etc, removed must be clearly given. In phrasing individual sentences, it is always clearest to work from the whole to the part. Poor specifications abound in such phrases as 'Fix salvaged basin taken down as elsewhere specified on east wall, and shorten or lengthen hot and cold pipes and waste branches, all as necessary', and 'Hang old re-used door from pantry in 4 in × $1\frac{1}{2}$ in frame in new opening in north wall with 6 in × 3 in lintel over.' It would have been more helpful to say, 'Turn off hot and cold mains, disconnect plumbing, remove and re-fix lavatory basin in new position on east wall; adapt and re-connect hot and cold water supplies and waste branch,' and 'In north wall, insert 300 × 150 mm lintel and cut away to form new doorway opening; line with 100 × 36mm rebated deal frame, primed for painting, to receive salvaged door from pantry.' Then the foreman knows just where he is, and with the least possible fuss. The word 'existing' should be retained for parts of the building which will remain existing after alteration— 'disused' or 'previous' or 'demolished' is otherwise less misleading for everyone.

The extent of detailed direction which the architect will wish to give, and conversely of initiative in dealing with day-to-day problems which the foreman is required to display, must somehow clearly be conveyed by the terms of the specification. Where work must be inspected before it is covered, this should be clearly laid down. Where samples of materials are to be approved, or qualities and colours selected before use, the specification must make this entirely clear.

Some typical general clauses useful in specifying repair work

CONTRACTORS AND SUB-CONTRACTORS: The whole of the work, including specialist sub-contracts to be carried out by nominated sub-contractors, is to be undertaken as the responsibility of the main contractor, Messrs —— ——. The main contractor shall be responsible for synchronising the work of all sub-contractors in such a way that the whole of the work is executed in the best, most efficient and expeditious manner.

PROTECTION: This house is of great architectural importance, and contains decorations and furnishings of the utmost value. It is essential, therefore, that the greatest possible care will be taken throughout the repair works to eliminate every possibility of damage to the fabric and contents from any cause whatsoever. Particular care will be necessary to avoid all accidental damage to original window glazing, by means of careful close screening and protection.

The contractor shall be responsible for arranging with the owner's agents for the removal, storage and replacement of all articles which would otherwise be exposed in any way to damage, and must ensure that this has been done before the relevant work is commenced.

The contractor is to provide and maintain, throughout the whole period of the works, all necessary supports, shores, hoardings, etc, necessary for the complete protection of the building, its decorations, contents and furnishings, and all persons from all harm whatsoever arising from the works, and is to be responsible for the complete repair at his own expense of all damage occasioned at any time during the progress of the work.

The contractor shall similarly throughout take all reasonable precautions to avoid damage to the adjoining properties and public or private roadways, to be made good promptly at his own expense.

RUBBISH: The building will remain inhabited, and every effort is to be made to reduce mess and disturbance to a minimum. All materials and equipment are to be inconspicuously stored and all rubbish cleared away at intervals, the building and environs being kept as clean and tidy as possible.

SCAFFOLDING: All scaffolding is to be non-ferrous. It is to be erected, securely constructed, maintained and carefully dismantled so as to avoid all damage whatsoever to the building, its decorations, contents and furnishings.

SALVAGE: Appropriate credits are to be allowed for all re-usable or saleable materials and fittings removed from the site; and all other salvaged items are to be stored as directed.

No salvaged materials whatsoever shall be taken from the site without written consent. Proper weighbridge certificates, witnessed by a representative of the estate staff, shall be obtained for all old lead removed, for credits at rates to be negotiated.

ACCESS: All parts of the site and buildings except those immediately under repair are to be out of bounds to all operatives. Access routes to roofs and all other repair works are to be strictly as agreed with the architect. All external doors are to be locked nightly.

The contractor will be responsible for keeping all persons under his control, including men employed by sub-contractors and all unauthorised persons within bounds, and will be liable for all damage for adjoining premises and property, estate roads and planting and vegetation, by lorries, workmen or any cause. Any damage occasioned shall be made good at the contractor's own cost.

FIRE PRECAUTIONS: Although insurance can cover financial loss, it cannot replace an historic building. Fully adequate fire protection is therefore to be discussed and agreed with the local Fire Officer and maintained throughout the works by the provision of plentiful hoses, fire extinguishers, and other equipment sufficient for any emergency which might arise. No smoking whatever shall be allowed in any building; and any operative not complying with this requirement shall be instantly dismissed.[1] Extreme care must be taken with blowlamps and similar apparatus, and when using flammable materials.

PROGRESS CHART: The contractor shall within four weeks of the date of the order to commence operations produce in agreement with the architect a detailed programme charting the whole of the works, to be followed in their subsequent execution. One copy shall be forwarded to the architect and one maintained on site and kept up to date by the prompt and regular recording of progress. All modifications subsequently found necessary shall be discussed and agreed with the architect at each site meeting.

PROGRAMMING: Dates of commencement and completion of each part of the work together with all anticipated disturbances or requirements shall be notified in advance to the architect in sufficient time for agreement with the

[1] Applicable where extreme care is necessary.

owner or his agent. The work shall be so arranged as to allow the most efficient use of equipment and interrelation of trades, for the best quality work, and with a minimum of nuisance to occupants and visitors.

PAYMENT: Fixed prices shall be negotiated for all measurable parts of the work; and in the absence of agreement, the employer reserves the right to obtain competitive estimates. Payment for all other work shall be based upon the contracted Schedule of Rates.

All daywork sheets, vouchers, receipts, weighbridge dockets and other records of time and materials spent and recovered throughout the works are to be submitted for inspection by the architect and/or surveyor with each certificate application, and no claim for payment will be entertained unless properly so substantiated. The contractor shall at the same time also render up-to-date itemised and detailed forecasts of future costs estimated for the whole of the remainder of the work, to include all contingencies. This is of the utmost importance as the total expenditure cannot be increased, and must throughout be regulated accordingly.

3.3 Selecting a contractor

The next architectural hurdle to be taken—always the most difficult at the beginning of a job—is, of course, the selection of suitable contractors.

The names of likely firms are usually obtained either (a) from personal knowledge of the architect or of his client, (b) from trade organisations, such as local branches of the NFBTE, or (c) by recommendation, eg of other architects or one of the specialist registers of bodies like those earlier quoted.

In either case a letter will next be sent to discover whether firms are interested in tendering, and inquiring what jobs of similar character have *recently* been done, and the names of architects from whom references may be obtained. A telephoned personal inquiry will then give a useful quick picture of a firm and its special characteristics and capacities.

The first and most essential criterion is complete reliability, since no matter how brilliant or cheap a firm may be, it is useless if promises cannot be trusted. Given this, the next requirement is a staff of suitable size, and including the right trades for the efficient execution of the particular job in hand. In a really large repair programme, a sizeable firm will have the advantage of being able to draw upon experienced tradesmen in a variety of fields, and upon a variety of plant such as scaffolding from its own yard. But too large an organisation will inevitably have a more commercial outlook and less personal interest in the job. It is almost always best to select a firm as small as possible, compatible with the work to be done. An interview on the site will meanwhile quickly enable the architect to gauge whether the local builder is potentially interested in the building as a building, or only the job as a job!

The key man in the whole operation will always be, the working foreman. It is impossible for the architect to be constantly on the site, and many important decisions in detail must be left to the man on the spot. In the smaller firm of some 20 men, the foreman may himself be one of the principals, fully cognisant with the financial side, as well as with every other aspect of the work. In any event, a high degree of intelligence and initiative will be called for. On the leader's attitude and cheerfulness will depend much of the attitude of the workmen. On a cold afternoon in miserable weather, decaying structure can be a depressing sight; and it is just then that, in the absence of someone really sympathetic to the needs of the job, valuable original work can all too easily be lost.

Is it best to entrust the repair of historic buildings only to contractors with wide experience of this type of job? Obviously where this can be done, and where the firm is really interested, good work is more readily assured. But if only 'known' firms are used, the difficulty of finding contractors is greatly intensified, and the incentives of free competition are lost. In special cases such as dry-rot eradication work, a specialist firm's guarantee may be sought. But except for extremely specialised work such as steeplejacking, most building firms of any repute should really be able to tackle the great majority of repair and restoration jobs. Further, it is always an incomparable advantage for an owner to have at hand in the future some local firm with real knowledge of and interest in a building. Maintenance, in a way, can then become something of a 'family concern', and a sense of responsibility and security will be encouraged.

Steeplejacking is dangerous work: cleaning the flaming finial of London's Monument

Where a firm has had no previous experience of work on old buildings, frequent site visits may at first be necessary; but once the principles of the work are grasped and appreciated, the workmen will enjoy their new sense of individuality and craftsmanship. The constructional repair of an old building indeed often provides quite a challenge to present-day skills. The opposite point of view, and one which equally has a place, appears in the formation of direct labour squads, rather on the guild pattern, with local trained craftsmen working together and moving from job to job as a mobile *corps de secours*. There are also individual travelling craftsmen in trades such as roof plumbing, masonry and wood carving, who specialise in work on old buildings, moving around the country and

Lead: a roof plumber's forecast of his workmanship

living in close touch with their work. Every effort should clearly be made to encourage this very desirable practice. For personal and family reasons, the arrangement is usually more successful when there is sufficient work of a given trade within a small geographical area. This is not always easy to achieve; and when too long deprived of contact with his fellows, there is also a tendency for the lonely worker to develop a kind of 'outcast virtuoso' complex. The guild or group system is generally the best. For particularly specialist work such as the repair of stained glass, organs, clocks and the like, it is usually necessary to call in a specialist, to be employed under a sub-contract to the main local builder. Registers of craftsmen are maintained by bodies such as the Council for Places of Worship and the Council for Small Industries in Rural Areas.

Is it generally advisable to sub-contract lead recasting, masonry and similar trades? If the work is sufficiently complex, the equipment and stockyard facilities of a specialist single-trade firm may enable them to quote competitively for this aspect of the work. But the main contractor should also be given a chance of tendering, if he is really capable of the work, if only to avoid any suspicion of partiality on the part of the employer or his architect. In the later stages of a contract, especially when economies are having to be made, it is so often difficult to avoid jealousies, in which the other firm is always the profiteer.

Then there is the question of geographical location. What is a reasonable daily travelling distance? Thirty miles is generally regarded as a maximum radius: but the just-around-the-corner firm has a great advantage. A vanload of highly-paid tradesmen in a traffic-jam is neither productive nor economic. Many firms whose work is widely spread are in fact now maintaining a trained itinerant labour force, who stay on the job during the week. The cost of accommodation may balance favourably with the cost of travel, when a longer and more undivided day can be worked. Living conditions are important, and somewhere warm, dry and sociable in free time is essential. To meet the lodgings difficulty, many firms are now providing caravans for their operatives. Good living conditions are an essential background to good work.

3.4 Clerk of works

Another question is 'should a clerk of works be employed?' The answer must depend on the nature and the extent of the works, and the quality of the contractors. If a really extensive and concentrated programme of work is being undertaken, the clerk of works will be invaluable in giving day-to-day decisions in the architect's absence, and in keeping a watching brief over the interests of the owner. But a clerk of works, with his accommodation and facilities, is a large bird in the nest. The expense of his retention must clearly be justified in terms of commensurate savings, if this luxury is to be afforded. Generally the smaller or slower job cannot stand the additional overheads, and the whole burden of responsibility and supervision must be shouldered by the architect. The ideal case occurs where, by virtue of a busy maintenance programme on many buildings in a single ownership, an organisation can afford to retain a clerk of works permanently on its staff. He then, as well as supervising general maintenance works under direct labour, can also be responsible for the daily visit and occasional tricky decision which the smaller job may need.

Enquiries regarding the recruitment of clerks of works may be made from the Institute of Clerks of Works,[1] which maintains a Register of current vacancies. The Institute is an examining body and has published a salary scale, recommending graded salaries depending upon the intricacy and size of the contract. There is no Code of Practice for Clerks of Works; but the Institute has issued a useful guide to the duties and responsibilities which its members are expected to undertake.

3.5 Architect and builder

As in all building work, it is always good practice to meet each firm separately on the site before prices are tendered. Special difficulties, such as access for machinery, the disposal of demolition products and the avoidance of disturbance, can then be discussed, and the scope and details of the work clearly understood. The remainder of the tendering process follows the normal pattern, separate dates being allotted for visiting, and the drawings and specifications returned with the tender. Even more than in new buildings, contractors should be made to feel welcome to suggest any variations which their own staffing or special facilities may suggest, and which might have a significant effect on the cost of a job. Secondhand materials or fittings may, for example, be available, and possibly very suitable for re-use in an existing building. Specific dates for the work must be stated or tendered. If identical tenders are received—as not infrequently occurs with cost-plus rates—contractors should be given an equal chance of re-tendering, which gives fair opportunity to any firm particularly keen on the job.

In notifying the acceptance of a tender to all the contractors, it is usual to give the figures; and any proviso such as the obtaining of Grants should always be mentioned. It is too often forgotten that a contractor takes much unpaid trouble over a tender; and it is only fair that he should be promptly and properly thanked for his work.

Where the fixed-price contract is adopted, it is, of course, notorious that any 'extras' are always more expensive than work originally tendered for; and in compiling the bills for this type of contract, the greatest care must be taken

to check and countercheck the inclusion of every item which is likely to be needed.

3.6 Phasing of work

Where for reasons of urgency part of the work must start immediately, it is sometimes possible to divide the job into more than one contract, competitive tenders being obtained for each in turn. The preliminary contract can, for example, deal with demolition and site clearance and the salvaging of useful materials, while that for the main work is still being negotiated. Even this cannot be done efficiently until a fairly clear idea is obtained of the eventual programme; and great care is needed to prevent over-lapping, or the inclusion in earlier contracts of work which may later have to be altered or undone. Really urgent work, such as the repair of a fast-leaking roof, or the eradication of dry rot, often cannot wait for quantities and must be done under the best terms negotiable. But usually the reinstatement of finishes is then easy to measure, and is best taken to tender.

In general, despite the demoralising effect of the mounting spiral of wages and materials costs, it is always an economy to avoid rushing into bricks and mortar until the ultimate scope of works has been decided in detail. Conversion work demands the most careful planning, and cannot be properly done in haste.

3.7 Forms of contract

What form of contract is most appropriate, for work on old buildings? Where the Survey has been a thorough one, there are very few instances where a Lump-Sum contract cannot be applied. This must include clearly stated item prices, set out either against a Bill of Quantities or, in smaller jobs, a suitable Schedule of Works. In the latter case, it is essential to secure and agree in addition a really adequate Schedule of Unit Rates.

As in the case of a Specification, the Bill of Quantities is best dealt with room-by-room. This assists in identifying individual items necessitating remeasurement, whose amount rather than definition it may later be found necessary to vary. A dayworks item will be included, and can advantageously be substantial to attract competitive pricing, in preference to a high contingencies allowance,

[1] Institute of Clerks of Works of Great Britain Incorporated, 6 Highway Court, London, N5.

which is merely a stated financial provision without any competitive pricing element.

The Schedule of Works must again be as detailed as possible, defining each building operation in a clear-cut fashion to make everything easily identifiable. The Schedule of Rates can well be supplied by the architect, for the contractor to price on a comparable basis: this will be applied for variations (including contingencies) but not for dayworks.

For Contracts on a lump-sum basis, always greatly to be preferred, the RIBA Standard Form (with or without quantities) is applicable. A decision must be taken on whether or not to delete the 'fluctuations' clause, making the threat of rising prices in effect an incentive to early completion, but bearing in mind that the contractor who lacks this protection must cover himself otherwise in tendering. The real object of any good contract is after all, to reduce and as far as possible avoid all uncertainty. The Small Works form can be a useful if less specific basis for signature in appropriate cases.

In occasional instances, it may well be that from an unavoidable lack of professional involvement and hence of data, or from considerations of extreme urgency, only a Cost-Plus Contract can be agreed. In this instance, the RIBA Standard Form can only with difficulty and much ink-work be suitably doctored.

Rarely, a Cost plus Fixed Fee contract is applicable. The Contractor is in this way assured of least a minimum return, while he is offered an incentive to keep within the contract total: but again, no standard form is available.

Should the client be a Government Department, special forms are applicable; and payment is authorised by certificates and by the signature of the nominated architect (defined as the 'supervising officer').

3.8 Cost control

The aim should always be a firm, Lump Sum Contract, restricting dayworks to a minimum.

In instances where cost-plus arrangements are unavoidable, detailed daywork sheets provide a mine of information about the work—and the workmen—and it is the architect's duty not only to check the figures, but by analysing the sheets to find out exactly what is going on.

Throughout any job, it is important to keep the client properly informed of financial progress, not only in terms of money spent but by up-to-date estimates of future expenditure. A regular system of financial statements and cost reports should be insisted upon, in the spirit of control rather than crisis and cure, and the client kept fully posted of anything unexpected. 'Contingencies' under the contract must be clearly understood, in fact, as a specific provision for unforeseen changes found necessary to complete the work as originally contemplated—not merely as a handy pool of reserve money to meet additions in the scope of the work. When there is a fixed budget, arrangements can be made for the most important or difficult works to be done first, and if necessary for compensating the estimates as work proceeds by less important omissions from the initial programme. In old buildings work, the greatest problem is always 'to know just where to stop'.

The duration of a job is sometimes even more difficult to control than its cost. The 'liquidated damages' clause of the RIBA contract is always a difficult one to enforce, owing to the constant occurrence of the expected but unforeseeable problems and difficulties which almost inevitably arise—perhaps more in old buildings work than in any other—and can then always be quoted against it.

When the architect is fortunate in maintaining a practical working partnership with reliable and experienced quantity surveyors, a great deal of this control will be a matter of understood and joint routine.

The estimating and contract side of old buildings work is so much a matter of experience, and life is so short, that it does seem a pity that the practical experience of the profession in this respect cannot in some way be more effectively pooled. Careful analytical study of the up-to-date comparative costs of such jobs as the re-laying of copper or lead on roofs would be of value to everyone. There should be little difficulty in maintaining an index of current repair and maintenance prices for the most repetitive jobs and typical trades, in terms of unit rates. Such an analysis would be of the greatest possible value both to individual architects and surveyors, many of whom may receive only the occasional large repair job on which to judge other estimates, and also in the much greater problem of assessing the cost of repairs for the nation.

3.9 Site organisation and control

In the early stages of any job, but particularly where an occupied existing building is concerned, there is a great deal of preliminary organisation detail to be agreed on the site by the architect; and in this respect there is no substitute for frequent personal visits to the site.

It is, however, important to consider which points are the architect's responsibility, and which will be left to the contractor. The architect's first concern will be with the convenience of his client and the scope and quality of the work in progress. The contractor is a specialist in organising building operations, with regard to maximum efficiency and economy. Between them, and with the quantity surveyor if there is one, the two form a working team, each accepting certain responsibilities. In this there is a distinction between the new building and the repair job. In the new building, the contractor tenders against measured quantities of labour and materials of a specified standard; and the architect's main duty is to ensure that these are supplied. In repair work, on-the-spot decisions must be given regarding the work as it develops; and it is the architect's job to give technical advice, to see fair play and to ensure good work.

A distinction should here be drawn between the fixed price contract and the cost plus or direct labour job. A builder who has undertaken to complete specified work at a fixed price will wish to carry the entire responsibility for organising the work in the most efficient and economical manner. The architect need then satisfy himself only that his specification is complete, and that the order of work is in the best interests of the building and of his client. But with work on a time-and-materials basis, where there is no financial incentive to the builder to economise, the architect must himself ensure that the work is being carried out in the most expeditious way; and it is his business to assist with the actual organisation of the job. In either case, the terms of the contract and specification must make it entirely clear at whose door each responsibility lies. There are, in effect, three spheres of responsibility. It should not be necessary for the architect to inquire about such items as workmen's insurances, which are entirely the concern of the contractor. The responsibility for fire precautions and for all protection and shoring must also rest with the contractor: but since neither insurance repayments nor the contractor's reinstatement can replace an old building, the architect will wish to assure himself that every proper care is in fact being taken.

Insurances against possible fire and theft in an existing building are the responsibility of the employer; but it is the architect's duty to make sure this is fully appreciated, and clearly stated in the contract.

The first point to be settled on the site is the question of site facilities for workmen. In an occupied building, the architect must make sure that the minimum of disturbance will be caused thereby to his client. Permanent or temporary latrines and their siting will be agreed, and a suitable site office and telephone arranged. A supply of water and possibly a gas ring below stairs will be earmarked for the contractor. Access routes to all parts of the work will be agreed and, if possible, reserved for his use and control. Storage facilities under lock and key are extremely useful, and should particularly be allocated when valuable materials such as old leadwork are on site: in an inhabited building, the key to this can well be in the charge of the owner. On a deserted site or an empty building in built-up areas, it may be an economy for the contractor to engage a night-watchman: if irreplaceable old work is endangered, the architect may wish to insist on this as a condition of contract.

In work on occupied buildings, it is more than ever essential for the contractor to maintain a close co-operation with the owner and occupiers. Building work is dirty and tiresome to the house-proud; and plaster dust finds its way through every crack and crevice in the most unbelievable way. Building equipment must be kept out of harm's way, and paths kept clear for tradesmen and family visitors. Poisonous chemicals and vapours must be kept away from foodstuffs, and diplomatic relations maintained with the children and even the household pets. Most building

Pinnacle in splints at Westminster Abbey

contractor: but the architect must ensure that the maximum care is taken of an old building. Features such as valuable old stained glass and statuary are often irreplaceable, and must be carefully shielded from harm by stretched tarpaulins, close boarding or by padding with sacks of straw. Vulnerable materials such as roof leadwork must be protected from damage by nailed boots and dropped tools, and here again close boarding is the best defence. Adequate and inexpensive shoring may call for a good deal of resourcefulness. Quite light structures of boarding and wire ropes can be of great value, if only they are in exactly the right place. A firm frame of struts must somehow be contrived to give the maximum support, either from the ground or from firmer parts of the structure. If the shoring is efficiently designed on a triangulated system, the joints can be merely pinned like Meccano; or non-ferrous tubular scaffolding may be used. When the two faces of a wall have become dissociated, it will, however, be necessary to provide continuous support by means such as close boarding on one or both faces of the damaged area. In general, it is always wise for shoring to

Crown glazing has an inimitable 'life' and sparkle and can no longer be obtained. It demands screening to avoid damage during building work

occupants, however, are only too willing to help with facilities for preparing tea and the like, and to take an interest in the comfort of the workmen. Indeed for all the difficulties, it will often prove that work in an inhabited building is very much more amenable than in a gaunt and deserted one.

Shoring and protection are the legal responsibility of the

Rede Church, Suffolk; raking shores support close-boarding to retain the parting outer face of flint walling

err on the side of over-generosity, for prevention is the only possible cure.

In an existing old building, it is essential that the contractor should be taking extreme care against all possibility of fire. Firstly, the local fire officer should be contacted: he is always glad to advise without charge on the fire risks and fire-fighting provisions which should be made. Whatever extinguishers and equipment are recommended should be constantly in good repair, and 'at the ready'. Workmen must be trained not to throw matches about; and when particularly valuable work is concerned, or where flammable insecticides are being used, it may be necessary to ban smoking altogether. It must be made someone's responsibility to ensure that everything is in order every time the site is left for the night. It is impossible to be too careful: Coleshill was lost to a small blowlamp—and what is gone is lost for ever.

3.10   Use of scaffolding and plant

In cost plus or direct labour contracts, the architect will interest himself in matters which are normally the contractor's sole concern. The actual programming of the work can make the greatest difference to its ultimate cost, and the extent and utilisation of plant are worth careful thought.

If electric light is eventually to be installed, it is always an advantage to take the opportunity of providing the service at the outset. Adequate light is invaluable: it is impossible to do good work under dim lighting, and what may at first appear to be a positive profligacy in this direction will be found to repay handsomely in terms of time saved and quality of work. Electric hand-tools can save a great deal of time, and may sometimes be the only means of reaching inaccessible corners.

Another decision will be whether or not to use scaffolding.

Ingenious and economical access scaffolding enables a church to be entered from a clerestory window and is suspended from the vaulting

Fire precautions are essential during any contract. Coleshill, a major monument of British domestic architecture, is said to have been lost to a decorator's blow-lamp

Again, while not cheap, this does enable such savings in time and labour that it is usually worth while, especially where any heavy work is concerned. The general contractor may possess or hire his own scaffolding, or a specialist subcontractor can be invited to do the job. In the latter case, although the scaffolding will be erected with astonishing speed, some form of understanding is needed regarding minor alterations once it is in place. These may be frequent, and should not have to wait for a specialist visit, when much time can be wasted. Scaffolding contractors are naturally anxious to guard their responsibilities regarding extensive alterations; but it should be possible to reach agreement on this point. The scaffolding may be erected in slightly higher stages than are usual in new building; and care must be taken to avoid damage by the movement of loose members, or chafing of ropes during the work, and especially during the delivery and dismantling of scaffolding. Where very extensive scaffolding is employed, it may be an economy to speed up the programme in view of the reduction in hire charges.

Another device worth considering in roof repairs is the temporary cover roof. Constructed of tubular scaffolding or timber framing, and covered in corrugated iron or perspex, this obviates the need for tarpaulins and provides free access to the whole of a roof for uninterrupted work. When serious and expensive harm might otherwise be caused to internal finishes by rainwater, the cost of the added security and convenience is amply repaid. Two disadvantages should be mentioned: in summer, a cover roof is hot, and may make the use of insecticides uncomfortable; and in winter, care must be taken to prevent the whole roof acting as a sail and 'taking off', with possibly disastrous results. Sometimes, only a part of the cover roof need be used at a time: the disposal of rainwater must then be carefully arranged, during any periods while normal roof gutters are temporarily out of service.

The safety of his workmen is a paramount concern for the contractor—or in direct labour work, for the employer and his architect. All ladders must be properly tied for safety, as well as being padded to avoid damage to the building. Aluminium ladders, owing to their springiness and sharp ends, can mark stonework quite seriously if not protected; the rubber end chocks sometimes fitted are slippery in wet

Good scaffolding carrying a transparent cover roof, allows continuous work in all weathers

weather. Wooden ladders *must* be left unpainted, so that cracks can be readily seen. Incidentally, never climb a ladder holding the rungs: there may be one missing. Access and scaffolding boards 'walk' unless they are properly tied, and may easily provide dangerous traps and see-saws. Except in extreme circumstances, the use of lifts and hoists should be rigorously restricted to materials. There is no excuse for risking the lives of workmen.

Every precaution must, of course, be taken by the contractor to preclude danger or nuisance to the public and others, including any unwitting occupants of buildings who may thoughtlessly open windows in dangerous positions. Adequate close-boarded platforms and tarpaulins are necessary to prevent danger from flying chips and dropped tools. Proper warning notices are required by law, as are red warning lamps at night time on scaffoldings in any public way.

Everything possible should be done to encourage the co-operation of the individual workman. The personal interest of the owner and his architect in the way the work is done, and their sympathy with the difficulties and achievements of the job, are the workman's rightful due, and will be reflected in the quality of every detail. The architect, as well as the foreman, should know the names and skills of every specialist in the team. In the vast new building, this is impossible, but in the repair of a historic building, it is essential.

3.11 Drawings, correspondence and certificates

From the point of view of the architect's office arrangements, preservation work is broadly similar to new building. More site visiting is involved, and all instructions must of course as soon as possible be confirmed in writing. Sketch drawings and details are often more conveniently made on the site, and these and handwritten notes agreed with the foreman at the time of visiting are perfectly adequate if a copy is kept for filing purposes.

Although frequent and observant site visits are of more importance in old buildings work than chests full of drawings, a thorough survey-drawing is always worth the effort. Where conversion work is not extensive, the same survey negative may often later be adapted as a working drawing, if sufficient prints have first been taken off for all needs. Pencil tracings are easily altered but far less clear than ink negatives. Ink drawings may well be freehand and, if on heavy tracing paper, can be altered repeatedly without suffering overmuch. Another method of quickly revising a drawing is to obtain a true-to-scale print on tracing paper, from which unwanted detail can be deleted by the printer: the new negative can then be completed and printed with little loss of quality. The linen negative is rarely justified, except where great permanence is required. True-to-scale prints cost little more than dyelines, and give excellent service on the site. It is often convenient for drawings to be kept to a small and standard size such as A4 or A3, when they may be bound together with a Specification or Bill of Quantities. Drawings coloured to represent materials are always much easier to read than those with only varied hatching; and colouring, where not required as legal evidence, is quicker and cleaner in crayon than in water colour.

Site drawings are required to withstand rough usage, and should be clear and bold. Every essential dimension must be shown, so that nothing need be scaled from the drawing. To facilitate setting-out from an existing building, dimensions should always be shown from points which will remain, *after* preliminary demolition work has been done. Hidden features such as damp-proof courses, cramps, and supports must be clearly noted and indicated in writing; and explanatory border sketches and notes are often useful. Chalk is useful on site visits, when quick sketches may usefully be made 'on the wall'. If schedules are needed, these may be typed but are more easily copied, amended and kept up to date if handwritten on heavy tracing paper and printed. Extra copies of elaborate typed material can quickly also be printed with drawings, if an extra carbon copy has been typed on tracing paper.

Correspondence, certificates and accounts follow the usual pattern, except that it is always wise in cost-plus work to require an up-to-date forecast of future costs, as full details of past expenditure, from the contractor with each certificate application.

In the last stages of any job, a good deal of enthusiasm is needed to ensure that the interest of all concerned does not flag, and that every detail is properly carried to conclusion. When everything is finally completed, the contractor appreciates the personal thanks of an owner, as well as of the architect, on the dissolution of the team. Maintenance period inspections are made in due course, the usual period being six months from actual completion: in high quality work, twelve months is quite reasonable to ask. A large organisation may sometimes require to pay the contractor's accounts before the full maintenance period is complete, so as to allow settlement within a certain fiscal year. The contractor is usually in this case glad to accept settlement without prejudice to the correction of any little subsequent teething troubles requiring remedy; but in the normal event with a private client, the retention fund is a necessary security for the owner, and an incentive to the contractor to complete the fiddlesome list of minor repairs.

Professional fees for repair and conservation work to existing buildings are laid down in the RIBA Conditions of Engagement Para 3.3 and Table 2, which set out a minimum percentage fee varying from 13% to 10%, and decreasing with the total construction cost. Para 3.31 advises that higher fees may be appropriate for alterations to buildings of historic importance. A time-charge is applied (para 2.4) for making measured surveys and preparing plans of existing buildings, or (para 4.4) for building surveys and structural investigations. Out-of-Pocket expenses (Part 6) are reimbursed at cost.

It will be seen that, however interesting for the architect, conservation and alteration work is certainly not in the same financial field as the design of some types of new building; and on the smaller jobs, when grant applications and the like are entailed, the profit margin is often extremely slight. But old buildings are commonly set in a magnificent environment, with interesting owners, and one's work can sometimes be one's pleasure too.

4. The diagnosis

Before describing specific repair techniques, the author discusses the general diagnosis of the structural faults of an old building and the means at the architect's disposal for putting them right.

4.1 Structural movement

In examining any old building, the architect will often find a challenge to his imagination and ingenuity in deciding just what structural movements are going on, how significant they are, and what is to be done about them.

What principal agents of structural movement are likely to have been active? Firstly there are the external elements —wind and rain, temperature and ground movements. Secondly come the effects of human use and misuse. Thirdly there is the internal pattern of loading, thrust and counterthrust, active through history and derived from the building's own structural form. Lastly, structural movement is an inherent quality of the different materials which go to make up every building.

The external elements Most of the effects of wind and weather are all too familiar to architects. There is, however, one which applies particularly to old buildings, and of which too little account is taken. It is the differential settlement of foundations caused, not by mining subsidence, but by the ordinary operation of soil mechanics. A large building may occupy a site with varied subsoils, of different bearing capacities. For one reason or another, part of a site may settle—through the leaching action of underground streams or running water, or as a result of drainage improvements. A frequent cause of damage is the planting near buildings of quick-growing trees such as poplars: it is easy to forget when planting a small tree the astonishing volume of water which it will eventually draw daily from the ground and send into the atmosphere, drying and shrinking the surrounding soil.

All subsoils are also of course liable to seasonal variations, but some are affected by them more than others. Clay, in particular, shrinks appreciably and visibly in hot dry weather, and expands again in winter. Thus clay soil immediately surrounding a building will shrink and crack away from the walls. On the other hand, underneath a building the subsoil will be protected both from direct absorption of winter rain, and also from sunshine and evaporation; so that it will expand and contract much less. In consequence, a differential movement is set up, the external ground level rising and falling with the seasons much more than under the interior of the building. The movements which result are typified in an outward lean of the walls in the summer, when the garden is dryer than the subsoil, and a reversed tendency to lean inwards in

Looking downwards, the clockwise twist of this tower is clearly apparent on survey

Marks of a steeper gable on the east face of a church tower help to explain the full history of the structure and may give invaluable clues to earlier structural movements

winter, when the wet surrounding ground has expanded upwards, and the protected interior ground has not. The reappearance of cracks, rapidly increasing in a matter of weeks, can naturally be very alarming—especially if, for example, some grit should fall in the back of a church during prayers—so that this seasonal movement can assume a concern out of all proportion to its real importance. These effects are often added to and made more complex by human agency, as for instance when an old 'Tortoise' stove stands habitually in one corner of the interior. Faithfully stoked to red heat, it parches one small piece of floor and foundation while the rest is swollen with the rain of winter. A particularly delightful case is recorded in which the architect's answer to seasonal settlement was to send for the fire brigade, when the parched and shrunken clay was quickly hosed back to a more normal water content.

Damage by traffic

damage to building fabric by heavy traffic.

vibration

bulge

bulge

depression

Massive inverted reinforcing arches are given brilliant architectural expression at Wells Cathedral

Tie plates on a church tower showing characteristic systems of vertical 'ringing cracks'

Heavy additional buttress on a church tower. Tie plates mark the position of internal supports at the upper level

Human use The most spectacular case of movement resulting from human use to be found in old buildings is that caused by bell-ringing in a church tower. You have only to climb the belfry when ringing is going on, to feel the strain on the masonry of the rhythmic sideways battering of several hundredweights of bell. Even now, long-term damage may be a delayed result of wartime bombing. Equally important is the vibration caused by traffic, especially on cobbled roads. The pulsing of air set in movement by powerful organ pipes is another often-forgotten source of structural vibration. Perhaps the most damaging use of a secular building is the rhythmic pounding of dancing feet. But human use is really one of the less harmful causes of structural movement.

Settlement in tracery due to lack of abutment in an incompleted building (Cathedral of La Sagrada Familia, Barcelona)

Loading Every building has its own pattern of loading. The most clearly articulated are those of Gothic buildings, the only misfortune here being that the care with which the Gothic builders brought their loads down to ground level did not always extend to the foundations. To the inequalities of loading caused, almost inevitably, by structure, we must add inequalities caused by the unequal bearing properties of the soil. The science of structures in historical times was largely one of trial and error, and there are also a great many cases where utterly unexpected loads were subsequently concentrated on piers and foundations quite unprepared to receive them. When a building is new, both the spreading of the subsoil and all the little internal 'easings' and equalisings of loads will initially bring about a gentle 'settling' process involving compression and local movement. Many old buildings took decades or perhaps centuries to complete; and frequently additional wings have been juxtaposed, or additional floors added, at widely separated dates. The pattern of 'settling' and self-adjusting structure is therefore often complex. The result of initial movement in a new addition may in turn be to place an unequal loading upon its junction with existing work; and so a chain of movements may be set up through the building.

Materials Movements caused in buildings by the unequal behaviour of materials are likewise generally well known to architects. Wood is, of course, the commonest cause of this kind of movement, though fortunately it was a trouble of which traditional craftsmanship was fully aware. There were, however, certain very common practices which we now recognise as bad; as, for instance, the building of timber plates into masonry walls, where the timber will weaken the wall by shrinking and, in too many cases, by decaying. Another source of trouble is where materials of different hardness are bedded together, or where large units are bedded adjacent to small ones. Brickwork faced with butt-joined marble slabs, or the more frequent Early English example of a soft stone pier of many units, surrounded by a cluster of long Purbeck marble shafts, are typical examples of situations in which unequal materials are yoked together to their mutual disadvantage. Under load, the softer or many-jointed material compresses, and the load falls unfairly on the smaller and harder unit, which may then crack or spall.

From these four causes, every building is, as it were, structurally 'alive', with all its parts perpetually on the move. Indeed, one of the outstanding characteristics of traditional building techniques is their provision for this constant state of minor adjustment. In an old building which has been altered and added to at many periods in its history, the analysis of its structural movements may

Massive walls leaning through foundation settlement, are restrained by newer walling above

massy structures at which differential settlements and movements can congregate to relieve damaging stresses elsewhere. The first step is almost invariably—when justified—to reassure the owner where a structure is obviously not going to fall about his ears.

In next analysing the appearance of cracks, it must first be asked whether they are recent, or of long standing. This is not difficult to distinguish, especially in polluted city atmospheres, where old cracks will have been blackened by soot and dirt, and new ones will by contrast appear bright and clean. If a crack appears in a painted surface, close inspection will quickly show whether the movement occurred before or after the last repainting.

The next significant clue to the cause of a crack is its direction. Converging cracks, running upwards from the bearings of a lintel or from the springings of an arch, indicate a direct settlement of the lintel, or of the voussoirs of an arch due to its thrust. Cracks diverging upwards and outwards from the head of an arched opening may however indicate failure of the abutments, very possibly from foundation weakness. Stepped cracks in brickwork or coursed stonework will usually show wider openings, representing greater movement, in either the horizontal

be deceptively complex. How does one set about the diagnosis, and what cures can be prescribed?

Analysing cracks An owner will sometimes very easily take fright at a crack in walling, which may in fact be the best thing that ever happened to it. The crack represents a line of structural discontinuity, and while it may be a serious weakness in taut, tensely-stressed stonework such as window-tracery, it may provide a point in heavier,

A collapsing arch, its thrust released by a displaced abutment, also shows transverse settlement

or the vertical plane, thus indicating either a vertical settlement or a horizontal movement. One side of a crack may be in advance of the other, when a thrust at right-angles to the wall will be suspected. The wider end of a crack, representing the greater movement, may be either near or far from the source of the trouble, but will give valuable information on the direction of the movement.

The function of cracks and whether they are 'alive', may be readily checked by 'tell-tales' made of glass, cement or any hard material. Glass breaks definitely on any movement; but if the pieces are lost, the movement cannot be measured—occasionally also, one end may become detached without this being apparent. A dated cement stitch is the most useful, provided the masonry is well wettened so that no initial shrinkage cracking is caused. Flexible materials are of course useless—one case is recorded of tell-tales made of elastoplast! Clever new methods such as the use of plastic tell-tales viewed by polarised light are very interesting, but rarely applicable to the scale of movement which may be regarded as serious in old buildings. Often the best means of marking

Sagging courses of brickwork over a relieving arch

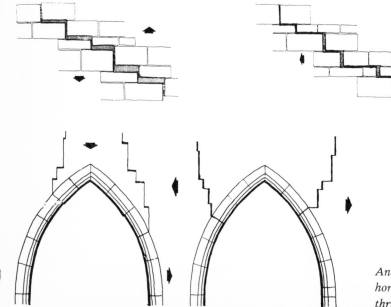

Analysis of cracks. Above, left to right: vertical settlement, horizontal movement, transverse failure. Extreme left: thrust and settlement of arch. Left: failure of abutments

A glass telltale affixed over a crack in flint walling

is purely to point up or plaster the area of walling concerned. Whenever tell-tales are fixed they should be dated, and their position recorded on a key drawing, safely filed for reference.

One can also use measuring instruments. Metal pegs may for example be inset into masonry on either side of the break, and their distance measured by means of a vernier scale. But usually, any really significant movement can be seen without mechanical devices.

Vertical departure from the plumb can easily be checked. A very fine plumb-line is best so as not to attract wind movement, and in gusty weather the bob may be hung into a bucket of water or oil. If the line cannot be completely stilled, it may be sufficient to take an average reading at the centre of its regular pendulum swing. Permanent marks may then be made on the wall at the top and bottom of the line for accurate future comparison. It is again important not to jump to conclusions: a marked departure from the vertical may be of no importance whatever—the structure may have been built like that. Many mediaeval walls have a 'batter' on the inner face

which has been wrongly attributed to an outwards lean—indeed, buttresses have sometimes ignorantly been built in consequence. The addition of buttresses is rarely either sound or necessary: being set on fresh, uncompressed earth they usually do more harm than good, and in settling may actively damage the wall they purport to assist.

Some points often invite cracks which may be of no significance at all. These include the line of junction between vaulting panels and walls, and between materials of different expansion and contraction rates such as carpentry and masonry, where movement must of necessity be expected and accepted. Everything in fact depends upon an intelligent analysis of all the structural history and movements of a building, viewed as a single comprehensive picture.

Foundation movement The great majority of walling cracks and failures may be traced to foundation movement. The subsoil under any wall will inevitably compress through the centuries, and a loose, sandy soil may run away from under loads. The heavier parts of a building will then settle relatively more; and the junction between light and heavy structure will show movement-cracks. It was because of this that the towers of mediaeval churches in fenland districts were so often constructed to stand independently of the main building. Under really concentrated loads, such as the later spire added to the central tower at Salisbury Cathedral, the overloaded piers have been visibly 'punched' downwards several inches. A simpler example is the apparent 'upwards' bow of many window sills, caused by the foundations under the windows being less heavily loaded than under the piers between, and resulting in differential settlement.

A frequent source of differential foundation movements is the building having partial cellars, with foundations set in deeper geological beds, more remote from seasonal movement than those near the surface. It is the bed of subsoil immediately under the foundations which produces the greatest movement. More serious is the case of buildings constructed on marshy ground and carried by heavy oak piles. So long as these were permanently saturated, little harm may have resulted; but there have been many cases of drainage 'improvements', where the subsoil water-table has been greatly lowered and the piles exposed to rot. The serious settlement and underpinning of Winchester Cathedral earlier in this century offers an example in point.

The remedy for foundation settlement may be found in careful underpinning. Local point loads are in this way spread over a greater area and either bridged over weak ground, or alternatively carried directly down to a deeper and more homogeneous stratum of the subsoil. But even with careful temporary shoring, the underpinning of a building can rarely be undertaken without risk of disturbing the upper structure. It is usually much better to accept and provide for controlled movement by means of straight or sliding joints. A perfectly sound and reliable mechanical solution can often be found at a fraction of the cost of tampering with existing foundations, and without the risk of setting up new problems worse than the first.

It is frequently possible to carry a structure over a weak patch by bridging loads across to sounder flanking sections in the actual walling—for example, by casting an *in-situ* reinforced concrete band in its thickness. A similar result in simple structures may sometimes be achieved by cutting away the walling and building in a deep bonding-

This fine photograph of West Walton church tower, taken by Samuel Smith in 1857, illustrates the understanding of marsh-land builders in siting a separate bell-tower independent of the structural movements of the church

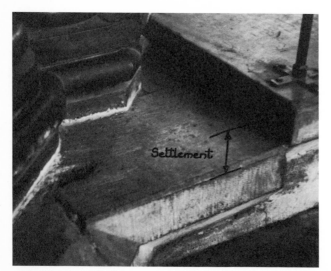

Differentiated settlement in a plinth under the point-load of the central tower at Salisbury Cathedral

course of strong tiles in cement mortar, forming a continuous beam through the full thickness of the wall. These methods may be combined with restraining measures against overturning thrusts or mechanical forces, as when a reinforced concrete wall-beam is used to spread the point-load from an arch or beam, or cracks in a bell-tower are stitched across by a concrete or tile band.

If underpinning is the only remedy, or if a continuous band must be formed in existing walling, the methods of operation are the same. The loading is first reduced as much as possible by carefully strutting the upper walling,

Reinforcement for a new in-situ beam linking a church tower and its flanking aisles

A network of tie-bars of differing dates in the central tower at Salisbury Cathedral

and any heavy floors and roofs whose load they carry. Sections of walling are next removed at equal intervals, leaving a longer section of sound structure between. The gaps are then carefully rebuilt, and the adjoining sections taken down and rebuilt in rotation, each bonded with its predecessor, until a continuous band of new walling or foundations is formed. A similar method is sometimes adopted for inserting a damp-proof course into existing walling.

Wall movements Movements are however not all due to foundation weakness. The thrust of an arch or an untied couple roof, exerted constantly on a wall for centuries, is bound to have results; and uneven loading of any kind is always cumulative in effect.

It is important to appreciate the distinction between a

dangerously tottering wall and a leaning tower. Pisa is quite safe (although recent reports suggest that shifting subsoil may make the tower insecure two centuries hence)—but a thin brick garden wall at a similar angle may be quite the reverse. The Tower of Temple Church, Bristol, is one hundred and fourteen feet high and leans five feet: it was for centuries a showpiece for important visitors, for whose delight small stones would be thrust into a crack at the base, and ground into powder by the ringing of the bells. Yet the story is told that in wartime after bombing, the structure was almost pulled down one morning by the military as a casualty, dangerous to the public. The Tower still stands.

The old rule of the 'middle third' is a particularly useful one. If the main weight of a structure, summarised as a

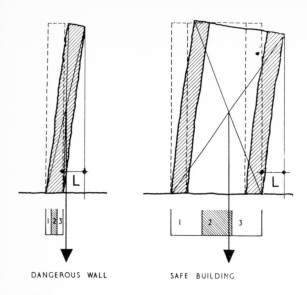

DANGEROUS WALL   SAFE BUILDING

The 'middle third' rule. Despite the fact that the extent of lean (L) is the same, the wall, left, is unsafe, but the tower is not

The use of a cranked internal buttress to arrest movement in an aisle wall. Ivinghoe church, Bucks (architect: John E. Macgregor FSA RIBA).

single force acting vertically through its centre of gravity, would bring the load beyond the middle third of its base, then there is a potential state of tension at its unloaded edge—and buildings are normally designed to resist only compression. But this rule cannot be applied to a single point in the wall of a leaning circular chimney, nor even to any wall which is tied into and buttressed by its neighbours. Provided the total state of loading of a building is well in equilibrium, its parts derive tremendous mutual support; and the whole context must be studied before any drastic remedies are indulged in. Perhaps all that may be necessary is the sound bonding of the member into existing stout cross-walls, or even the addition of an increased direct vertical load, acting on the principle of the mediaeval pinnacle, so as to bring the first load within safe limits. Further, where in a particular case it is desired to save a leaning feature, there is no

reason why even the middle-third rule need be followed, if proper provision is made for adequate tensional strength where it is needed.

The first decision in remedying wall movement is to enquire whether in fact it must be stopped at all, or whether its action can be localised harmlessly at certain points, on the principle of the sliding or expansion joint. Between unequally stressed parts of a live structure, relative movement is a perfectly healthy and natural phenomenon; and it is better to make reasonable provision for it than to 'set' a structure into a falsely stiffened state, which may often be a source of real weakness. If movement is to be checked, the next point to decide is the position at which restraint can most easily be employed, and to the maximum effect. Sometimes, only secure re-bonding to existing sound work is sufficient, once the cause of the movement has been eradicated. At other times, additional stays and supports will be essential.

Tie bars in direct tension offer great strength if their junctions with weaker materials are well spread. Iron should not generally be used in great lengths owing to its thermal movement, the effect of which may be considerable. If possible, a means of adjusting any tie, such as a collar with opposed threads, will always prove useful. Ties can sometimes usefully be linked at each end with the reinforcement bars of r.c. beams in the walls, when no visible tie-plates are necessary.

Compressional supports may take the form of *in-situ* reinforced concrete beams or struts, or sometimes of L-shaped ribs or stays between walls, or between wall and floor. Sometimes, as when a building is re-roofed, it is possible to combine structural reinforcement with new work. A reinforced concrete slab is often useful here, and may be tied right into the walling, if suitable gaps are left inside the parapets for any movement of the concrete during the setting period.

Very occasionally, strengthening may even take the form of bold flying arches and other new and striking architectural features of an interior, as in the Cathedrals of Salisbury and Wells. But usually, it is the unseen stay, quietly engineered in the thickness of walls, which offers the least conspicuous and most successful repair.

The 'correction' of movements. It is often asked whether or to what extent a leaning and crooked building should be straightened and corrected.

To the builder accustomed to new work, where straightness is constantly sought after, and any deviation from the true horizontal or vertical may represent bad building, it may have become a natural tendency to try and straighten everything in sight. Too often he wants to give a face-lift when all that was really needed was a good wash and shave.

In some circumstances, however, for one reason or another, it may be specially required to tilt back a leaning wall, or to jack up a sagging section of flooring. There is no reason why this should not be done. The first necessity is to ensure the homogeneity of the part to be moved: it must be carefully strutted or temporarily strengthened to withstand the hazards of moving. For example, a wall might have all windows and joinery removed, the

A concrete 'stitch' within insecure brick walling

Crenellated brick parapet leaning inwards

openings strutted and a stout framework of timber splints built up, perhaps on both sides, and tied through the openings. The two faces can even be close-boarded for added safety. Every care must then be taken to ensure that no train of movements can be set up, for example by the linked joints of a tenoned wooden frame transferring new stresses to a far end of the structure. The next step is therefore to prop or stay any other part of the building which normally derives support from the offending member, by means of shores placed so as to cause no interference with the work. After similarly ensuring its own stability, the wall can at last be dissociated completely from all its erstwhile surroundings. By means of jacks, block-and-tackle, levers, wedges, a Spanish windlass or any other gentle but powerful persuasion—even by inflating bladders full of air—the whole unit can then be carefully moved, strutting and all, to its new position, and the structure re-bonded together and its temporary supports removed. Here, as always, when new work is bonded into old, provision should be made in the jointing for a little spreading and settling of the new work, and for the initial compression of freshly loaded subsoil. This can for example be done by means of wide bed-joints under the toothings of new work, filled with a soft lime mortar to permit gentle settlement.

If the effort and expense are justified, the principle can be carried to extreme lengths, walls being tilted, raised or lowered, and indeed even whole buildings 'boxed' with a framework of temporary stays and moved bodily on rollers, or hoisted by crane to entirely new sites. Needless to say, this is a job for careful and intelligent labour under particularly watchful and resourceful direction, preferably by an architect with very considerable experience of old buildings: but it can be done, and may offer a solution when the only other answer might be the demolition of a valuable building.

4.2 Decay

If a building is alive, it is also mortal. From the moment it takes life, its various materials each begin at their own rates to wear away and to decay.

This constant process brings with it most of the problems of an ancient building. Unlike a plant or animal, a building cannot help itself by replacing its own worn parts. True maintenance consists not only in renewing evident decay but also in preventing it, the key being an intelligent appreciation of the very distinct life-cycles of different building materials.

It is often not appreciated by the layman that each of the various parts of a building has its own life-span, higher or lower in the scale of permanence. The most frequently renewed material is paint, requiring attention at intervals of a very few years. Flaking paint is an eyesore, a symbol of neglect, while fresh paintwork is universally attractive, as every Estate Agent knows.

Further along the scale are the short-lived materials like

Glass quarries released by decaying lead cames

thatch, roofing felt and, at some remove, asphalt, all of which require relatively frequent replacement. Next come the metals—copper and lead roofing especially. Copper requires renewal, and lead can either be renewed or simply recast and made up with new.

After the longer-term but periodical replacements, like roof battens, a new problem enters the picture. Stonework indeed decays, but so slowly that it becomes somehow identified in the public mind with the building itself—so much so, that piecing with obviously new stone can sometimes seem almost an affront. The problem of replacing worn-out materials is therefore immediately complicated by considerations not only of utility and decay, but of identity. To quote an absurd example, it would be possible to renew every unit of an ancient building wholesale, either by taking down and erecting a copy in entirely modern materials, or even by copying it utterly, piece by piece, *in situ*. But the new building thus erected will be a modern copy, and will never look or feel like anything else. How far are we to go?

It must first be admitted that the occasional case does occur in which the modern copy is defensible or even justified. No one is likely to suggest re-erecting an exact copy of the Parthenon in Hyde Park or even on the Acropolis. But there have been countless buildings in which a lost wing of a symmetrical pair, or several bays of an arcade or colonnade have subsequently been replaced with new work to universal approval—it was the only thing to do. The tenacity of sentiment is however by no means always so reasonable; and proposals have been quite violently defended for the rebuilding of buildings destroyed, in the self-same jumble of original 'styles' which was merely an accident and expression of their genuine history. The desire to rebuild a memory can be very strong, even to the extent of building an absurdity. Even the best modern copy has about it something self-conscious and unreal. The decision must nevertheless somehow courageously be taken. At some stage in history, every part of every building dies. Stucco has a short life; marble has a long one. Except in the extreme case, the modern copy is a lie, and the decision can only be taken, with courage and conscience, to rebuild in the spirit of our own time.

The difficulty lies in knowing just where to draw the line.

Castle Howard, Yorkshire: the dome of this magnificent Vanbrugh house was re-constructed after fire to an outline accurately plotted from old photographs by means of photogrammetry

All the world will agree to a fresh coat of paint, but few to a fresh stone facing. The one is an accepted periodical maintenance necessity—the other may be seen as the destruction of something irreplaceable. What are the criteria? Where is the line between replacement and destruction, and between maintenance and the modern copy?

The first element which must be acknowledged is that of original craftsmanship, as in an elaborate or characterful stone carving; this can rarely be replaced, and the only

Buried rectangular downpipes set into brick walling at Burton Constable, Yorkshire

thing to do is to save as much as possible, and then to give some modern craftsman a chance to show his own hand. Carved details and craft-work of any kind can rarely be copied without some feeling of faking, or at least of intrusion. In the case of features such as a well-authenticated classical moulding, for which even the original drawings or templates may still be available, the repair of a damaged or missing section is far less offensive, for the 'craft' element is no longer articulate, and its differing dates do not obtrude.

The second criterion is the importance of the actual materials themselves. Stonework may come from a quarry which is now closed and cannot be matched. Crown glazing is not made today and even if it is cracked, cannot be replaced by new glass without losing something valuable of its period. On the other hand leadwork does not, as is sometimes said, contain a significant amount of silver or anything else valuable; and if it is perished, it is a simple matter to recast it. Further the principle extends not only to the visible but to the normally unseen parts of the building, if these are of sufficient interest. It would be

nonsense to replace a uniquely interesting roof construction by steel trusses; and vandalism is not diluted by being out of sight.

The final element is that of architectural necessity. If an essential part of some outstandingly beautiful feature is missing, making nonsense of the whole, there is sometimes a strong case for local renewal. If one arch or pier of a series is missing and a fine symmetry thereby destroyed, there may be justification for replacement. Every case must be very carefully considered on its merits.

The new addition or replacement need not be deceitful: where an essential part of a fine rood-screen is missing and has to be re-carved, there is no reason why the new work should not bear its date. On the other hand there was until recently so necessary a reaction to the 'restorations' of Victorian times that patching was often done not only obviously but even assertively, to the detriment of the building. A building is not only a 'dig' for some future archaeologist but a piece of architecture today and tomorrow, and the chief concern of repairs is that they should either be quite inconspicuous, or else contribute in a positive way to the true architectural effect which the builders intended.

It has been suggested that the whole process of decay and renewal might be likened to the life of a landscape. Every year, leaves fall to the ground unlamented, to be replaced by new. At intervals, branches fall; and at longer intervals, trees fall. But as long as the intentions of the original landscape artist are carefully followed, it is the same landscape. The parallel is not exact, but the principle of the relative decay of leaf, branch and tree, and the necessity of periodic renewal and replacement are a valid lesson if old buildings are to live long.

4.3 The control of damp

Almost every trouble found in buildings can be attributed in one way or another to a single factor—damp. Damp is the prime vehicle of decay. It weakens the physical endurance of materials and their resistance to frost and erosion, it softens timber and attracts pests, and is an essential condition of fungal growth. The protection of old structures is very largely a question of controlling natural moisture travel through the fabric, and directing it into the healthiest and least harmful channels.

The first point to determine in analysing structural damp is to locate its source. Apart from damage due to defective plumbing, unwanted dampness may appear either (a) from the ground, or (b) from rain and weather or (c) from atmospheric humidity.

Once admitted to the building, water will thereafter travel either by gravity or by capillary suction, especially where there are considerable differences in evaporation potential on the two sides of a wall. Moisture therefore generally moves either downwards, or else towards any drying element, such as an exposed corner swept by the wind, or the warmed air currents from an internal radiator. In combating moisture travel, the most useful remedy may be found either in a barrier or in a counter-attraction. The most impervious barrier is any form of structural discontinuity; and the most tempting counter-attraction is proper ventilation. From an intelligent combination of these two, the answer to almost every problem can be found.

Rising damp Ground water is everywhere present in some degree, and is generally 'on the move' through the sub-soil. After rain, it will be penetrating downwards; and at other times, evaporating upwards to the surface. The lateral flow of ground water follows the configuration of the ground, unless underground rock strata slope and lead it in other directions. Rising damp may thus appear even on a very dry day, if the ground itself is sufficiently wet.

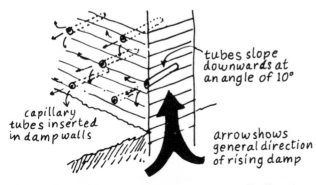

High-capillary tubes set in the base of a wall allow it to breathe and discharge rising damp

It may be more marked on the 'uphill' side of a building, or anywhere near a spring or watercourse.

Often, the underground water-table can be lowered by improved site drainage, when no work to the building may be necessary. It is virtually impossible to 'dam' underground water movements; and all that need be done is to provide an easier and more tempting route, either by open ditching or preferably by means of proper land-drains.

Frequently the only improvement needed to dry out a damp wall itself is plenty of fresh air. A narrow external dry-area or trench against the foot of the wall will often provide sufficient ventilation to dry the damp outwards, before it can rise to the level of vulnerable internal decorations. Ready drying out is much more effective than any impervious renderings. Indeed if, as often happens, a mediaeval timber framed wall has been faced with Georgian brickwork, it may be positively unwise to trap the rising damp in this way, when a serious threat could be caused to timbers buried in the walling.

The commonest cause of rising damp is the wall without any damp-proof course, in which moisture is drawn up by capillary attraction and by the heat of the interior, bringing with it salts harmful to masonry, softening timber into beetle-fodder and ruining decorations and finishes.

The classical remedy for rising damp is to build in a damp-proof course. This is a laborious operation, and was traditionally done by shoring up and removing alternate sections of the lowest courses of walling, rather as in underpinning, and rebuilding them complete, incorporating a damp-proof course of blue brick, slate or a similar material. The remaining sections are then removed and rebuilt in turn until a continuous barrier is formed. The method is extremely expensive, and a number of new solutions to the age-old problem have been developed during the last few years.

One method earlier recommended by the Building Research Station as being suitable for regularly coursed materials like brickwork entails progressively sawing a slot in walling, into which a metal damp-proof membrane can then be driven, a section at a time.

As with any damp-proof course, the membrane should be at least 150mm above the external ground level to avoid splashing. It may only be practicable to make the cut

A rectangular lead downpipe, shaped over mouldings, has become damaged and discharges over stone walling

An untended square lead drainpipe set in an angle, soaking the walling on both sides

Parapet gutters require a good outlet and emergency discharge spout

above floor level, when the vertical face of the wall between the new damp-proof course and the floor should be protected with two coats of bitumen paint. Especially where the floor is itself of impermeable material, the skirting should then also be of a material unharmed by moisture, such as one of the plastics.

The damp-proof membrane must be absolutely continuous, and should be continued through chimney breasts and similar features. Walling in poor condition or with a loose rubble core cannot be treated by this method. A slight settlement of a millimetre or two is inevitable, but in practice this is unlikely to have any significance.

A newly-developed method of great interest is the impregnation of a complete course at the foot of a wall with a silicone water repellent. The brickwork or stonework is first drilled at frequent intervals with lines of small holes leading down into the heart of the wall, when one of the proprietary solutions can be poured in or injected under pressure until saturation point is reached, and a continuous water-barrier formed. Little is yet known of the permanence of the system, but especially in soft brick walls, any method calling for so little structural disturbance must offer very great possibilities, and deserves more research and experiment than it has so far received.

Particularly fascinating experiments have been made more recently with electrical methods of repelling damp. The theory is that if an electrical potential can be encouraged between a building and the earth, moisture can be induced to flow from the one to the other. Only a small amount of current is said to be required; and the installation involves virtually no structural disturbance. If this method is satisfactorily proved on test, it might indeed prove to be very valuable: but care seems needed, to avoid undue reliance upon 'test-bed' results under ordinary knockabout building site conditions.

Rainwater penetration The source of penetrating damp is usually obvious. The direct effect of weather may be more pronounced on the western side, or facing whichever is the prevailing wind, and irrespective of ground layout. Water penetration will certainly also occur whenever any large impervious surface discharges over a less resistant one. Defective gutters and downpipes are at the root of three-quarters of the damage from this cause.

Very few walling or even roofing materials are themselves, however, literally *impervious* to damp. Almost all absorb and carry moisture to some extent; and the successive movement of water into walling, followed by its drying-out and evaporation, produces in effect a kind of structural 'breathing' inherent in all materials.

This alternating moisture-movement takes place firstly in the bolder pattern of units and joints, and secondly in the actual pore-structure of the materials. Both processes are conditioned by the position and exposure of the materials concerned. Copings, parapets, cornices and projecting

Wet walls betray an untended gutter above a party wall

Inadequate outlet in a lead parapet gutter. The tell-tale pools of standing water suggest rot in the timber beams and the wallplates beneath

ledges must stand up to a great deal of weather, and indeed for long periods may be almost permanently wet.

Modern experiment has taught that traditional building practice with regard to the jointing of materials had a very sound scientific basis. As a general rule, unit materials were almost always set in a softer and more porous jointing material, as occurs with brickwork and stonework set in lime mortar. Not only does the walling then adapt itself naturally to loading, without damage to the stones, but also moisture travel is controlled and localised at the joints, so that deleterious salts are deposited harmlessly in the softer material. In the jointing of materials, there is often no sounder guide than traditional practice.

Within the materials themselves, the pattern of moisture travel is governed not only by the total volume of the pores, but also by their relative sizes and arrangement. The fine pores generally draw from the larger ones. The actual capillary 'suction' of a material varies with its moisture content, and cannot be judged only by its total thirst or saturation capacity. More research is needed on this point.

From a dignosis of causes, the next step is to consider suitable remedies. In situations where it can be accepted that saturated walling is suffering no harm, although discomfort is nevertheless being caused to a building's occupants, the inner face may sometimes be lined with a separate and impervious skin, isolated from the face of the wall by a continuous, ventilated air-space. This means was adopted in many Victorian houses, when walls were often battened and counter-battened internally before being faced with lath and plaster. A ventilated cavity will carry away moisture and stop its travel more surely than any barrier, and by equalising the evaporation rates from the two faces of a wall, will remove the chief initial cause of travelling damp. The best example of ventilation against damp is, of course, the continuous air-space behind tile-hanging, by which a supreme degree of efficiency in weather exclusion is achieved by a quite absorbent facing material, allied with proper ventilation. Slate or tile-hanging is still an effective if drastic treatment for any wall which is not man enough to keep out the weather. The weight of slates is liable to pull out their fixing nails

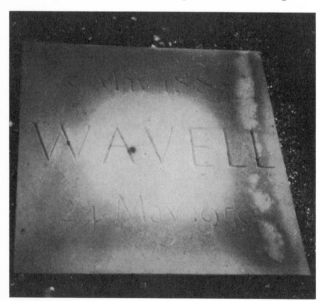

A memorial stone set in a low-lying cloister, draws water inwards from its outer edges in a constant cycle of evaporation

unless they are centre-hung. Tiles are eminently suitable; and an ingenious variant is the 18th century 'mathematical tiling' sometimes encountered, and which on face looks exactly like brickwork, until the outer angles are examined. The corners of buildings where tile-hung faces abut at an angle may need careful treatment; and with a single face, the ends of the battens must be protected by some form of cover-flashings.

There are some circumstances in which really thick and long-established ivy creeper, having damaged walling almost beyond recall, nevertheless now shelters its host in rather the same way as tile hanging, and may be trimmed back and suffered to remain as the lesser of two evils.

Any continuous 'skin' of waterproofed rendering is always in principle unsound, since once it is cracked by any movement of the structure behind, rainwater penetration will be canalised into severe local points, where little can be done to remedy it.

Over small areas, a remedy often advanced is the lining of the wall internally or externally with an impervious but flexible material such as an impregnated felt of keyed pattern, subsequently rendered with a flexible lime plaster finish. The life of impregnated felts in such a position is not known, but should not be unduly short. The internal lining of wet walls generally with metal foils and barriers nevertheless almost always acts only as a dam, and drives the moisture path to its unprotected edges. To 'tank' the internal surface of a wall satisfactorily in this way is extremely difficult; and very often moisture is only driven into the wooden linings of doorways and openings, where it may set up timber decay in the frames, and soak back around the architraves to soil the finishes and decorations. The only really satisfactory check to damp is structural discontinuity, allied with adequate ventilation.

Waterproofing solutions Several products are marketed for application to walling, which the makers claim to form a protective waterproof 'skin'. The most obvious form of coating is oil paint, renewed at frequent intervals.[1]

There is a long tradition of protecting walling by means of periodical coats of limewash. Particularly in the case of a rather shaggy random stonework, this treatment can be

[1] A waterproofing solution recommended by the SPAB for brickwork is a mixture of petrol and linseed oil, in equal proportions.

most effective in appearance. The broad texture of the material strikes through its coating, and the weathering effect is not displeasing. In point of fact, there is probably little chemical preservative action, but a good deal of the daily weathering is borne by the limewash. The general physical effect is in fact rather that of a close and absorbent overcoat, needing renewal every three or four years, but meanwhile giving valuable protection at quite low cost.

Experiments have also for centuries been made in the use of solutions leaving wax deposits in the surface pores of a material. Paraffin wax cannot, however, easily grip anything but a completely dry stone, and an excess of wax does tend to attract surface dirt. Although these applications can do no chemical mischief, and no doubt help to fill the larger surface pore spaces and cracks, they must still be physically foreign to the normal drying process of any walling material. Shellac varnishes and resins have proved even less successful, owing to the deleterious effects of light and water, which quickly make them useless.

It is now thought that part from a surface coating such as paint, the best waterproofers may be those which repel moisture without clogging the pores: to this end, the silicone water-repellents have recently been developed. Their action is to coat the walls of the surface pores of treated walling with a material of low surface-tension, so that while air can still pass, the water is repelled into globules which run off the material as off a duck's back. The silicone water repellents have the added advantage of discouraging dirt adhesion, so that soot and other sources of chemical attack are not given the opportunity to gather on the treated surface. After many years of experiment, silicone water repellents are now in commercial production; but they are by no means cheap, especially since they require periodical renewal, at intervals depending upon their original penetration and the conditions of subsequent exposure. Their cost is therefore prohibitive for the treatment of whole buildings, but they are claimed to be the only material so far developed which combines the advantage of protection, safety and invisibility.

There is still the danger that apart from helping to exclude external weather, any means whatsoever of increasing the water-repellence of surfaces will also operate in reverse, and check the natural drying-out of moisture from inside the wall. Any salts in solution can then be concentrated at the inside of the barrier, where they will crystallise and bring about the spalling of the face.

Airborne moisture A great deal of damp in buildings is caused by condensation, especially from warm, moist spring air striking cold and massive walls with great thermal capacity. The only real remedy is to provide a separate lining, insulated from the cold wall, and incorporating an airtight barrier to prevent the condensation from occurring behind it. A further source of dampness, which may persist in walls which have once been saturated for any length of time, is the presence in wall plaster of deliquescent salts. These are chlorides and nitrates brought to the surface by the evaporation of contaminated moisture, which in humid conditions attract and absorb atmospheric damp. This then appears as a patchy staining with no apparent cause. The only way of removing the salts is to strip the offending plaster; and since the moisture is absorbed from the atmosphere rather than driving through the wall, this is one of the few cases in which an impervious lining of foil or waterproof paper may also be useful.

Dampness due to deliquescent salts may usually be detected in wet or humid weather, particularly just before rain, and in atmospheres just insufficiently damp to cause actual condensation. Where expensive wall linings are impracticable, some measure of superficial protection can be given by an 'overcoat' of highly-absorbent anti-condensation paint. Very little can be done to prevent condensation on glazing; and the most practical remedy is to ensure that running moisture is effectively led away before it can cause any harm.

5. The repair of old roof coverings

5.1 Repair, or renewal?

The repair of roof coverings is of paramount importance in all building maintenance.

In examining the condition of an old roof, one must first recall its detailed function—the collection of rain and snow, to be shed from the building at predetermined points—and how this is achieved. This may be either by a system of overlapping small units such as tiles or slates, or by means of a continuously jointed surface such as sheet metal. In either case, the effectiveness of the roof is chiefly limited by its behaviour at certain 'danger points', the most pronounced of which are the following:

(*a*) The fixings holding the roof covering to the structure.

(*b*) The joints in its materials, such as drips and welts.

(*c*) Points of maximum exposure or mechanical wear, such as metal slopes facing the sun, or at the foot of a rainwater pipe.

(*d*) Inaccessible and unattended points—especially internal valleys and secret gutters.

(*e*) Interruptions such as skylights and chimney stacks.

(*f*) Abutments against other structures, either more or less rigid than the roof itself.

Besides watching these points, useful information can also be achieved by interrogating the building's inhabitants, whose evidence will usually not be lacking, although it may be overstated.

The architect must, however, concentrate not only upon locating the points at which water is actually penetrating, but upon assessing the whole general condition of the roof covering. Present water-tightness is not the only criterion. It may, for example, be found that a slated roof which at first sight is perfectly sound is laminating so badly at some points that it cannot long remain so, or that lead shows fatigue lines which must very soon become actual fractures. Or, on the other hand, poor roof design may be causing local weakness which could now be remedied in such a way as to make the structure perfectly sound and lasting.

The first question which must be asked is whether the existing covering can be patched, or must now be renewed. In the latter case, there will be the problem of the possible substitution of different materials. The main issues in taking these decisions can usefully be summarised as follows:

(*a*) What is the condition and remaining life of the materials? Is it economic to patch them any more, or would renewal now be cheaper in the long run?

(*b*) How serious and costly would further leaks be? Would they merely make a patch on a ceiling, or might they set up dry rot before being noticed? Does the interior contain valuable decorations and furnishings, whose protection should be taken into account?

(*c*) Is the material one which *can* be patched, or can it only be renewed as a whole?

(*d*) Is the roof covering material the same as the original? Does it form an integral part of the building's architectural appearance?

(*e*) Is the present covering potentially an efficient one, suitable to the building which it protects? Should the old material, although it was perhaps the best or cheapest available when it was laid, be replaced now by any other, more suitable and effective?

(*f*) What budget, labour and materials are at present available? Will any anticipated future demolition work realise useful replacement materials, such for example as stone slates?

(*g*) How much maintenance would a particular roof covering need, and how much is it likely to get?

(*h*) Above all, which is the more economic in the end—present repair, or deferred expenditure on roofing but with consequently increased maintenance costs? If roofing repairs are deferred, other less urgent work must also wait its turn.

The repair of existing materials brings mostly technical rather than aesthetic problems. Almost always, it is in fact neither necessary nor desirable to introduce 'foreign' materials into a roof; but difficulty may sometimes be found in obtaining matching materials such as individual tiles. If different materials are already present, the change may be simpler to make—for example, ridge tiles and bonnet hips may often inconspicuously be used to replace defective leadwork dressings.

The nature of the roof covering material itself may dictate whether repair is possible or not. For example, cracks in reasonably sound lead may be satisfactorily repaired by 'burning', but it is not possible to patch copper in this way. Inevitably, cases will occur which are on the borderline between repair and replacement. Thus old tiled roofs are found from which the tiles fall like leaves in early autumn. Inspection generally reveals that this is due to the corrosion of ungalvanised wire nails with which the tiles were pinned. In such a case the only permanent remedy is to strip and re-hang all the tiles, even though the great majority of them are apparently hanging on grimly, and may be years in their final decline. Cost is usually the main factor, and the architect's only course is then to try to influence the client to see his bank manager. Otherwise, he can only stress that replacing the tiles as they fall is purely a first-aid measure, and that the cost of replacing the roof entire must still loom large on the near horizon.

It is when complete stripping and re-covering are necessary, that major complications are more likely to arise. The simpler cases are those in which the covering material itself is largely sound and re-usable, but must be stripped because of the failure of its fixings; for example, in the case of a tiled roof in which the pegs or battens have perished. There is unfortunately almost always a large proportion of wastage in removing the old covering, and new material must be added when re-covering. Ideally, the new units should closely match the old: but sometimes this is impossible because of cost or short supply. In these cases it is usually wisest to gather the old materials together to the most important section of the roof, and to use the new tiles or slates for slopes concealed from view.

A variety of roofing techniques at Winchester College: tiles, machine and hand-made, sheet lead and stone roofing in diminishing courses

If modern tiles have to be introduced, it is better to choose a good sparkling bright type than to attempt an exact match, which will often darken to a depressingly drab colour in the course of time. On a building with high parapets, it is sometimes possible to re-use the old tiles or slates for the upper parts of the roofs, and to confine replacements to unseen positions below. This is well worth the effort, for many an old building has been ruined by the hard appearance of patches of machine-made tiles.

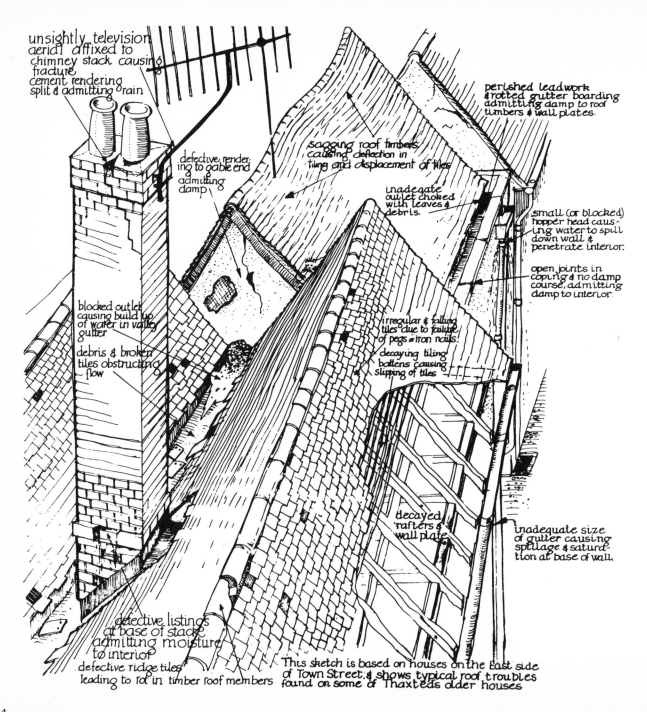

unsightly television aerial affixed to chimney stack causing fracture cement rendering split & admitting rain

defective rendering to gable end admitting damp

perished leadwork & rotted gutter boarding admitting damp to roof timbers & wall plates.

sagging roof timbers causing deflection in tiling and displacement of tiles

inadequate outlet choked with leaves & debris.

small (or blocked) hopper head causing water to spill down wall & penetrate interior.

open joints in coping & no damp course, admitting damp to interior.

blocked outlet causing build up of water in valley gutter

debris & broken tiles obstructing flow

irregular & falling tiles due to failure of pegs or iron nails.

decaying tiling battens causing slipping of tiles

decayed rafters & wall plate.

inadequate size of gutter causing spillage & saturation at base of wall.

defective listings at base of stack admitting moisture to interior

defective ridge tiles leading to rot in timber roof members

This sketch is based on houses on the East side of Town Street & shows typical roof troubles found on some of Thaxted's older houses

94

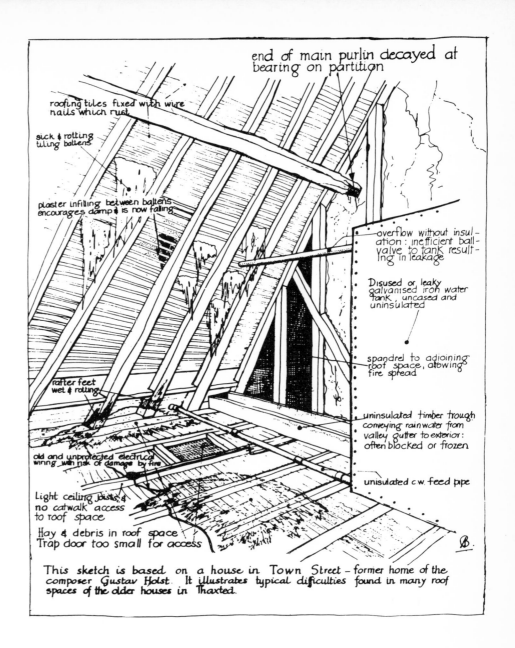

end of main purlin decayed at bearing on partition

roofing tiles fixed with wire nails which rust

sick & rotting tiling battens

plaster infilling between battens encourages damp & is now falling

overflow without insulation: inefficient ball-valve to tank resulting in leakage

Disused or leaky galvanised iron water tank, uncased and uninsulated

spandrel to adjoining roof space, allowing fire spread

rafter feet wet & rotting

uninsulated timber trough conveying rainwater from valley gutter to exterior: often blocked or frozen

uninsulated c.w. feed pipe

old and unprotected electrical wiring with risk of damage by fire

Light ceiling joists & no catwalk access to roof space

Hay & debris in roof space Trap door too small for access

This sketch is based on a house in Town Street – former home of the composer Gustav Holst. It illustrates typical difficulties found in many roof spaces of the older houses in Thaxted.

Typical roof defects noted in Town Street, Thaxted: the troublesome chimney stack in the external diagram could well be removed, if it is no longer required or architecturally significant

95

Failing tiling: here the fault seems to lie in inferior modern tiles and not in the fixings

These attractive clay pantiles are now rarely made, but they may be permeable by driven snow

old; and here the change in the appearance of the building, as well as the introduction of a material of perhaps lower standard, are matters not to be undertaken lightly. The extreme example of this type of substitution may be seen in almost all country districts, in the rusting corrugated iron which now covers so many a once-attractive thatched cottage. Another problem is the possibility of substituting copper for lead, for reasons of cost. On concealed roofs, this may not be a matter of architectural moment; but on roofs exposed to view, the changed appearance is a public concern; and it is thus vital to be conscious of one's responsibility to the building, and certain of the result. This part from practical questions of durability, which must also be weighed in the balance, and of cost, which can best be investigated by obtaining actual alternative estimates. Generally speaking, the use of substitute materials should only be resorted to when economic factors make the change inevitable, or when the original material has shown itself

Cast sheet lead: best of all roof finishes, but less suited to steep pitches like this at Ely Cathedral

The most careful thought is needed when the old covering is so unsound as to be unusable. It may then be necessary to consider substituting a new, cheaper material for the

Roof lead-work being renewed with standing welts

to be in some way seriously unsuitable for the building which it covered. In many old buildings, the roof contributes so much to the interest and attraction of the whole that the use of incongruous materials can mean utter spoliation.

5.2 Sheet roof coverings

The durability of all metal coverings is dependent upon: (*a*) their degree of exposure, particularly to acid-charged droppings and to sunlight, and (*b*) their means of support and fixing, with special regard to provision for thermal and structural movements. The most frequently used metals are lead and copper.

Lead The great virtue of lead as a roof covering is its ease of dressing and adaptation to irregularities of shape, and its very great durability when properly supported and fixed. Its one disadvantage is a liability to 'creep' when improperly used, so that if the material is denied its natural

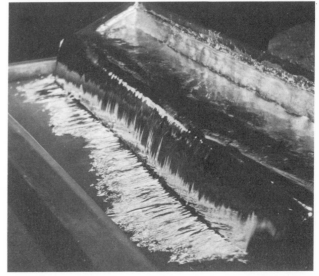

Molten lead runs from the heat-pan in a silver stream on to the casting table

freedom, thermal movements may accumulate without returning to their original position.

Recasting sheet lead In historical times, cast sheet lead was widely used; and this is still the longest-lived roofing material. Old leadwork, whether cast or milled, may be melted down and recast, either on a casting-table erected at the site, or at the centralised workshops of one of the several firms specialising in this type of work.

Milled lead is a perfectly good material, easier to dress than the cast sheet, but slightly less stiff. It is, therefore, at a disadvantage in exposed positions such as cornices and places where rigidity is sought. A debatable point is whether milling actually reduces the life of lead by re-arranging its crystalline structure; this is often claimed, but scientific proof has never been given. Since in recasting lead, the old material is all re-used without complexities of salvage and financial credits, cast lead is, however, in fact no more expensive in renewing old work, especially in relation to its undoubtedly longer life. The old lead re-moved from the building should first have all soldered patches cut out—other impurities can then be skimmed from the surface of the molten metal in the 'pot'. Stories that old leadwork contains any really significant amount of valuable silver are mostly apocryphal, and there does not seem to be any special reason for setting aside old lead for return to its own particular building. If interesting old inscriptions are found, these may be cut out and saved for display. Otherwise the old material is all melted down, and a proportion of new pig lead added as may be needed. The finished lead can be varied from 6 lbs to 9 lbs in weight, and cast lettering and ornamental devices can readily be formed by pressing patterns into the sand.

Re-laying roof leadwork Sheet lead must always be firmly and continuously supported, and the boarding carefully overhauled and prepared. An underlay of building paper facilitates natural thermal movements, and may help to even out minor irregularities of the boarding. Lead should always be protected in this way from contact with oak, so as to prevent attack by tannic acid.

Whatever the original arrangement of the roof, the new sheet sizes and lengths must be carefully restricted, to localise movements and provide plentiful expansion joints. A maximum area of 2·20m² must normally be strictly

Leadwork, inadequately fixed, has sagged into the eaves gutters and probably exposes gaps under the slating

insisted upon, with individual sheets not more than 3m in length. Under proper supervision and in very sheltered situations, particularly for internal leadwork protected from sunshine, these sizes may be slightly exceeded. But no single cause has so much reduced the life of ancient leadwork as its layout in sheets of excessive size. If through this fault in the past, old lead has suffered premature decay, it is essential to remedy the design and to limit the sheets to a proper size. This is not always easily done, since the sheet sizes govern the position of 'drips', whose number may in turn be limited by the available fall, for instance behind a parapet. In tapered gutters, too, an increased number of drips, the depth of each of which has also sometimes to be increased for safety, can result in embarrassingly wide gutters climbing far up the roof slopes. But much can be done by re-planning the layout of drips and rolls to new falls, designed upwards from the outfall, and by introducing additional upper drips as economically as possible. Sometimes, excessively large sheets adjoin unnecessarily small ones, when their sizes may be averaged out; or a very large slope can be re-laid to cross falls in the shorter direction, with rolls laid diagonally or crosswise. If a slope falls in more than one

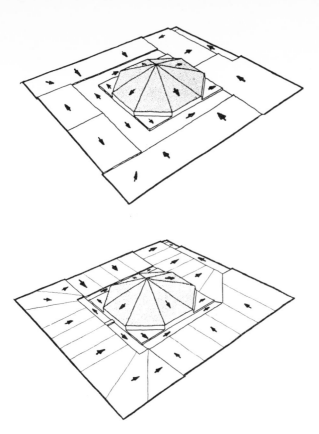

Flat roof redesigned to allow proper sheet sizes. Top, diagram showing the original layout of the leadwork. Note size of sheets and absence of drips in internal gutter, making no allowance for expansion. Below, diagram showing the layout as redesigned.

direction, the roll should be formed with its open side on the more sheltered face; and if a roll cuts diagonally across a vertical drip, it must always be set with the open side downwards.

In relatively flat surfaces such as gutters, trouble from inadequate drips is common; these should indeed preferably be no less than 65mm deep. If, however, as frequently occurs in old buildings, this depth is unobtainable, the drip may be reduced to 40mm, if some means of capillary check is provided in the vertical face. One way of doing this is to chamfer off the lower edge of the boarding before

Acid rivulets from tiling, especially where lichen is present, can cut deep runnels into leadwork

it is fixed, forming a groove into which the head of the lower sheet can be dressed; the foot of the cover sheet is afterwards dressed vertically past and down on to the flat. In specifying joints between the sheets of re-laid lead, a choice must be made between lapped junctions over a wooden roll, and tightly-dressed open rolls or standing welts. Where heavy traffic is anticipated, or when future replacement of individual sheets may be required, the wooden roll has the advantage. In this case, intersections and the ends of rolls are 'bossed'. Generally otherwise the open roll is best, and on any degree of slope, its tight and continuous grip is a great help in restraining any possible slipping of sheets. This method of fixing was general until the 19th century; and thanks to the firm grip of the curved, open rolls, leadwork of the upper part of Robert Adam's dome at Kedleston Hall was found to be almost free from movement after 200 years.

The head of each sheet on sloping surfaces is usually fixed by two staggered rows of copper nails; but on steep slopes, additional support can sometimes be obtained by turning the top of each sheet over the boarding, and securing it by nailing to the back. Whatever was there before, proper soakers and cover flashings are the only satisfactory way of protecting the junctions between roofs and walls or chimneys, where any kind of fillet is bound to crack away. It is useful to remember that sheet lead dressed into a hollow box such as a sump is strengthened by dressing, and that it is weakened by working when beaten over a projecting arris. Proper fixing clips, lead 'dots' and cover flashings must never be skimped, and a typical specification for the renewal of roof leadwork is given below.

A difficult problem, for which no really satisfactory remedy has yet been produced, is to prevent damage to lead-work by the acid-charged washings from lichen growing on slates. A lead gutter immediately under stone slates is often found to be deeply scored by this acid, in narrow 'rivulets', entirely distinct from the shallow depressions left by mechanical wear or constant dripping water. The damage is believed to be caused not so much by heavy rain as by the more heavily charged dewdrops, whose action is not diluted by washing. Since stone roofs under copper telephone wires may often be observed to be lichen-free, it has been suggested that one expedient may be to set a copper strip at the ridge, or in the slope itself. Evidence of the practical effectiveness of this method would be most valuable. The only alternative seems to be either to set an extra renewable overcloak at the point of maximum wear, in which case provision must be made to resist capillary attraction, or to reduce the width of outer lead sheets against the foot of roof slopes, regarding them as expendable. In this case, the use of wooden rolls will enable individual sheets to be renewed without damage. It is a pity that no more satisfactory solution has yet been found. Small dew-gutters have been rejected as being awkward and unsatisfactory, and perhaps the only remedy may be the introduction of an eaves course of some kind of absorbent tiles. Other ideas would be welcomed.

The high salvage value of lead makes it a temptation to theft, especially in isolated and unprotected positions. One of the best and most economical precautions is by regular floodlighting during hours of darkness, at any time buildings are particularly at risk.

Repairs to old leadwork should always be made by lead burning and never with solder, which has a different coefficient of expansion and will break away. Temporary stopping of lead cracks with the various mastics and bituminous compounds is all a very doubtful business, and really cannot be relied upon. In practice it usually only conceals the trouble, while inviting further damage as soon as the lead starts again.

Outline specification for re-covering roof in recast lead in accordance with architect's detailed site direction

1. STRIPPING AND RE-CASTING: Carefully strip old defective lead from roofs where directed, load and transport from site and credit certified weights at rates to be agreed.

Cut out and remove all solder and impurities. Carefully cut out any inscriptions, records of previous re-castings, etc., and set aside for re-use as directed.

Re-cast all remaining to the following weights, making up as necessary with virgin English lead:

Cornice	8 lb. (BS 8)
Roofing generally	7 lb. (BS 7)
Dressings to wooden sills	6 lb. (BS 6)

Cast new inscription and date into one sheet, as directed by the architect.

New milled lead to be used for soakers, is to be best English milled, of 4 lb. (BS 4) weight, uniform in thickness and texture, and free from defects.

Transport new sheet lead to site, unload and store as directed by the general contractor.

2. RE-LAYING LEADWORK: Except where otherwise agreed by the architect, the work throughout is to be carried out only by registered plumbers. All new lead to be well and neatly dressed without injury, in sheets of specified sizes, securely fixed with copper nails and lead or copper tacks, joints where necessary being welted or 'burned' and not soldered, and proper provision being made for expansion and contraction. Detailed site instruction on the work will throughout be given by the architect.

3. SPECIAL PRECAUTIONS: Where excessive hammering, etc., is liable to cause damage to internal plasterwork or finishes, special precautions are to be taken to avoid vibration, including the use of screws instead of nails wherever directed.

4. SHEET SIZES: The previous excessive sheet sizes are not to be reproduced. New sheet sizes are not to exceed 24 sq ft (2·20m²) in area, nor 10 ft (3m) in length, except where specially directed by the architect.

5. BOARDING: Boarding of all flats, gutters, etc., is to be carefully adapted by the general contractor, with revised and additional drips in positions to be directed by the architect. All projecting nails to be driven well home and edges and irregularities planed off to provide a continuous, smooth supporting surface. After the architect has approved the repaired substructure, an underlay of stout waterproof building paper, with

smooth surface on both sides, shall then be laid over the whole substructure before the lead is laid.

6. FIXING: New sheets are to be fixed at the head with two staggered rows of copper nails with 10mm flat heads at 75mm centres and 75mm apart. Drips at the joint between the top of each sheet and the foot of the next are to be provided, each of depth at least 65mm whenever the old boarding layout allows. Where existing boarding does not permit drops of this depth and cannot be adapted to provide it without raising gutter heads to an impracticable extent, or increasing gutters to an uneconomic width, drips may be retained where directed at a minimum of 38mm deep. The top of the lower sheet must, however, in this case be dressed into an anti-capillary groove half-way up the vertical face of the drip, the foot of the upper sheet being dressed past and down on to the flat.
On inclined roofs exceeding 15 deg. in pitch, drips may be replaced by overlaps, to be at least 150mm deep, measured vertically.
The sides of all sheets are to be fixed with lead or copper tingles 65mm wide, securely nailed down and turned into hollow rolls. Alternatively, where directed, fixings may be made by dressing around wooden rolls, with bossed ends and intersections. The foot of each sheet more than 750mm wide is to be similarly supported by lead or copper clips.
Lead 'dots' are to be formed to support all vertical faces as directed, and whether or not these were originally so provided, and wiped over countersunk brass screws and washers at centres not exceeding 750mm in any direction.

7. VERTICAL ABUTMENTS: Against all vertical abutments, form 150mm upstands and protect with cover-flashing inserted 25mm into walling, new grooves being cut for the purpose where necessary. Cover-flashings are to be secured with lead wedges at 450mm to 600mm centres, pointed in with cement mortar, and dressed down at least 100mm over upstands. Sheets are not to exceed 2·4m length, to be lapped at least 100mm, and supported at intervals of not more than 750mm by means of 65mm lead or copper clips securely fixed to walling and turned down behind flashings, then dressed back 25mm over outer face.
Secret gutters against abutments are in future to be avoided. Where specially permitted, they are to be formed of 6-lb (BS 6) lead, copper-nailed to roof boarding under the last slate, dressed over a tilting fillet and across the gutter, then turned up and protected as described above.

8. VALLEYS: Valley boarding, adapted and repaired as directed, is to be recovered with 7-lb (BS 7) lead, dressed to slope of boarding, turned over tilting fillets at each side, and carried up under re-fixed slates to a distance of at least 75mm measured vertically. Upper end of each sheet to be close copper-nailed and lower end lapped at least 150mm, measured vertically.

9. RIDGES AND HIPS: To be covered with 7 lb (BS 7) lead in sheets not exceeding 2·4m in length, with 150mm lap at joints, dressed over rolls and 150mm to 165mm down slates on each side. All dressings to be firmly held at 750mm intervals by double lead clips 65mm wide, fixed under rolls and carried down under wings, then dressed back 25mm along upper face.

10. GUTTERS: Tapered gutters are to be reformed by the general contractor in accordance with the architect's detailed site instructions, with drips at intervals as specified above, and from width at least 230mm at lowest point. Before refixing of slating, re-dress gutters with 7 lb (BS 7) lead carried 150mm up slope and over continuous tilting-fillet. Form upstands and cover-flashings at abutments as specified above.
Downpipe boxes to be re-formed where directed, and of dimensions at least 230 × 230mm × 100mm deep. Cut away masonry of parapets and provide 7 lb (BS 7) lead overflow spouts to each box as directed, discharging through parapet and clear of wall externally. Back-gutters behind chimneys to be re-dressed with 7 lb (BS 7) lead dressed at least 100mm around each angle of chimney.

11. DORMERS: Boarding to be made good by general contractor all as directed, and any particularly uneven old boards faced with approved outdoor quality hardboard, securely nailed down.
Cheeks to be recovered with 6 lb (BS 6) lead dressed over top board and nailed thereto on reverse and also supported by wiped lead 'dots' as specified above. The front edge to be dressed around the corner post, securely copper-nailed and welted back over nail heads. Tops of dormers to be re-covered with 6 lb (BS 6) lead as for flats, with lead or copper fixing tabs at all exposed edges.
Dormer and chimney aprons to be dressed at least 100mm around angles, and to have 230mm inclined apron supported by lead clips at not more than 750mm intervals. Soakers against dormers and chimneys to be 25mm longer than slates and turned

up under cover flashings and dormer cheek leadwork.

12. DRESSINGS TO CORNICES AND LEDGES: Whether or not these were originally so provided, all cornices and water-holding or permeable ledges of stonework are to be carefully dressed with 8 lb (BS 8) lead with welted expansion-joints at 2m to 2·5m intervals and dressed at least 20mm into joints of walling. All ledge and cornice dressings are to be fixed by lead dots at distances not exceeding 750mm, utilising original mortices where possible. Where possible damage to stonework would be avoided thereby, old 'dots' may with the permission of the architect be cut off flush, and fixings obtained by large-headed, coarse-threaded brass screws and washers driven into the retained lead plug, the upper part of the new 'dots' being wiped around them.

13. REPAIRS: Thoroughly inspect and check over all remaining existing leadwork to roofs throughout and repair as directed in detail by the architect.
Cut out all soldered or inadequate patchings, iron nails and other temporary fixings; and repair by burning-in new pieces all of weight to match existing. Re-dress and re-fix all loose and displaced leadwork as directed, making up with new lead or copper clips, and copper fixing nails where these are deficient or inadequate. Where severe acid cutting is apparent on sloping faces (e.g., under drips from slating at heads of dormers) these are to be reinforced where specially directed by temporary 4 lb (BS 4) milled lead over-cloaks.

14. DUCKBOARDS: Overhaul and renew all duckboards as directed in creosoted deal, so as to permit free flow of water from melting snow. Repair and replace all defective and deficient guards to downpipes and other constricted points as directed where blockages could otherwise be caused by leaves and rubbish.

15. COMPLETION: All roof plumbing works are to be approved in detail by the architect before the operatives leave the site. Leave all leadwork in a sound and weather-tight condition and remove all tools, plant and equipment and unused materials. Carefully clean out all gutters with wooden shovels; wash down and leave all tidy on completion.

Copper Copper has been used for roofing buildings for many hundreds of years. The green 'patina' which the material develops is itself an attractive and important feature of many architectural exteriors; and copper is much lighter than lead. It is also cheaper, although enjoying a slightly less venerable old age than its sister metal.

The greatest danger to copper on a roof is from excess working, either when it was originally dressed, or through 'drumming' due to inadequate support. This causes fatigue and eventually cracking, and the Copper Development Association recommend that sheets should not be repaired with soldered patches.

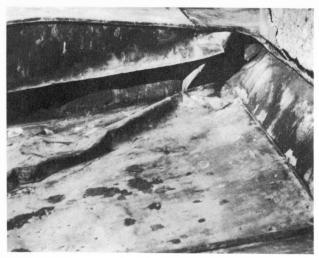

Wotton House, Buckinghamshire: Soane's copper roofing in sheets of excessive size, has now buckled by thermal expansion

Where a copper roof has failed in any degree, therefore, it is usually more economic to strip and re-lay it throughout. The boarding can also then be overhauled and repaired, with particular regard for the smooth and continuous support which the metal requires. The substructure should be closely examined by the architect before the new covering is laid. Felting is desirable to prevent chafing, but should be non-bituminous: it is laid with butt joints and fixed by copper nails.

Copper for re-roofing should be thoroughly annealed and of 22 or 23 gauge. Samples may be tested by weighing and by a 'double-bend' test described in BS 1569. Although old copper can in fact be re-annealed, this is seldom worth while. The new metal is fixed in sheets not more than 1·8m to 2·4m long, jointed head-to-foot by double welted seams. The area of sheets should not exceed 1·30m^2; if sheets of greater size are used, there is a risk not only of drumming and fatigue, but of thermal movements lifting whole sheets of copper from the roof.

For the side joints between sheets, there is again the choice between standing seams and welting over wooden rolls. Flat-topped rolls are better than the pointed type, in forming which the sheets may accidentally be dressed up and away from the substructure.

A system of 'economy' copper roofing was at one time developed, in which sheets of extra size were held in place by sliding clips, permitting ready expansion and contraction. Where for any reason the traditional layout is impossible, the method may enable a defective copper roof with excessive sheet sizes to be relaid, without entailing extensive carpentry alterations to the boarding system or substructure.

Copper must not be jointed or patched with solder, which has a different expansion rate and will come away. On the flat, a fall of at least 1 in 6 is recommended, with drips at least 50mm deep at every 3m: the rolls are usually staggered at the drips to facilitate working. A Scandinavian practice is to paint the joints with raw linseed oil before welting. The re-laid copper roof should be very closely examined on completion, with special regard to the absence of working cracks, and to firmness and continuity of support. Lastly, as with any metal roofing, it is particularly important to prevent damage during adjoining works, as can so easily happen from a dropped chisel or an in-trodden nail: really adequate protection of the finished job is quite essential.

A typical specification for re-covering roofs in copper is given on page 103.

Other substitute materials Aluminium is a young material, and has not yet had the opportunity to show its paces for such long periods as copper and lead. It dresses well and when proved by time, may well earn a place alongside the other metals suitable for re-roofing old buildings. The chief drawback at present is the practical difficulty of any simple kind of jobbing repair except the replacement of complete individual sheets.

Other useful materials where only a limited life of a generation or so is called for include the various rubberised and reinforced bituminous felts. The latter can be readily dressed when heated, and hold their shape well once set in position. But in the repair of old buildings whose life is commonly measured in centuries, such materials cannot, of course, hold comparison with metals such as lead and copper.

The various types of asphalt are nowadays used on old as

Outline specification for re-covering roof in sheet copper in accordance with architect's detailed site direction

1. STRIPPING OLD COPPER: Carefully strip old defective copper from roofs, etc., as directed, load and transport from site, and credit certified weights at rates to be agreed.

2. NEW MATERIALS: All new copper used shall conform to the requirements of BS 1569: 1965, and shall be of 24, 23 or 22 standard wire gauge, except as otherwise directed, and of dead soft temper.
Throughout the entire new copper roofing works, no iron nails shall be used in contact with the copper as before. All copper shall be fixed with copper nails or brass screws.

3. RE-LAYING COPPERWORK: The work throughout is to be carried out by experienced plumbers or recognised copper-roofing specialists. The whole of the work in connection with the new copper roofing is generally to be carried out on the site, and in accordance with detailed instructions to be given by the architect.
All new copper sheet is to be laid truly flat, flattening being carried out on the bench. Before laying, the material is to be prepared by cutting, bending and seaming to fit accurately into the bay of the roof for which it is intended: thus avoiding unnecessary forming, dressing and cold working. Due allowance is to be made in all dimensions for expansion and contraction.

4. SPECIAL PRECAUTIONS: Where excessive hammering, etc., is liable to cause damage to internal plasterwork or finishes, special precautions are to be taken to avoid vibration, including the use of screws instead of nails wherever directed.

5. SHEET SIZES: The previous excessive sheet sizes are not to be reproduced.
Except where specifically directed otherwise, new copper sheets are not to exceed 600mm in width. Areas of individual sheets in 22, 23 and 24 s.w.g. copper are not to exceed 1·30m^2 and in 26 s.w.g. sheet where used, 1·11m^2 each.

6. BOARDING: The boarding of all flats, gutters, etc., is to be carefully adapted accordingly by the general contractor with new drips wherever necessary, in positions to be directed by the architect. All projecting nails are to be driven well home, and edges and irregularities planed off to provide a continuous, smooth supporting surface.

7. FELT: After detailed approval of the repaired substructure an underlay of felt is to be laid over the whole of the boarding to receive the new copper. The felt is to be type 4A (ii) brown impregnated flax, known as inodorous felt No. 1, 23kg per roll, conforming to BS 747: 1968/70. Alternatively, Fibirine Felt may be used.
The felt is to be laid butt jointed, and secured with copper nails.

8. SEQUENCE OF OPERATIONS: After the roof surface has been prepared, it is to be brushed clean and laid with sufficient felt for a day's work. The prepared new copper is then to be laid in the following sequence:
(a) cesspools;
(b) gutters;
(c) drop aprons;
(d) main roof sheeting;
(e) cover flashings.

9. FIXING: All free edges of the new copper are to be properly secured by means of copper cleats as directed by the architect. These cleats are to be not less than 50mm in width, and secured to the roof boarding, or passed through slits or joints in the roof boarding and secured on the underside. Cleats 50mm wide are to be fixed at 380mm centres in all joints from eaves to ridge, at 300mm centres on verge edges, and two per bay at drips, eaves and ridges generally. Transverse joints are to be fixed with one 75mm wide cleat in the centre of each double lock cross welt, and two 50mm wide cleats in each single lock cross welt. Each cleat is to be fixed close to its right-angled turn by a minimum of two copper nails or brass screws; the tail end of the cleat is then to be turned back to cover the heads of the nails or screws so as to prevent all abrasion of the under surfaces of the copper when any movement takes place.
Ridge to eaves joints are to be formed with standing seams or batten rolls as directed. Standing seams are to be formed to a nominal height of 25mm and are to be spaced generally at 540mm centres. Batten rolls are to be formed to the following minimum sizes: Height 38mm, width at base 45mm, width at top 32mm. The finish of batten rolls at the eaves may either be splayed or vertical, as directed on site.
On roofs not exceeding 5 deg. in pitch, transverse joints are to be formed with drips not less than 50mm in height. On roofs between 5 deg. and 60 deg. in pitch, double lock cross welts are to be used for transverse joints, and are to be staggered in alternate bays. Transverse joints to roofs exceeding 60 deg. in pitch may be single lock welts.

10. VERTICAL ABUTMENTS: Against all vertical abutments form 150mm upstands and protect with cover flashings, joined to upstand by means of 25mm single lock welt where practicable. Alternatively, the cover flashings may be beaded and held to the wall by means of a copper strap, fixed behind upstand and turned down behind the cover flashing and welted round its lower edge.
Secret gutters against abutments are in future to be avoided. Where specially permitted they are to be formed of 26 s.w.g. copper, copper-nailed to roof boarding under the last slate, dressed over a tilting fillet and across the gutter, then turned up and protected as described above.

11. VALLEYS: Valley boarding is to be adapted and repaired as directed, and suitable tilting fillets provided to enable the sheeting in the gutter to be joined by means of a single lock welt to a continuous fixing strip, nailed to the tilting fillet so as to allow for free movement of the copper in the gutter.
Lengths of copper in valley gutters are to be joined by double lock cross welts where pitch is 60 deg. or less. For steeper pitches, single lock welts may be used.

12. RIDGES AND HIPS: Ridges and hips to all roofs formed with standing seam down-joints are to be finished with standing seams welted in, or with ridge rolls, as directed.
On roofs formed with batten roll down joints, the ridges and hips are similarly to be finished with batten rolls 65mm to 75mm in height and approximately 50mm wide at the base.

13. EAVES: The eaves are to be finished by means of a separate and continuous fixing or lining strip cut from half-hard copper strip, secured to the fascia by copper nails or brass screws.
A drop apron made from dead soft temper copper is to be secured to the bottom edge of the lining plate, and at eaves level is to be turned outwards at 90 deg. to the fascia. Cleats 50mm wide, two per bay, having previously been fixed to the roo decking, are to be folded over this 90 deg. flange. The roofing sheets are then to be turned over and under this projection, and finally dressed down to form a single lock welt on the fascia.

14. GUTTERS: Tapered gutters are to be reformed as necessary by the general contractor with drips at intervals of from 2m to 3m and from a width of at least 230mm at the lowest point. Detailed site instruction on the whole of this work will be given by the architect.
In long gutters from 6m to 15m where excessive expansion takes place, special expansion joints are to be formed in the new copper to accommodate such movement, as shown in the graph in CDA publication No. 42, *Copper Weatherings and Flashings*.
Re-line gutters with new copper sheet, with upstands and flashings as described above.
Reform downpipe boxes where necessary, of dimensions at least 230mm × 230mm × 100mm deep. Cut away masonry of parapets as directed and construct overflow spout to each box, of 26 s.w.g. copper, to discharge through parapet and clear of wall externally. Back-gutters behind chimneys are to be dressed at least 100mm around each angle of chimney.

15. COMPLETION: All relaid copperwork is to be approved in detail by the architect before the roofers leave the site, and left throughout in a sound and weather-tight condition. Remove all tools, plant and equipment and unused materials; carefully clean out all gutters with wooden shovels, wash down and leave all tidy on completion.

Longstraw thatch, shorter-lived and many times re-coated

Reed thatch with 'eyebrow' dormer and sedge ridging

well as on new roofs; but doubts have been raised in many minds by the impossibility of being able to guarantee the roof for any really adequate period, in relation to the life of an old building. Continuous materials of this nature must be supported absolutely firmly; and such details as the function between a wooden roof and a vertical wall are always danger points. Where a more permanent job is impossible however, asphalt makes a sound job for its own life span, and may usefully be employed to protect an ageing roof for 20 or 30 years.

5.3 Unit coverings

Thatch Many more medieval roofs than would now appear so were originally covered either with thatch or oak shingles. Nowadays the use of thatch is mostly confined to rural situations, owing mainly to the cost factor, and to the risk of damage by fire. Thanks largely to the encouragement of the Council for Small Industries in Rural Areas, the craft is nevertheless very much alive and has many young apprentices. A thatched roof indeed offers the best insulated covering available; but it must be carefully maintained, and renewed at relatively frequent intervals. The simple, unelaborate shapes of old thatched roofs, formed of rough rafters and unwrought spars, are a perfectly adequate and suitable substructure; and there is no need to regularise and sophisticate them. Overhanging eaves and verges are generic to the material; but internal valleys, parapet gables and back gutters are not, and should be removed whenever possible. Eaves gutters are best avoided altogether.

'Longstraw' thatch is the least durable of the family and with a life of only 20 to 30 years, it also requires the steepest pitch (about 50deg). The material is cheap, but machine thrashing, which damages the straw, and rising labour costs have made straw thatch an increasingly uneconomical material. Reed thatch is, however, a horse of a different colour: it is tightly 'sprung' into position so as to present only the butts of the reeds at the surface, and if re-ridged at intervals, may last easily 70 or 80 years. Combed wheat reed is a little less durable, with a life of 35 to 60 years. There is no more depressing sight than worn-out thatch; and periodical repair and attention are essential. Damage by birds and vermin can be minimised by wiring over the roof with a stout galvanised mesh.

Nowadays roofing battens are usually pre-treated and fixed over roofing felt

Northumberland stone roofing-slab released by a twisted fixing peg

Thatch may also be fireproofed by treating it with a solution of sulphate of ammonia, borax, boracic acid and alum[1]; but the treatment is simpler for new than existing thatch, and needs periodic renewal. Experiments are being made with a fireproof blanket underlay, fixed over the rafters to protect the interior; and if successful, this method may easily help to reduce the chief hazard of the material.

Tiles Clay tiles were imported from the Low Countries during and after the 13th century, and their use became compulsory in London in 1212. In historic buildings they are usually hand-made, and held in place by means of oak pegs hung over riven oak battens. Except when iron fixing nails were used and have been eaten away by tannic acid, the battens are usually the first casualty needing replacement.

In rebattening a roof, the old tiles should be carefully set aside, and the battens stripped and replaced by new ones, usually of heavy gauge deal. It is false economy to skimp

batten sizes; and to preclude corrosion, they must be securely fixed to the oak timbers by copper nails. If these will not penetrate the ancient and hardened timber, extremely strong aluminium alloy nails can now also be obtained.

Tiles may be re-hung either from oak pegs, as they were originally, or by means of stout copper, aluminium alloy or galvanised-iron nails.

Where the pitch is adequate, roofing felt under the battening is not really necessary. It may, however, be found a great convenience in keeping the structure watertight during the course of operations. Otherwise the additional ventilation admitted by the unfelted tile roof is all in fact a credit on the health account. Pantiles are indigenous to some parts of the country, but elsewhere are too assertive for use as a substitute material.

Slates Stone slates are common in some areas, and vary enormously in quality and characteristics. Some are liable to damage by frost, especially in the upper half, which is kept wettened by contact with the slate above. For all stone slates, a very heavy roof construction is needed. The lowest courses of a roof, where there is the most water to

---

[1] Recipe recommended by Council for Small Industries in Rural Areas: 28 lb. sulphate of ammonia, 14 lb. carbonate ammonia lump, 7 lb. boracic acid and 14 lb. alum lump, dissolved in 50 gallons water. Coverage 500 sq. ft.

Slating in bad shape at Gamul House, Chester: the battening appears to have been remarkably slight

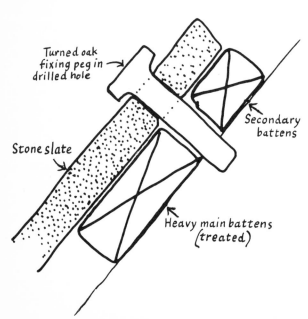

Double-battening to prevent the twisting of fixing-pegs at Blanchland, Northumberland

Turned oak fixing peg in drilled hole

Secondary battens

Stone slate

Heavy main battens (treated)

A rare and engaging interlocking ridge treatment

be combated, are first laid with the heaviest and largest slates, the remainder being laid in succeeding courses, decreasing gradually in weight and pitch until the smallest offcuts can be utilised at the ridge. When cheap rail transport became available in the 19th century, the smooth, black Welsh tiles, drab in appearance but amenable to pitches of as little as 22deg, easy to lay and predictable in performance, to a great extent supplanted local stone, and were often used for replacements. It is however always

Duckboards, cat-ladders and access ways need regular maintenance

through the slots and laid flat on the underside. The slate may then be slid up into position, with the tabs in place, to be turned down over the battens from inside. This is only practicable when there is reasonable access to the roof-space. The common but bad practice of drilling and screwing tiles into place with brass screws and washers, covered with mastic, is a fundamental error and can never make a good job.

Shingles Oak shingles are now rarely found, and have been almost entirely ousted by cedar, which is an excellent material for the purpose. The life of shingles is limited to some 40 or 50 years, after which considerable repairs begin to be necessary. Swarming insects behind shingles also sometimes attract damage by woodpeckers. On the rare occasions when shingles are to be renewed in oak, the nail-holes must be burned with a hot iron, as protection to the nails against tannic acid attack.

Duckboards Although scarcely a roofing material, these are an important provision under this heading. Proper means of access over roofs should always be arranged, so as to avoid any damage to delicate slates and tiles. Duckboards in gutters are useful in supporting melting snow, while allowing the free passage of water beneath. They should be carefully designed to avoid interference with the flow of water, and must be of wood such as cedar or utile, or of creosoted deal, and not of timbers harmful to metal like oak. Care should also be taken in the placing of nails and screws to avoid harm to the metal. An adequate supply of wooden shovels or cleaning boards must lastly be kept at hand in any ancient building, to encourage snow clearance without unnecessary damage to the roofs.

possible, where expense permits, to obtain a high-quality stone slate of a closer match. Where an area of slating is to be cut out for repairs, this may be achieved by working diagonally upwards from the eaves so as to damage the fewest possible fixings. The support of individual replaced slates by lead tabs turned up at the bottom is an unsound practice, since the tabs gradually open and release the slates, and are especially liable to damage when the roof is being brushed clear of snow. Copper tabs are stronger; but the best device of all is to slot the slates at their fixing holes, where they will later be protected by the course above, and to hook in stout copper tabs, tucked

Outline specification for repair of slated roof in accordance with architect's detailed site direction

STRIPPING: Strip all lead dressings and leadwork from gutters, dormers, hips, valleys, ridges, etc., of slopes as indicated on the plans, by section as directed on site, and cart away and credit.

Any leadwork in good condition may be salvaged for re-use if approved by the architect. Carefully remove existing stone slates to roof slopes as indicated, and set aside as many as possible for re-use.

Strip old battens and cart away, and remove boarding where existing, for re-use as directed.

Shore as necessary, and remove all disused, seriously damaged and useless timbers. Cut out or remove all

timbers found heavily infested with beetle, and thoroughly treat remainder with '. . . . .' or other approved insecticide, all as directed.

Cart away all rubbish with minimum disturbance and mess, and protect interior from damage whilst un-roofed.

Replace all deficient and inadequate rafters, purlins and other roof members with new well seasoned deal of similar scantlings, all as directed by the architect.

It is not intended to renew or straighten old and crooked structure, but rather to set the roof in sound and healthy repair. In general, timbers are to be

inspected and repaired individually and as far as possible in position, with a minimum of replacements and renewals. All 'live' structural movements must be resolved, design defects such as insufficient drips or falls properly remedied, and beetle infestation cut out or thoroughly poisoned. Exact symmetry and straightness are, however, not sought after, and irregularities which are not unsound or unsafe are to be retained. Detailed instructions on all points will be given on the site by the architect.

continued . . . .

FELTING AND RE-BATTENING: After approval of repairs to each section of roof carpentry, lay '. . . . .', ... quality or other equal and approved roofing felt over rafters, lapped sheet over sheet, and batten with . . . . deal battens securely fixed with . . . . nails at . . . . in. centres.

LEADWORK: All leadwork to gutters, hips, valleys and dormers, and all dressings, soakers, etc., throughout are to be renewed in accordance with the attached Specification for leadwork, and as directed on site.

SLATING: On all external slopes visible from the ground, the existing slates are as far as possible to be re-used, made up as necessary with new '. . . . .' slates or other equal and approved, of nearest possible match to the old, as directed. Carefully relay . . . . face with new or salvaged slates as directed, in regularly diminishing courses from eaves to ridge, to present an unbroken face of similar slates towards this side. Elsewhere the slates are to be kept as far as possible of a single type within each roof slope, changes being confined whenever possible to the lines of hips, valleys or verges.
On unseen slopes where indicated on the drawings, ... quality '. . . . . . .' slates are to be used equal to a sample to be approved by the architect.

FIXING: Slates to be of random width, laid to regularly diminishing courses, as may permit the maximum re-use of existing slates. No slate to be cut to a width of less than half its length. Only wide slates to be used at the hips and verges.
Each slate to be securely fixed by two stout copper nails, equal to sample to be submitted to and approved by the architect. Slates to be accurately cut to rake of roof on dormer cheeks and at valleys, hips and verges. Nailing to be clear of woodwork. Lay double course at eaves and verges and point up verges in water-proofed cement mortar, struck off smoothly.
Against raking parapets at . . . . gable where there is insufficient upstand for lead soakers, slating is to be carefully flaunched with fillets of water-proofed cement, weathered away from stonework. Elsewhere against abutments, insert 4 lb (BS 4) lead soakers 25mm longer than slates, turned up under proper stepped or raking cover flashings as specified.

COMPLETION: On completion and approval of the roofing repairs, remove all rubbish from roof and attics.
Carefully vacuum clean attic spaces and leave all clean and tidy.

Notes on re-thatching

Thatching being a specialist craft, no specification is usually issued; but the following notes are of guidance.

NORFOLK REED: All old thatch must be completely stripped; to attempt encasing old reed roofs is never satisfactory.
New reed thatch should generally be 300mm thick, reduced to 250mm at the verges. For every 'square' of 10m super, about 100–120 bundles of best Norfolk reed (or in poorer work, 'mixed' reed) will be needed. The reed is laid in courses, 'sprung' into position and held down by hazel rods some 1·5m to 2·5m long at 1·8 to 2·0m centres. These are stitched to the battens with stout tarred cord, or secured by pointed iron hooks 200mm to 300mm long, driven into each rafter. In completing the ridge, a reed 'roll', 100mm to 200mm in diameter is first laid, and then covered with 150mm of sedge, held with rods and herring-bone cross spitting, and patterned to design.

In roofs open to view from below, a woven mat of reeds is sometimes used in place of battens.

COMBED WHEAT REED: Wheat straw instead of being threshed can be passed through a reed combing machine, when being unbroken it can be used for thatching like reed.
Old work may be cased, when a 300mm new coat is sufficient; otherwise if it is completely stripped, 300mm to 450mm thickness is required, calling for approximately 20 bundles or 'nitches' (12·7kg) of the combed wheat reed, 25 spars and 25 four-foot 'binders' per square. The finished roof is often completed by trimming with clippers.

THRESHED LONG STRAW: All eaves and verges should be stripped, together with any superfluous and decayed old thatch, down to a sound foundation of the original coat. The wheat straw should be of good quality and is prepared in 'yealms' or layers 350mm to 450mm wide by 100mm thick, well wettened and laid to a thickness of 250mm to 300mm. The verges and eaves may be increased to 300mm or 380mm. The straw is held in place by 'brotches' of split hazel or willow 600mm to 750mm long, pointed at each end and twisted in the middle to form a staple. Exposed rods are finally fixed over the straw to hold down the eaves and verges.

Timber structures, fungi and pests

5.4 Repairing timber structures, roofs and woodwork

The successful repair of ageing timber structures, perhaps more than any other type of old buildings work, demands of the modern architect a real appreciation of the structural and design principles employed by his professional ancestors.

The timber framed structure, indeed, often has as much about it of engineering as of architecture. The first thing to do is by analysing the construction in detail, to reach a real understanding of the stresses and loading pattern involved. Sometimes the part which each structural member fulfils is clear enough. Often too, for example in elaborate mediaeval roofs, one will find all manner of complications to unravel, before the cobwebs can be brushed from one's hair.

Timber framing will usually be either of Tudor date, with post and lintel framed storey by storey, each floor overhanging the last, or of the later fully framed, diagonal-braced type in which the main posts run the full height of the building. The reasons for overhanging storey construction were partly practical, the lower storeys being thus protected by the upper, and the maximum accommodation crowded into the walled-town sites, and partly structural, as the weight of the walls in fact 'pre-stresses' the floor beams as well as reducing their span. Where the ground-floor of this type of building has been enlarged to match those above, the structure may be greatly weakened if internal posts are removed. Similarly, upper floors may be weakened by the removal of projecting gables which balance and tension them.

Roof construction at first consisted of coupled pairs of rafters, laid 'flat' and pegged at the apex: later, integrated systems of transverse trusses and longitudinal ridge-boards and purlins were introduced.

Timber trusses were often prefabricated, then taken apart and re-assembled on the site; and the identifying numerals of each member may often be found cut into the timber at the joints.

Mediaeval timberwork was always heavy and usually very lavish: our forebears apparently had no appreciation of the principle of the thin, deep beam. In consequence there is often an enormous factor of safety, and even fairly wide-spread depredations of rot and beetle can be accommodated without real danger. The timber used was usually oak which, although often full of shakes and holes, becomes iron-hard with age and will suffer little harm from the elements, even out of doors. Chestnut may also be encountered; the theory that it is impervious to beetle attack is, alas, a fallacy. Elm was frequently used for floor boarding.

During the 17th century imports of foreign deal began, but by this time the great period of timber building was on the wane, and it is rare to find a framed old building constructed with softwood.

It is important to remember that movement plays a large part in the life of any timber structure, and is a natural part of its history. Oak, in particular, moves fiercely for many years after felling. It is thus more often than not a mistake to attempt to straighten up a framed building which has come to rest in an eccentric posture, provided only that its individual parts are sound, and the structure not so distorted as to be unsafe. Similarly, one must beware of doing anything which may violently alter the conditions to which timbers have become accustomed over several centuries. Thus the practice of stripping and exposing previously plastered timbers, 'for effect', is questionable on structural as well as aesthetic grounds.

Having got to know his building therefore, from the viewpoint of what makes it stand up, the architect must be very

Here at Langley, Shropshire, a building's entire biography may be read and understood in its ancient timber framing

Timber framing: the structural logic of a Suffolk oak-framed building. Each bay and member is clearly articulated in relation to its purpose

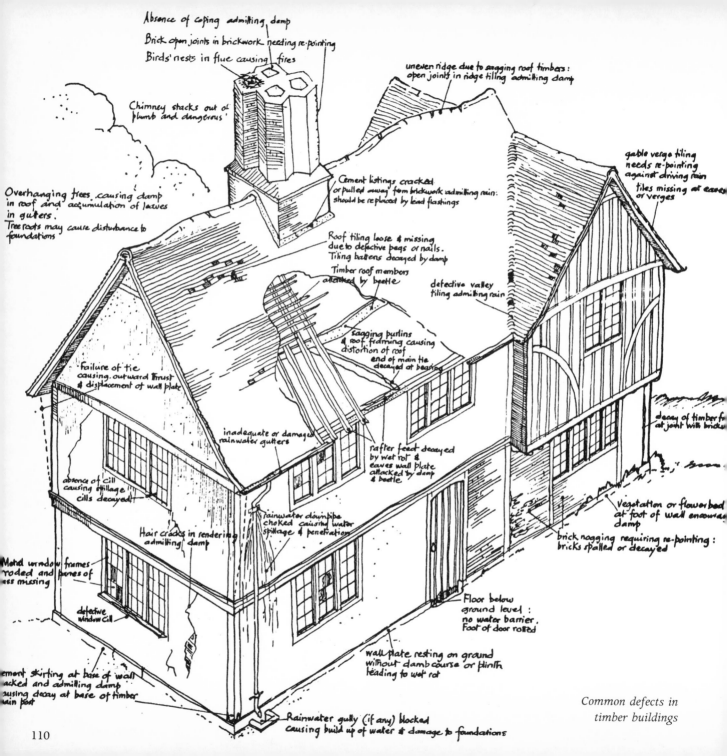

Absence of coping admitting damp

Brick open joints in brickwork needing re-pointing

Birds' nests in flue causing fires

Chimney stacks out of plumb and dangerous

uneven ridge due to sagging roof timbers: open joints in ridge tiling admitting damp

Overhanging trees causing damp in roof and accumulation of leaves in gutters. Tree roots may cause disturbance to foundations

Cement fillings cracked or pulled away from brickwork admitting rain: should be replaced by lead flashings

gable verge tiling needs re-pointing against driving rain

tiles missing at eaves or verges

Roof tiling loose & missing due to defective pegs or nails. Tiling battens decayed by damp

Timber roof members attacked by beetle

defective valley tiling admitting rain

sagging purlins & roof framing causing distortion of roof

end of main tie decayed at bearing

Failure of tie causing outward thrust & displacement of wall plate

inadequate or damaged rainwater gutters

rafter feet decayed by wet rot & eaves wall plate attacked by damp & beetle

decay of timber fr at joint with bricks

absence of cill causing spillage cills decayed

rainwater downpipe choked causing water spillage & penetration

Vegetation or flowerbed at foot of wall encourag damp

Hair cracks in rendering admitting damp

brick nogging requiring re-pointing: bricks spalled or decayed

Metal window frames corroded and panes of glass missing

defective window cill

Floor below ground level: no water barrier. Foot of door rotted

cement skirting at base of wall cracked and admitting damp causing decay at base of timber main post

wall plate resting on ground without damp course or plinth leading to wet rot

Rainwater gully (if any) blocked causing build up of water & damage to foundations

Common defects in timber buildings

110

Historical features previously hidden: a delightful lath-marked hammer-beam truss, invisible on survey, but later discovered in a bedroom partition

Dropped and propped: a parted purlin in this fine oak roof may be capable of jacking back into position when the outside is re-thatched

careful in deciding which of its many apparent faults are harmless eccentricities and which are active and dangerous defects, requiring a remedy.

As a general principle it is best to renew carpentry with carpentry, provided no assertive 'faking' is thereby entailed. Furthermore it is usually best also to use the same species of timber as the original, always provided that really well-seasoned stuff is available. Quite often, and especially in the country, second-hand oak can be found, which if sound is ideal for repairs.

There are times, however, when the extensive shoring and dismantling, and perhaps the disturbance of moulded plaster finishes which would be necessary to reach and replace defective timbers, may justify the use of metal plates and splints instead. It has been said indeed that some ancient buildings have now structurally a metal roof, merely faced with the relics of ancient timberwork. The architect must therefore consider very carefully whether the historical interest of the work requiring repair is sufficient to pardon this structural dishonesty. A possible compromise where decorative detail is seriously damaged is to gather all original surviving work to a single part of the building—for example, to the bay nearest the chancel in an old church roof.

When it is decided to strengthen a beam with steel plates, these may be applied on the same principle as on a rolled-steel joist, either at top and bottom or even only on the tension face. If much heavy metal is added to an already sagging floor, however, its weight may cause further deflection unless the existing structure is first jacked up to an equivalent extent. Occasionally it may be possible to stiffen a beam from above, suspending it by hangers from some other part of the structure. In this case it is vital first to analyse what new stresses will be set up in the building as a whole, and to ensure that the suspending member itself is a rigid anchor. For example, it is useless to attempt to support a sagging beam by means of a tie-rod suspended from another timber which is itself subject to movement.

Replacement by timber is usually less difficult, assuming that a sufficiently strong member can be accommodated, but alternatives may sometimes have to be found to achieving this with a single beam, owing to the impossibility of tenoning it into existing mortices in fixed members at both ends. For example, it may be found possible to replace one beam with two, inserted alongside each other, each tenoned into one end and subsequently bolted together.

Where metalwork will be exposed to view, wrought-iron is less foreign-looking than steel. The tannic acid in oak will attack small iron fixings unless they are protected, for example by bitumen, but will not seriously weaken stout metal bolts.

The weakest links in any timber structure are the joints, which should always be carefully examined. The oak pegs pinning mediaeval tenons are frequently found to have perished, and must then be drilled out and renewed—the new pegs should be left projecting, and not trimmed off flush. Failure of the tenon itself through decay or fracture is fortunately less common. Where it is possible without excessive cost or disturbance to remove the affected beam for repair, it may be possible to contrive the insertion of a false tenon, well and tightly housed into it. Otherwise the defective junction may be strengthened by means of metal angles or plates, securely bolted to it and placed to 'bridge' the point of maximum weakness across to solid members.

Carpentry need be no more sophisticated than its history and situation warrants—for example, unshaped larch poles may be perfectly adequate for a thatched roof.

Actual physical failure of a timber member due to over-loading is comparatively rare, unless it has been weakened by some external influence. The thoughtless removal or maiming of a strut or brace, or even of a whole load-bearing partition, during the course of some ill-contrived past alteration, may sometimes have caused sagging or even

Raking archbrace indicates earlier end wall of an oak-framed Kent building, extended later in its history

collapse; and no architect needs to be reminded of the depredations of amateur electricians. Empty mortices give a useful clue to missing members; but their presence does not always indicate a lost link, for secondhand timbers were frequently used by the old builders. If over-stressing is definitely found to be due to the removal of intermediate supports, they should undoubtedly be reinstated: but since more often than not, a post or partition was removed simply because it was in the way, a similar fate may sometimes be confidently predicted for the replacements. As it may be impolitic for the architect to insist on his client's parting with the offending Bechstein, ways may have to be sought for giving the structure new courage. If the over-stressed member is in a floor construction, it may be possible to stiffen it by bearers from its better-blessed neighbours. Alternatively the effective span can sometimes be divided by inserting additional beams in the opposite direction—for example by cutting the member and inserting a steel joist, carrying the cut ends by means of a plated lower flange. Complete replacement of a beam by steel is usually a last resort, as complicated bearing problems will almost always be involved. An interesting example given by the SPAB is the typical case where tie beams of a mediaeval house have been cut away to give increased headroom: here it is sometimes possible to overcome the inclined thrust of the rafters by trussing the ridge in the other direction, lengthwise from gable to gable.

In all timber repairs it is important to remember the special propensity of timber to adjust its dimensions under unequal loading. Thus a beam whose bearing has no 'slack' will jam itself tightly between the walls when expanded during damp weather and may actually compress itself between them. If the end or the joint of a timber member is repeatedly blocked from natural expansion by dust or grit and rubble, it will compress when damp, and then shrink further upon subsequent drying. In time, these cumulative shortenings may become quite appreciable, often reducing the bearing area of a beam with disastrous effect. For this reason, the wedging of timber members 'for rigidity' between walls or other fixed structures is quite useless, and may well be actually harmful. Timbers can be blocked up with hardwood wedges to give a uniform bearing, but the wedges in compressing uniformly easily fall out, and should be nailed or otherwise fixed in position.

The most common cause of weakness in structural timbering is, as always, damp and its resultant evils, fungal and beetle attack. The end of a timber particularly is its Achilles' heel and should be well protected from weather penetration. For this reason, too, even in dealing with a sound timber structure, every opportunity must be taken to provide adequate ventilation, and to introduce adequate damp-proof courses between timbers such as wall-plates and damp walling. Timber ground floors were often set directly on damp earth. In cellars where the floors above have suffered from damp and lack of ventilation it is often possible to reduce the span of damaged and sagging beams by supporting them intermediately on new brick piers incorporating proper damp-proof courses. New timbers should never be set alongside, nor in close contact with damp walling.

Defective timbers under parapet gutters are a source of disaster and the bearings of trusses are frequently found in a precarious state of decay. The classical remedy is to shore up the structure and to scarf on a new length of timber, carefully jointed to the old. Both tie beam and

This tie-beam has been cut through at some time to give extra headroom

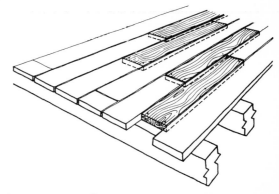

When repairing floors it is important to preserve the continuous joint lines between boards, without patching across them

The new fibreglass cornice at Wotton House: the acorn pendants are original timber coated with fibre-glass

principal rafter may be treated in this way so that the triangulation of the truss is restored *in situ*. The usual procedure is to cut away the decayed end of the beam until structurally sound timber is reached, allowing a diagonal cut to be made, with a length of approximately three times the depth of the beam. Feather edges at top and bottom should be avoided by cutting stopped ends to the main diagonal. The new timber end is then cut to match and bolted on and the joint may be further tightened by driving wedges from each side into a socket cut equally into the old and new timber half-way along the diagonal cut. Structurally this type of joint is strongest if the bearing end of the timber is sloped to 'carry' the remainder; but the scarf may perhaps be reversed in favour of the saving of ancient mouldings upon the under side of the old beam. The job may be further strengthened where necessary by plating the joint with steel, bolted closely right through the beams.

Alternatively, the load of a truss may sometimes be carried to the wall by new concrete corbels, set well into the masonry so as to avoid overturning, or by means of metal hangers. If this type of repair is adopted, great care must be taken to maintain the triangulation of the truss. Sometimes timbers in concealed, damp situations such as

parapet gutters are best completely removed and replaced with concrete; but in this case it is essential to avoid subsequent damage to leadwork by irregularities or direct contact with the concrete, by means of careful screeding and heavy building-paper underlays.

Joinery and floors The repair of joinery is not usually a difficult matter. It is generally sufficient to cut out rotten sections of woodwork, and to piece in new wood, securely jointed home. Where decayed wood is difficult to remove— for example when glazing bars containing valuable glass are beginning to fail—it can often be strengthened by plates of brass or other non-ferrous metal, housed into the surface and secured by countersunk brass screws. In repairing doors and other joinery, it must be remembered that wood requires room to move, and that joint lines give it just this facility. The foot of a vertically boarded door should thus be pieced board by board, maintaining the joint lines between them.

Timber floors in old buildings are usually of wide elm boards, or occasionally of oak. Floors are one of the most rapidly worn finishes in a building, and may have been frequently renewed. Very often, damaged boarding will be found to be cased with new deal, the old beetle-infested woodwork being left as a source of hidden trouble. Occasionally a good original elm or oak floor with only local patches of damage may have been cased in the same way, and can now be opened up and properly repaired. In repairing timber floors, each board should be treated individually and cut away and pieced, the joints between the boards being maintained. Even if two adjoining boards are pieced, the patches should still be individual to their boards, and movement and shrinkage thus confined to the regular pattern of original joint lines. Loose and squeaky boards are often the product of careless electricians, or may give a clue to structural failure. A whole floor which has dropped slightly, leaving a wide gap between the boarding and the surrounding skirtings, is always suspect as a possible case of dry-rot, with attendant shrinkage and collapse of hidden wallplates.

It is important not to misjudge a floor in a superficially tatty and neglected condition: if it is structurally sound even the most irregular and unprepossessing boarding may be capable of polishing beautifully. As with many other

Fungal decay spreads rapidly

The spreading mycelium of merulius lacrymans

'finds' in an old building, a feature which many would not have looked at twice may yet so easily again become an object of value and pride.

5.5. Eradicating timber fungi and pests

All timber pests are fundamentally nature's forest scavengers, whose function it is to break down and convert dead trees into soil, and allow new trees unimpeded growth. Once a tree is felled, whether by age or by the axe, the timber is, from a natural standpoint, 'dead' and ready for destruction. The fact that wood has been shaped and re-used as a building material is of no interest to a fungus or a beetle, whose ambitions culminate in costly damage to old woodwork.

The fungi are parasitical, and can only live by feeding directly on organic matter, such as wood and leaves. They breathe in oxygen and give out carbon dioxide, and are thus vulnerable by respiratory toxics. Some may spread to dry wood and others cannot, but all require an initial host with a moisture content of some 20% for germination. Although in a new house, the moisture content of timber may for a while be as high as 18%, this is soon reduced in normal circumstances to some 12-14%, so that in fact, a sound, dry building has nothing to fear.

Identifying merulius lacrymans The most serious and devastating fungus from the point of view of the building owner and also, unfortunately, the species most frequently found in old buildings, is *merulius lacrymans,* or weeping merulius. Paradoxically, the fungus is usually known as dry rot, the name being something of a misnomer, except that the infection can spread to dry wood, and leaves it arid, dead and brittle.

The life-cycle starts with a spore, of which there are many millions in the atmosphere. They are remarkably resistant to physical extremes of heat and humidity, and very long-lived. A spore landing on wood with a moisture content of about 20-25%, in a temperature of 7°C to 27°C, and preferably in a still, stuffy atmosphere, can germinate, and then throws out hollow strands known as hyphae. Hair-like and fine at first, these seek their way by thrusting and branching gently into the wood. Timber consists of approximately two-thirds cellulose and one-third lignin; and it is on the cellulose that the growing hyphae feed, their enzymes converting it into sugar, digesting it and reaching on to new wood, leaving behind a dry and desiccated framework of lonely lignin. The hyphae unit into a rapidly-spreading cotton-wool like structure known as mycelium, which is at first white, and develops yellow and purple spots on exposure to light. In later stages of the attack, strands called 'rhizomorphs' develop from the mycelium, and it is these which convey moisture from the decomposing wood to sound timber many feet beyond, weeping tears on it until it too is subjugated and ripe for attack.

When the attack is sufficiently well established, the fungus will produce a 'sporophore' or flower—a fruiting body which produces millions of spores or seeds. The sporophore is at first a whitish grey, like an unwholesome fleshy growth, and gradually becomes more leathery and clammy. The spores are a bright rusty red, and unbelievably numerous—a sporophore may give out from two to five million spores per square foot, for several days; and these are carried everywhere as a fine red dust in the air, to germinate in damp timber elsewhere and start the process afresh.

Dry rot exhibits an uncanny knowledge of the presence of timber, and can thrust through brickwork and over walls for great distances to reach and consume fresh food. An attack in a damp cellar may often spread in wall linings to seek the timbers of a roof, or from one building through brick party walls into the next. The whole process is entirely voracious and obscene.

The symptoms of dry rot are quite unmistakable, and may be suspected from any of the following symptoms:

(*a*) amusty, frowsy smell,

(*b*) the appearance of fleshy, spreading mycelium or in severe cases, of actual fruiting bodies,

(*c*) cracking and bulging of joinery (skirtings, panellings, linings, etc) caused by shrinkage of hidden timbers attacked by the fungus.

(*d*) loss of nature in the woodwork, which gives a dead, hollow sound when tapped and offers no resistance to probing,

(*e*) the characteristic, hungry destruction of timber, with deep cracks, especially *across* the grain, giving a cubed appearance.

Once *merulius lacrymans* has been discovered and identified, the only remedy is an utterly ruthless, detailed campaign of extermination, coupled with careful remedy of the unhealthy conditions which started the attack. The fungus has no heart and no Achilles' heel, and unless completely destroyed to the last limit, it will gather its forces and start again more virulently than ever. Fortunately it may readily be poisoned, once its entire extent has been discovered.

The architect charged with the responsibility of eradicating an attack has two alternatives open to him. He may either employ a local builder to carry out the whole of the work of opening up and eradication, or he may call in one of the numerous specialist firms to deal with the attack. If a builder is entrusted with the whole of the work, the architect must ensure by thorough briefing and supervision that only careful and conscientious workmen are employed, and that they know exactly what to look for and what is to be done. The advantage of employing a specialist firm for treatment is that the work of trained and experienced workmen is more certain to result in a thorough and successful job, reinforced in most cases by a guarantee.

Dry rot causes cross-cracking and cubing in boarded wall linings

Sterilising an attack of dry rot in soft brick walling

This is particularly valuable when, for example, a property which is known to have suffered from dry rot is shortly to be sold.

The resultant peace of mind, however, is purchased at a price, since any firm issuing a guarantee must inevitably err on the side of over-thoroughness, and will therefore of necessity be more expensive. It is of course impossible to lay down hard and fast rules as to when specialists should be called in: so much depends upon the convenience of the individual case. The cost of disturbance, for example, might be greater than that of actual repair, when complete eradication is essential at any cost. Or if a specialist firm is just around the corner, there may be little cost difference to be considered. If the architect is confident from his own knowledge and experience that he is master of the situation, and that good builders are available and can be relied upon to co-operate fully with him, success is assured. If, however, the attack is a particularly virulent and complicated one, or if there is no general contractor who can be given the job in complete confidence, it may be worth the extra cost to call in the specialist. Some of these firms make an initial charge for visiting and reporting on a building; but this is usually deducted from their account for any work subsequently carried out.

Eradicating dry rot The first step in eradicating dry rot is to find the heart of the outbreak, and to trace its extent with the greatest care and thoroughness. Each searching branch of the fungus must be systematically traced from its source to growing tip, and the finishes opened up for a foot or two beyond. Floorboards, plaster, joinery and finishes must be removed without compunction if there is the slightest suspicion that the fungus has penetrated beneath or behind them. Extreme care is necessary in examining the backs of timbers in contact with walling, and all vestiges of fixing and built-in timbers, along the back of which the hyphae can easily reach.

When the extent of the trouble is known, treatment can begin. If fruiting bodies are present, these should first be liberally treated with fungicide to prevent the spread of airborne spores. All infected timbers are next cut away: it is usual to require the removal of all infected wood to an arbitrary distance of at least 0·5m beyond the last visible attack. Where, however, important structural timbers are infected, but have not yet been actually weakened by the fungus, it is possible under vigilant supervision to poison them very thoroughly and retain them. All fungus-infected timber removed should meanwhile immediately be burned, together with all sweepings, dust, dirt, shavings and sawdust from the infected area. No attempt should be made to save any scrap, even 'for firewood'—for this is in effect a cancer, the last vestige of which must be totally destroyed.

All brickwork into which mycelium has spread, and any masonry or walling adjoining an outbreak, must next be similarly poisoned. Hyphae may be destroyed by heat, but the effect of waving a blowlamp over brickwork is very inconclusive. If a structural wall is too thick to absorb fungicide into its heart, it must be drilled with holes at intervals, into which the liquid can be sprayed under pressure, so as to permeate the entire material. In this respect, thorough heating with a blowlamp or with flame-throwers is useful in drying out moisture and making the brickwork receptive to the liquid: but care must be taken to avoid damage by fire, especially by charring the end-grain of cut timbers. Walls should whenever possible be treated from both sides. Volatile and flammable solutions cannot, of course, be used in conjunction with a blowlamp. Meanwhile the cause of the outbreak must be traced and rectified. The presence of any of the fungi is always evidence of an unhealthy condition, inviting further damage and decay. Leaking gutters, inadequate soakers and flashings, defective downpipes, earth piles above damp-proof courses, and all sources of dampness must be removed. Ill-ventilated and stagnant spaces must be opened up to a constant current of air, by the introduction of new ventilators and openings, since the fungus abhors fresh air; and even a vigorous growth may be arrested (but not killed) by exposure. If wall-panelling has suffered, it may be possible to introduce air-bricks so as to provide a continuously ventilated cavity behind it. If a spring or other source of moisture is traced, it may be possible to pipe the water safely away: water should never be blocked, but always encouraged to flow away by the easiest possible route. Ventilation must be continuous, and not dependent upon intermittent opening of windows or closable ventilators of any kind.

New timbers inserted as replacements should be thoroughly treated from every face against infection, and no unnecessary wood fixings or bonding timbers re-introduced into walling. A careful inspection must lastly be made to ensure that adjoining parts of the neighbouring buildings are free from infection.

The finishes can then be reinstated, and except for periodical future inspections in difficult cases, the attack can be confidently regarded as cured.

Eradicating other timber fungi The only other fungal decays attacking timber in buildings are relatively unimportant, since they have not the power of spreading to sound wood. They do however indicate the presence of unhealthy conditions, in which more serious trouble could well develop. These minor fungi are usually known somewhat loosely by the general name of wet rot.

Coniophora Cerebella or the cellar fungus is the commonest. It cannot live on timber with a moisture content of less than 25%, and is thus usually found in situations too damp for true dry-rot. The fungus can be identified by its fine dark brown or blackish strands, and the green and leathery, lumpy fruiting body. A paper-thin shell of sound wood is sometimes left on the surface of the timber, which shows deep cracks *along* the grain but rarely across it as in true dry-rot.

A robust lion carved on an oak wall-plate: note the death-watch beetle flight holes

Other wet rot fungi found in old buildings include *poria vaillantii,* the pore fungus, with spreading strands rather like string.

Eradication of all these less serious fungal varieties is usually a simple matter of cutting out and burning all the infected timber. It is however wise to treat the area with fungicide as a precaution against any subsequent outbreak of dry rot, which may otherwise easily occur during drying-out.

5.6   Timber pests

Beetle destruction in timber is rarely as dangerous as fungal attack, the reason being that an infected section is only weakened by the total cross-sectional area of the tunnels it contains—the timber around them remaining unimpaired

in strength. It is important to remember this in dealing with beetle attack in old buildings. In mediaeval structures particularly, the members are often of such massive sections that even the loss of half of their cross-sectional area may not result in any significant weakening relative to the strength required of them.

Beetle attack which is expended need receive little attention, except for any necessary strengthening of the damaged timbers. Active attack should not however be left unattended. Current infestation is easily identifiable by the clean, bright appearance of recent exit holes, and by the little piles and patches of fresh boredust which fall from them. To assist in distinguishing the pest, a resumé of the life-cycles of each is given:

Identifying timber pests The chief insect destroyers of timber in buildings are the death-watch beetle and furniture beetle. Both are of similar family with a broadly similar life-cycle of egg—larva—chrysalis—adult beetle, and the two are often found together. It is at the larva stage that the boring and feeding of the grubs causes all the damage, for adult beetles do not eat, and their life is short.

The different species are identifiable mainly by the sizes of the flight holes, by the appearance of the excreta, and sometimes by the type of wood attacked. In early summer, the beetles themselves may also be found.

The *death-watch beetle* (*xestobium rufovillosum*) has a life-cycle of three to ten years, depending upon environment, from a damp, warm timber to old, hardened hardwood. The eggs are laid in clutches of about 70, in any cracks and crevices in suitable timber. Hardwood is preferred, particularly its outer, softer layers of sapwood next to the bark; and timber pre-digested by decay or fungus offers a special attraction. The attack is usually concentrated in the damp and more edible timber such as wall-plates, the feet of rafters and bearing ends of beams and trusses, and in all timbers buried in or set against damp walling.

Timber softened by fungal attack is particularly tempting to beetles of all kinds. The eggs of the death-watch beetle hatch out in about 2-8 weeks; and the larvae, which are curved white grubs with brown heads, select a suitable spot and then burrow into the timber. After a varying period of years, during which extensive galleries are eaten into the timber, the dust being emitted in bun-shaped pellets, the larva enters a pupal stage lasting 3-6 weeks, and emerges as a full-grown beetle. In the case of the death-watch beetle, this remains in its pupal chamber until the following spring, then emerges in April, May or June to seek a mate. During these months the characteristic tapping sound can be heard as beetles of both sexes rap their heads quickly—about eight taps per second—in short bursts upon the timber as a mating-call.

The full-grown beetle is about 6mm to 9mm long, brown in colour, with little patches of yellowish hair; and emerges through a flight hole some 3mm in diameter. The beetle often falls to the floor—once, one fell from ceiling beams on to my drawing-board—but can fly in search of a mate. An attack may die out if timber becomes sufficiently hard and unpalatable through age and proper maintenance. Softwood is rarely attacked.

The *furniture beetle* (*anobium punctatum*) may be found in both hardwood and softwood, again chiefly in the sappy layers under the bark, especially some 8-10 years after felling, and often in furniture. It is therefore a more serious pest in the lighter construction of post-mediaeval buildings where the proportion of sapwood is often high. Although the flight holes frequently appear in polished surfaces, the eggs are laid in cracks and joints and unvarnished recesses, in smaller clutches of 15-20. These hatch out in 3-4 weeks, and the larvae bore into the wood, first along the grain and later in all directions, forming cylindrical or oval pellets of bore-dust. They are whitish grubs with red-brown jaws, and shed their skin at intervals. After a shorter period of 12 to 36 months, the last 2-3 weeks of which are spent in a pupal stage near the surface, the larva becomes a full-grown beetle. Without waiting for the next season, this immediately finds its way to the surface and emerges to mate, a little later than the death-watch beetle, in June, July or August.

The flight-holes of the furniture beetle are smaller than those of the death-watch beetle and about 1·5mm in diameter. The beetle is about 3mm long, reddish to blackish-brown in colour, with short yellow hairs, and lines of marks along the wing cases. Both hardwood and softwood are attacked, but only when seasoned: wet or damaged timber is again attractive, but has by no means a monopoly of attention.

The *house longhorn beetle* Another insect pest, so far mostly confined in this country to areas of Surrey and found chiefly in timbers less than 50 years old, is the house long-horn beetle (*hylotrupes bajulus*). This is a much larger creature, up to 25mm in length, with a life-cycle of 4-11 years. The eggs are laid in large numbers—perhaps 100 to 300 per beetle—but singly and in pairs, and hatch out in 10-14 days. The larvae bore voraciously to and fro along the grain, often under a thin intact surface, and their activity is said sometimes to be plainly audible at night. The galleries are shallow and broad, up to 12mm wide, and packed with fine dust which makes chemical penetration less certain. After a pupal stage of some three weeks, the beetle emerges in June or August.

The full-grown longhorn beetle may be 19mm to 25mm long, and the upper part is heavily covered with grey hairs 'parted' in the middle. There are also four patches of grey hairs on each wing cover. The beetle emerges through few and scattered flight holes about 6mm to 12mm long, representing a relatively disproportionate amount of unseen damage. Only fresh, sound softwood is affected.

The *powder-post* or *lyctus beetle* attacks only unseasoned hardwoods, and thus is rarely found in old buildings, being a greater enemy of the timber yard.

Bats are an anemy of beetles, and an excellent scavenger of roof-spaces. There is a splendid story of a vicar who, discovering that bats could be frightened by noise, rode up and down the aisle of his church on a motor-cycle, sounding a high-pitched horn. But even after such drastic 'curative' measures, his church may still have been the poorer. Bats should never be destroyed without reason, since they certainly do more good than harm to a building.

Eradicating timber pests The eradication of timber pests in buildings is simplified by the fact that the different species all respond to the same treatment. The advantage to the architect of being able to distinguish the beetle is that it will enable him to make a more accurate assessment of the actual damage suffered by the structure.

As with the fungal treatment, there are specialist firms who deal exclusively with beetle eradication, carrying out excellent guaranteed work, but inclined to be expensive. The choice again then must be dictated by circumstance and preference, but generally in simple cases, a good local builder under proper supervision is quite capable of producing a completely satisfactory job.

The work of eradicating pests in an old building usually falls into three main phases.

As with fungal attack, the architect must first look for the unhealthy conditions which have encouraged the pests to feel at home, and cure them at source. Damp and lack of ventilation are again the enemies; and once these are dealt with, the beetles will feel less inclined to linger.

All dust, dirt and rubbish should next be removed, preferably with a powerful vacuum cleaner. This is necessary, not only to remove conditions favourable to the beetle, but also to facilitate the treatment which will follow.

Next, the extent of the attack must be traced and its severity assessed. The latter is often a most critical part of the work in old buildings, particularly in dealing with valuable carved or moulded work. The architect must differentiate between timbers which have been so badly eaten that their strength has been impaired to the point where replacement is necessary, and those which, although attacked, still contain sufficient sound timber to play their original rôles in safety. Beetle-riddled 'frass'—that is, timber which is so severely honeycombed that it is virtually useless—will usually be found to coincide with the sapwood areas of structural timber. Thus a beam which at first sight appears absolutely riddled and useless may be found to have a solid heart quite adequate for its work, the limit of the beetle damage being the clearly demarked surface of the heartwood. Extensive opening-up is not always necessary for the purposes of an insection as the beetle's flight-holes are of necessity always on outside surfaces.

Having decided upon the scope of the work, the actual treatment and repair can be started. Where damaged timbers of a roof or other structure are to be treated *in situ,* the first step is to seal off the area as far as possible to exclude dust and dirt from spreading elsewhere and to introduce as much as possible light and air for proper access and treatment. When a roof can be re-battened at the same time as the timbers are treated, a more thorough job can, of course, be ensured.

The most extensive and often the most expensive part of the work in severe cases is the initial cutting away of badly infested wood and beetle-riddled frass. The latter may often be removed simply by scraping or wire brushing: rather blunt tools should be used, to avoid damage to sound timber. All infested wood and fragments must then be cleared away and burnt—it is useless to leave them lying between attractive ceiling joists—and all accessible spaces again thoroughly cleaned with vacuum-cleaners. When the timbers are clean and accessible they may be treated with insecticide.

For the *in-situ* treatment of timbers in existing buildings, the most useful methods of application are brushing, spraying, and injection. Brushing should be regarded as a method of spreading the chemical lavishly over the surface and into the cracks. There is no 'brushing-out' as with paint. Spraying should be carried out with a coarse spray at fairly low pressure, rather than as a high-pressure atomised mist, which is wasteful and inefficient. Where the bearings of timbers are inaccessible, it may be necessary to drill deep holes and to saturate the buried wood by injection. Since flight-holes must connect with the sub-surface 'galleries' of borings, injection into these is also a valuable means of reaching hidden timber with insecticide where it is most needed. Gas treatments, at one time recommended by the authorities, involved the sealing of an interior and saturation with methane gas or gammaxene smoke sublimate, but are far less effective than thorough treatment with insecticide liquids.

Whatever method of treatment is adopted, very much depends on the skill and intelligence of the operatives, the degree of supervision and their working conditions. A good operative must be honest and thorough, and must have a proper knowledge of the enemy, and of his ammunition—slapdash and clock-watching personnel are useless in this class of work. The architect must be vigilant and co-operative, and must personally know exactly what is being done in the most inaccessible places. Cramped, stuffy spaces in a vapour concentration, with inadequate access, are extremely uncomfortable and unlikely to be as thoroughly treated as they deserve: plenty of light, air and access are essential to proper treatment. Where flammable liquids are being used, fire extinguishers should always be provided.

Any new timber introduced into the 'danger areas' in repair or replacement work should also be treated with insecticide. This is best carried out before it is fixed. Timbers may be vacuum impregnated in sealed cylinders, or treated by the 'hot-and-cold' process, when they are heated in a tank of liquid, or by cold 'steeping' (from minutes to 72 hours) or 'dipping' (from 10 seconds to three minutes). With hardwoods such as oak, maximum penetration can be achieved by steeping; but with softer timbers a greater penetration of the insecticide is assured by these methods than usually results from simple brushing or spraying.

It must be admitted that however thorough the treatment of a structure may be, it is physically impossible to guarantee that every single egg, grub and beetle in the timber has been utterly eradicated. But if the roof has been made inhospitable by thorough ventilation, the drying of sound timber and the removal of damaged wood and frass, and if all accessible timber has been saturated with a suitably toxic and permanent insecticide sprayed over it and injected into the flight holes, cracks and joints, the chance of any further serious weakening of the timbers by beetle should be very remote for many years to come.

Fungal poisons and insecticides The architect who has to deal with combating fungal and beetle attacks in old buildings cannot complain of a lack of choice when it comes to selecting a poison or insecticide for any particular case. Indeed, the very multiplicity of these products may almost prompt him to pick one with a pin and hope for the best. However, it is of the first importance that the particular poison selected should be based on ingredients of known and proved efficacy, and any firm unwilling to provide this information should be treated with suspicion. The qualities chiefly required of an *in-situ* timber preservative are:

Ease of application.
Deep penetration.
High toxicity to insects and fungi at low concentrations.
Permanence.
Absence of smell and colour.
Harmless to operatives, paint and furnishings.
Non-corrosion of metals.
Preferably non-flammability.
Reasonable cost.

No single preservative combines all these virtues, but the best have most of them. There are basically three types of wood preservatives:

(*a*) those based on tar oils,
(*b*) those based on water-borne salts, and
(*c*) the organic solvent type.

The organic solvent type are those most used for the *in-situ* treatment of existing timbers. They are based on either a rapidly evaporating vehicle such as white spirit, naphtha or one of the petroleum distillates, or alternatively, a penetrating non-volatile base, which is usually a petroleum fraction such as diesel oil or gas oil.

The fungicides incorporated are usually either
(*a*) pentachlorphenol, or
(*b*) copper or zinc napthenate, or
(*c*) chlorinated napthalenes.

Pentachlorpenol is a crystalline solid, used as a 5% solution: to prevent surface crystallisation, some non-volatile as well as a volatile solvent is generally used. It is highly toxic to plants, and also a little to humans. It is, however, non-corrosive, chemically stable and odourless; and the timber treated can subsequently be painted. Water-solubility and volatility being very low, it is very permanent.

The metallic naphthalenes have a powerful fungicidal and insecticidal effect, and are chemically stable and of low water solubility and volatility, so that they too are of high permanence. Care is sometimes necessary in the treatment of painted timbers, or in repainting treated woodwork, especially with the lighter colours. Copper naphthenate is light green, and the more powerful of the two. Zinc naphthenate may be used where a colourless fluid is required, but is somewhat less potent. Both are non-toxic to plant life, and are therefore suitable for timber in greenhouses and similar situations. Admixed with pentachlorphenol, their effect is even more potent than either chemical alone. Chlorinated naphthalenes may be either liquids or waxy solids, both of which are toxic to humans by virtue of their chlorine content.

Either together with the fungicide, or as a separate fluid, powerful insecticides may also be included in a timber preservative. The most common and effective are benzene hexachloride, DDT, and dieldrin. Generally, more than one line of attack is used, the insect being subjected to contact and stomach poisons, and the timber made repellent to the female for the laying of eggs.

The solvent base may be either volatile or non-volatile. The volatile types are mostly petroleum or coal-tar distillates, which are clean and non-staining but highly flammable. These carry their 'passenger' chemicals into the wood; and then quickly evaporate outwards again. The other types are the less volatile petroleum fractions such as gas oil and diesel oil, which are cheaper and at least as effective, since their penetration is continuous after application and does not depend upon immersion time. They are, however, only generally suitable for non-painted timbers where discoloration and a slight oiliness and odour are not objectionable, and must not be used near plaster, along which they creep and stain. Aqueous

Fume treatment against timber beetle at Westminster Hall

solutions may cause damage by swelling timber, and are less desirable in buildings. It is always wise to test samples for their staining effect before any fluids are used.

Fumigant insecticidal processes are generally suitable only for objects which can be comprehensively treated in a fumigation chamber. Smoke treatments, by which a suspension of contact insecticides may be disseminated, are useful in inaccessible places, although they are effective only if carried out at the right time of year, when the adult beetles are emerging. There is no residual effect, and frequent repetition of the treatment will be necessary.

Recently, poison has been produced in two new and ingenious forms, designed to protect uninjured timbers. One manufacturer now produces solid sticks of water-soluble fungicide which can be built into a wall, and are designed to impregnate any rising damp with its own defence against the fungal attack of timbers. Special surface paints are also now made which are designed to release a gradual surface 'bloom' of contact insecticides over a long period, thus obviating the need for frequent spraying, for example in the tropics: the 'bloom' is of course self-renewed whenever it is cleaned or rubbed away. These are doubtless the advance guard of other interesting new methods of prevention, but vigilant maintenance must always remain the soundest defence against every harm to which buildings are heir.

Outline specification for fungal eradication in accordance with architect's detailed site direction

Preliminaries

Preliminary Clauses as for General Contract.

General

FUNGICIDE: The fungicide to be used throughout is to be '........', obtained from Messrs .... of ...., and used strictly in accordance with the makers' instructions. A fugitive dye is to be incorporated if required by the architect, to enable the extent and penetration of the fungicide to be traced.

SHORING: The contractor is to provide and maintain all necessary shoring, propping and other temporary supports as necessary, to ensure the stability of the whole of the structure during the works.

FIRE PRECAUTION: Special care is to be taken to provide and maintain adequate fire extinguishers, as directed by the architect in consultation with the Fire Officer.

TEMPORARY SCREENS: The sections of the building in which fungal attack is known or suspected are as far as possible to be isolated from the remainder by means of temporary screens, tarpaulins, etc., maintained throughout the course of the works. Operatives working upon fungal eradication may enter or pass through sound sections of the building only when absolutely necessary for access and as sanctioned by the architect.

DISPOSAL OF INFECTED MATERIALS: All infected timbers and materials are to be removed as directed in detail on the site by the architect, carted immediately from the infected area to an agreed site outside the building, and there burned without delay.

SALVAGED MATERIALS: Any re-usable materials such as floor boards, linings, panelling, etc., removed for purposes of tracing fungal growth, but which themselves appear sound and unaffected by attack, are to be stored outside the building for the architect's detailed inspection and disposal instructions.

Order of works

REMOVAL OF INFECTED MATERIALS: The architect will direct each stage of the work in detail on the site and no stripping, eradication or remedial work is to be done without such detailed instruction. Eradication work will commence at the heart of the fungal outbreak; and the first stage to be directed will comprise the tracing of each line of fungal spread from its source to its farthermost limit.
Remove and cut out, cart away and burn all infected timbers, joinery, flooring, etc., as directed in detail by the architect on the site. Similarly take up floorboards, remove wall plaster and finishes as directed, tracing all visible signs of fungal spread until the limits of each strand are reached. Continue stripping of all finishes to points at a distance beyond these limits to be directed in detail by the architect.

CLEANING: If fruiting bodies are present, these are in no circumstances to be disturbed until their inspection by the architect, and will then be liberally sprayed with fungicide before any cleaning is undertaken. When the full extent of the fungal attack has been traced and all affected timbers removed as directed, thoroughly clean down all surfaces, remove all loose material and clear out all dust and debris prior to treatment, cart away and immediately burn.

TREATMENT: A brazier's blowlamp is to be played upon walling wherever directed in the area of fungal attack, until the surfaces become too hot for the hand to be held on them in comfort. Immediately afterwards and while the surfaces are still warm, spray or brush on liberal applications of fungicide, all as directed by the architect.

Where further directed, drill 6mm diameter sloping bore-holes in large timbers, and in all thick walls adjacent to area of infection, to facilitate penetration of fungal poison to their interiors. Very thoroughly irrigate these drillings with fungicide, fed by means of large funnels, and continue as directed until lack of absorption indicates that penetration is as complete as possible.
Liberally spray or brush all timber and other surfaces in area of attack with applications of '........' fungicide, paying special attention to the backs of timbers, and to ends of beams, etc., where exposed end-grain is favourable to deep penetration by the poison. The architect will give detailed site direction on the whole of this work.

NEW WORK: Make good removed timbers with new construction as directed. All new timber used is to be impregnated with '........' preservative by the .... process before fixing. Wherever possible, hidden members will be replaced by inorganic materials, e.g. timber lintels by concrete and timber fixing blocks by breeze.

REMEDY CAUSE: Trace and remedy the cause of the outbreak, all as directed by the architect; building in new damp-proof courses, additional ventilators, etc., to ensure the proper prevention of any further trouble. Detailed direction of this work will again be given on the site by the architect, without whose instruction and approval no work is to be done.

REINSTATEMENT: Clauses as for General Contract.

Outline specification for pest eradication in accordance with architect's detailed site direction

Preliminaries

Preliminary Clauses as for General Contract.

General

INSECTICIDE: The insecticide to be used throughout is to be '...........' obtained from Messrs .... of .... and used strictly in accordance with the makers' recommendations.
A fugitive dye is to be incorporated if required by the architect, to enable the extent and penetration of the insecticide to be traced.

SHORING: The contractor is to provide and maintain all necessary shoring, propping and other temporary supports as are needed to ensure the stability of the whole of the structure during the works.

FIRE PRECAUTIONS: Special care is to be taken to provide and maintain adequate fire extinguishers, as directed by the architect in consultation with the Fire Officer.

DISPOSAL OF INFESTED MATERIALS: All infested timbers, frass, etc., are to be carted immediately from the infected area to an agreed site outside the building, there to be burned without delay.

SALVAGED MATERIALS: Any re-usable materials such as floorboards, linings, panelling etc., removed, but which appear either free from attack or else to contain sufficient sound material to permit their re-use after repair and treatment, are to be stored outside the building, pending the architect's detailed inspection

and disposal instructions.

Order of Works

REMOVAL OF INFESTED MATERIALS: The architect will direct each stage of the work in detail on the site and no stripping, eradication or remedial work is to be done without such detailed instruction. Cut away and remove plaster and finishes as directed and clean out all surface rubbish from the area to be treated.
Trim of all 'frass', (i.e., surface wood so heavily riddled that it has lost its usefulness) from the timbers by means of wire brushes or blunt scrapers, until structurally sound timber is reached, all as directed on site by the architect. Open up existing structure as necessary to permit free access for treatment to hidden faces of all timbers; and remove or cut out all heavily

infected timbers as directed.

Thoroughly clean out all accessible spaces with vacuum cleaners; and leave the whole as clean as possible for detailed inspection prior to treatment with insecticide.

TREATMENT: All infested timbers, and sound sections immediately adjacent, are to be thoroughly treated with the specified insecticide as directed in detail by the architect. This is to be applied liberally, wherever possible by brushing, the liquid being run into the flight holes, and elsewhere with an approved coarse spray. Particular attention is to be paid to shakes, joints and other crevices in the timbers, and generous treatment given to ends of beams etc., where end-grain is favourable to deep penetration by the insecticide. Wherever directed drill 6mm holes downwards into inaccessible timbers and inject insecticide into them until lack of absorption indicates that saturation is complete.

NEW WORK: Repair or replace timbers with new, securely scarfed and jointed into the existing. All new timber after cutting and before being fixed is to be thoroughly impregnated with '. . . . .' preservative by the . . . . process, as a protection against further pest attack. Detailed direction of this work will again be given on site by the architect, without whose instruction and approval no work is to be done.

REINSTATEMENT: Clauses as for General Contract.

5.7   Walling, stonework and rendering

Walling decay Decay in walling may have taken one of two chief courses: either the whole wall, its facing, core and jointing may have deteriorated, or else the individual units such as bricks or stones may themselves have suffered damage. The remedies are distinct, and the problems of 'walling' should be considered separately from those of the individual stones.

Old walling may have been constructed in one of two ways. Either the stones were laid in courses the full thickness of the wall, or else the two faces were constructed separately, with a rubble core between. The first method is constructionally sound; but the second is not—hence the early collapse of many a heavy Norman tower.

In faced walling, however attractive at the surface, the weight of internal floors is often concentrated upon the inner face. If the infilling shrinks or settles, a further load is also placed upon the two outer leaves of the wall. The loosened rubble of the interior progressively drops into any interior spaces behind the two faces, further separating them so that eventually a loose wedge of free rubble is driven steadily down the inside of the wall, bulging and separating its outer faces.

Solid, coursed walling is free from this trouble and is more likely to have been damaged either by structural movement or by persistent saturation. The most vulnerable situation in any wall lies in the topmost few courses, where the most water can penetrate and there is no superimposed load to hold the structure together. Rainwater can damage walling in two chief ways—by washing out the mortar from the joints, and by expanding into ice and forcing the stones apart. Another trouble-point occurs where, from a lack of supporting partitions, or from the placing of

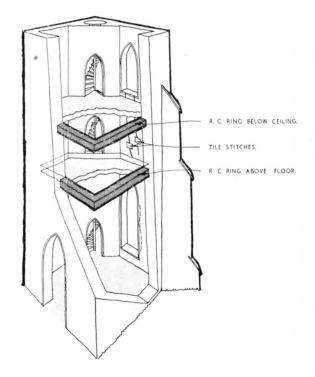

R. C. RING BELOW CEILING.

TILE STITCHES.

R. C. RING ABOVE FLOOR.

Diagram showing strengthening of stone tower by inserting r.c. ringbeams and by tile stitching of vertical "ringing cracks"

window and door openings too close together, or from structural settlement, the joints of masonry have opened to admit weather penetration.

Flint walling presents special problems, since the unit is so small and smooth, and offers so little key for proper bonding. When the faces are finished with knapped flints,

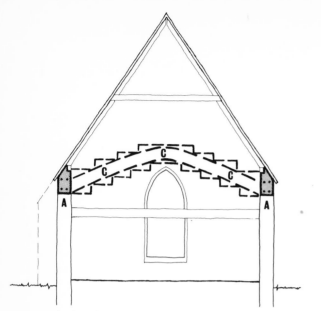

Five methods of restraining live roof thrust. Above: r.c. eaves beams (AA) spanning between end walls; for use where the masonry in the gable wall is itself defective—ties in the gable wall (CCC), used with eaves beams

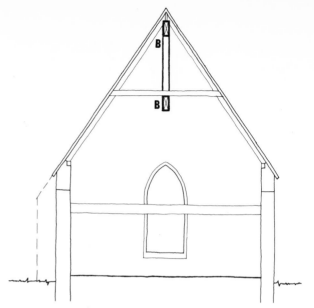

Construction of a trussed ridge (BB) spanning between end walls

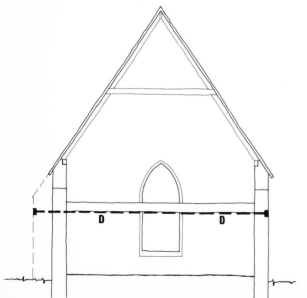

A tie dropped to immediately below first floor (DD)

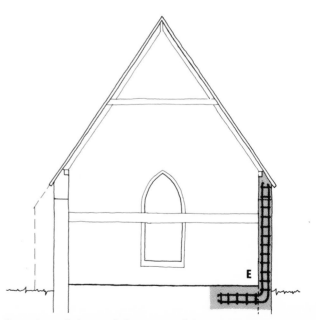

Insertion of internal buttresses (E). Diagrams based on materials supplied by SPAB

Good repointing of flintwork

Keat's House, Hampstead: painted stucco forms an essential architectural element of many such Regency and Victorian houses

Kedleston: frost damage to a brick ha-ha

the facings are particularly liable to part from their rubble backing. Since flint-knapping is a dying art, this type of walling is increasingly of historical importance. The flints themselves are practically indestructible, but their hard and non-porous nature precludes any real 'grip by mortar' and may provide hard-lined water channels into the walling, offering free inroads for frost and erosion.

Apart from damp, a frequent cause of damage is the movement of dissimilar materials built into walling, as when timber bonding members and lintels or wall-plates

Should buildings wear buttonholes? A wisteria creeper graces an ancient archway to The Close, Winchester

Iron grille rusting at the point where it is set into stonework

have shrunk, and no longer give proper support to the stonework above. The rusting of iron ties and cramps has probably resulted in more damage to walling than any single other cause.

Lastly, a great deal of damage is caused by the roots of vegetation on walls. Some creepers are harmless, while others are not. Virginia creeper attaches itself to a wall by means of suckers, and except when it spreads into gutters, hopper-heads and the like, does relatively little harm. Ivy, on the other hand, sends deep roots searching into the joints of masonry, loosening the mortar and weakening the structure. Lichens and mosses, where the air is sufficiently pure to permit their growth, are also harmless; but the presence of moss will usually indicate an extremely

damp patch, such as might be caused by a leaking gutter. Tree branches, shrubs and undergrowth of all kinds should be kept well cut back from buildings, which they damage not only by harbouring moisture but sometimes by physical beating and scratching as well.

Repairing damaged stonework In setting about the repair of any wall, the first step is to remove all plants, creepers and vegetation whose roots are causing internal damage. This should be carefully done; and ivy, in particular, must but cut at the roots and poisoned at least six months and preferably a year before the repair, when the dead creeper will have lost its grip and can be gently lifted away. It may be necessary to dismantle the topmost stonework courses so as to be able to grub out all the roots which otherwise might grow again.

The next stage in cases of serious failure, and where the heart of a wall has perished, is either to dismantle and rebuild all defective sections, or to strengthen the wall *in situ* by careful internal grouting. The decision must depend upon how serious is the condition, and how important the identity of the walling as being itself of special character or interest.

Bad repointing which makes nonsense of the pennant stone walling over which it has been applied

A neatly re-pointed tower: Church of St Mary, Twickenham

In grouting a decayed wall it must first be carefully shored and supported, where necessary by means of close-boarding. After any damaged upper courses have been removed, the interior is next washed out by copious hosing with clean water, to remove loose dust and rubble from within. Grouting is usually carried out in stages of two to three feet at a time, from the bottom upwards. Lines of vent holes are driven into the heart of the wall and a liquid mortar grout is then poured in to fill and consolidate the interior spaces. As the grout begins to appear at each line of vent holes, these are stopped up in turn until the whole of the spaces have been filled.

The mix for grouting may be either a strong portland-cement mortar, or a weaker lime mortar, depending upon the materials and structure of the wall. Care must in all cases be taken to avoid disfiguring the face by overflow-marks at the vent-holes.

If the core of a wall has burst it so seriously that it cannot be grouted, whilst either the external stonework or interior finishes such as wall paintings are to be preserved, it is sometimes feasible to save one face, and to rebuild the other. The structure must in this case be carefully shored, and the face to be rescued may need continuous support from close boarding. In rebuilding, the two faces can be reassociated by through-stones properly bonded into both sides: these may sometimes be achieved conveniently at old putlog holes. In cases of minor movement, it may be possible to give support by short metal ties between the two faces, carrying generous tie plates: but this is at best a time-honoured expedient rather than any real remedy.

The final resort for walling whose heart has failed is the local rebuilding of offending areas. Where this is done, a record photograph should first be taken of rubble walls, or a numbered elevational drawing made of ashlar work. Most of the materials may be suitable for re-use; and salvaged brick or stone from the interior of the wall may be useful for new facings.

A stone column, earlier patched by plastic repair, is given a stone collar to maintain its correct jointing pattern with *a minimum of structural disturbance*

Less serious is the case where it is the face of the walling, and not its inner core, whose joints have failed. These should always be raked out to a depth of at least one and a half inches: superficial repointing is soon fetched out by frost, and the last state may then be worse than the first. To ensure proper adhesion, it is most important to ensure that the brickwork or stonework is extremely thoroughly wettened. Repointing mixes should wherever possible match the original mortar in density, and should on no account ever be harder than the material being pointed. The amateur mason must be restrained from spreading the pointing over the face of stonework like butter; and it should be stressed that it is the individual units—the stones and bricks of the wall—and not the pointing lines which must take the eye. 'Ribbon' repointing is incredibly widespread and equally hideous; and the mortar must be kept back to show the arrises of the courses above and below. On no account must joints ever be widened 'to take the pointing' as some inexperienced builders will suggest. If surface joints are too deep for normal repointing, they may sometimes be repaired by surface grouting: this more frequently occurs with very random rubble stonework in exposed positions. In this case the wall is again thoroughly hosed and wettened, and any insecure stones temporarily blocked into place with wooden wedges. The joints are then stopped with tow, leaving small holes through which the grout may be poured. The tow is in due course removed, and the repaired walling repointed in the normal way.

In walling of flint and similar hard materials, the joints are the only part of the wall which may 'breathe', and a soft mortar is essential. Where individual flints have fallen from the faces, these may be replaced; or sometimes, over-large areas of surface mortar may be 'galletted' with small pieces of flint, to good effect.

Shafts and mullions in dressed stonework should ideally have the same number of joints as the stonework in which they are set. In practice, and especially in 13th century work, this is rarely the case. The shafts of Purbeck marble which cluster around Early-English piers, and window mullions of all periods cut from long stones and set alongside many-jointed rubble walling, are often found damaged as a result. Where it is possible to contrive new mortar-joints of extra depth to accommodate the extra settlement, this should always be done. The spalling arrises of the longer, harder material can otherwise only be repaired by replacement or piecing. Similarly, the cast-iron shafts and balusters which are sometimes found to have been introduced into stonework will inevitably be 'foreign' to the construction, causing extra damage unless provision is made for their differential movement. In external work, the expansion and scaling of ironwork features due to rust is almost unpreventable, unless the fixings have been very carefully sheathed with lead. The only possible remedy is periodically to clean off the rust and scale, rustproofing the metal where accessible, and to point up the surrounding expansion spaces with waterproof mastic. Galvanising is not permanent, and iron in contact with stonework should whenever possible be replaced by non-ferrous metal.

Some iron ties are impossible to remove, owing to the extent of structural disturbance which would be entailed: these can only be cleaned very carefully, rustproofed, and as far as possible protected from moisture penetration—for example by bitumen paint and additional damp-proof courses. Mortices can also sometimes be cut in surrounding stonework to permit their future expansion. But where it is practicable to remove iron ties, they should always be replaced by harmless materials such as the non-ferrous metals—bronze, copper or delta metal—or slate, according to the needs of each particular case.

If it is desired to remove vegetable growths, the Building Research Station recommend that this may be done by spraying with a $2\frac{1}{2}\%$ solution of zinc or magnesium chloride; unless actual harm is being caused however, chemical treatments are really best avoided.

5.8 Stonework decay and repair

Stone types In understanding the weathering of stonework in old buildings, it is essential to distinguish between the different stone types and their structure. In outline only, these may be recalled as follows:

Granite Formed by the crystallisation of cooling molten minerals: granite is therefore unlayered, and consists of an irregular close packing of grains or crystals of quartz, felspar and mica. Its hardness relates largely to the condion of the felspar grains, but is of the highest order. Granite is virtually insoluble under normal conditions, as well as being practically impervious to moisture.

Sandstones[1] Consist of individual calcareous or silicous sand grains, united by cementitious materials, which may be either carbonates (soluble) or silica and iron oxides (acid- and water-resistant). Since sandstone is 'laid down', the structure is stratified, with a natural 'bed'; and sometimes there is a considerable clay content. Of variable permeability.

Limestones Principally carbonates of lime, laid down in prehistoric sea-beds. Limestones have a pronounced natural bed and often contain numberless fossils and shells. They are slightly soluble, especially by water carrying carbon dioxide or sulphur dioxide in solution. The magnesian or dolomitic limestones are compounds of carbonate of lime with carbonate of magnesia: they are particularly vulnerable by sulphur. These differing constituents and properties of the various natural stone types govern their

---

[1] The name 'freestone' usually refers to a sandstone, but is merely a non-specific term for an easily wrought stone, in which the sedimentation layers are not pronounced, and such as may be used for dressings.

Raby Castle, County Durham: weather has reduced these stone mullions to a feather edge and they cannot long survive

and pavings in old buildings are not always of the most suitable stone, and may have received more wear than they were designed to receive. Damage by point loads and knocks is also frequent, especially in positions facing motor traffic. Wind erosion is sometimes marked, especially in corners where little eddies and 'whirlwinds' are found. Trees planted near buildings may take them unawares, lashing and scratching any soft stonework within their growing reach. Schoolboys' penknives are another hazard. Although the cause may no longer be

Wind erosion of stonework allied with saturation from a leaking gutter

weathering and decay in buildings, and give the key to their behaviour in any particular situation.

Identifying the cause of stonework decay The chief agents of erosion and decay in stonework are:

(*a*) external physical abrasion;
(*b*) internal disruption by frost;
(*c*) internal disruption by crystallising salts;
(*d*) direct solution by rainwater and airborne chemicals;
(*e*) faulty materials and craftsmanship.

External physical abrasion Stonework, like any other material, is liable to wear by friction of any kind. Steps

The West Tower, Bristol Cathedral: stone erosion hastened by fumes from a local gas-works

will result. But if, whether from an extraordinarily damp and unventilated situation, or from the use of stones of inherently excessive suction, the pore spaces are themselves already full of water, then freezing can only in turn disrupt and burst the stone.

Damage by frost is usually therefore found in positions where stone may be completely saturated, while being at the same time exposed to extreme cold. Small chips and fragments of stone at the foot of walls during frosty weather, and the little clean scars on the stonework itself

Certain very soft sandstones are liable to damage by nesting mason-bees

apparent, the effects of physical damage are usually easy to identify.

An interesting but rarely found cause of damage to stonework is the mason bee. This insect enlarges holes in the softest sandstones found in certain parts of the country (notably in Lincolnshire) and nests in them. The damage done may be quite extensive; but the mason bee most commonly attacks only the very softest of stones.

Internal disruption by frost When water expands into ice, it increases in volume by one-tenth. If the pores of the stone contain sufficient room for this expansion, no harm

St Neot's, Huntingdonshire: natural washing of a stone bridge by a river in flood

in exposed positions, will usually give the clue to mischief from this cause.

Internal disruption by crystallising salts The other cause of internal expansion and bursting of stones is the crystallisation of salts. These may have been introduced with actual building materials, such as unclean sand, or absorbed from the ground and atmospheric soot deposits. The natural moisture rhythm of the stone carries them with evaporating moisture, to be deposited just beneath the surface, where they crystallise and expand, bursting successive layers from the face of the stone. Close examination will sometimes show even the crystals themselves, on the line of fracture.

The worst offenders against stone are the sulphur compounds. Sulphur is almost always found in soot deposits, but the resultant damage tends to show different forms in town and country. In heavily polluted areas, soot generally tends to collect wherever stonework is unwashed by rain. The sulphur content combines with atmospheric moisture, firmly attaching the deposits to the unwashed stone, and building up into thick encrustations of heavy, form-destroying dirt. Stonework protected from normal washing is particularly vulnerable when allowed to become saturated with water from other causes, such as leaking gutters and flashings. This happens for example when the lead dressings on a stone cornice have perished, and the moulded console brackets beneath are frequently saturated, without ever being properly washed.

In the less polluted country areas, there is less visible soot deposit; but sulphur gases are still present in the atmosphere, to be carried into the stonework by rainwater.

In limestone, these sulphur deposits react with the natural carbonate content to form sulphates, crystallising and producing the characteristic blistering and scaling of the surface. A hard and shiny 'skin' of calcium sulphate is sometimes found on limestone in unwashed positions: at one time, this was thought to protect the stone, but it is now realised that by first cracking at the arrises and then gradually separating away, this 'case-hardening' is as harmful a product of sulphur as any other.

A particularly violent type of damage by sulphur compounds may be seen in some old buildings of magnesian limestone, such as York Minster. Where the stonework is

Stonework made architecturally unrecognisable by atmospheric pollution

not regularly washed clean, it may be eaten into cavernous holes by magnesium sulphate derived by the sulphur from the stone.

The harder sandstones and granites show less serious damage from atmospheric pollution. They do not build up the limestone pattern of cleanly washed and gently eroded highlights, backed by deep and soot-encrusted shadows. Instead, they tend to gather a thin and extremely hard black film on both exposed and sheltered surfaces, which although chemically less harmful, is an architectural detraction, and may be much more tenacious and difficult to remove.

Direct solution by rainwater and airborne chemicals Finally with certain stones, erosion may be caused not only by the internal bursting forces of ice and crystals, but by an actual dissolving of the cementing element which binds the stone grains themselves. Even pure rainwater, allied with the natural moisture rhythms, can gradually dissolve the bonding agent of some stones. Sometimes this in turn is carried back to the surface of the stone, where it is deposited by evaporation to form a hardened 'crust', closely following the shape of the stone, and from which it will eventually crack and separate: the whole process then starts again.

More frequently, this 'dissolving' of a stone is aggravated by chemicals absorbed by the rainwater from the atmosphere. Limestone especially is soluble by water carrying carbon dioxide or sulphur dioxide. Carbon dioxide is a natural constituent of the air, being given to it by the breathing of all animal and plant life. Sulphur compounds in coal are either sent into the air as smoke and soot, or else combust to make sulphur dioxides. In this respect, slow-combustion stoves are indeed almost more damaging than open fires, for even where there is no smoke, there may well be sulphur dioxide.

Faulty materials and workmanship Apart from chemical causes, stonework may suffer from defects either in the stone itself or in the position and method of its use.

A common cause of unequal weather, common in stones from certain quarries such as Ham Hill, is the presence of visible 'soft beds', which erode more quickly than the rest. On a small scale, the alternation of hard and soft layers merely produces a slight surface roughening, which may be of no consequence. Any deeper beds of soft stone will, however, bring serious faults and failures.

Another stone defect is the presence of minute fissures, originally caused by earth movements and later re-sealed by deposits of calcite. In elaborately carved stonework, such 'vents', as they are called, can cause serious weakness, as occurred in the Anston stonework of the Houses of Parliament.

From a craftsmanship point of view, the commonest error found in masonry work is incorrect bedding. All sedimentary rocks, laid down on the ocean bed, have a laminated structure, with a more or less pronounced pattern of layers. They are strong in compress, but weak in shear along the lines of lamination. The stones may have been laid in the building correctly, or with a vertical bed, either at right angles to or parallel with the face. In general vertical bedding is durable only in moulded work such

as stringcourses, which might otherwise lose projecting members, and for members like arch voussoirs. Face bedding is usually encountered as a device for utilising stone from thin beds in deep stonework courses. It is useful to be able to distinguish the effect of 'bruising' caused to stonework by its original dressing. This produces a result rather similar to face-bedding, but which a good mason will clearly identify.

Other masonry faults are of course legion; but a particularly interesting cause of occasional failure is the juxtaposition of sandstone with limestone in such a way that water drippings from the latter have apparently attacked the limestone. Nevertheless, it must be admitted that limestone and sandstone were not infrequently laid down in geological juxtaposition, without apparent ill effect! It seems likely that the true cause of the phenomenon is again either the crystallising of soluble salts, or the dissolving of the cementing material in the sandstone, by impurities in moisture 'drawn' by the more porous material into itself. In this case, the effect is yet one more example of the unequal yoke.

Other physical phenomena which must have an effect on the life of stonework are the varying temperature movements of its mineral constituents, and the differences in thermal and moisture movements between exposed and protected stone. It may readily have been forgotten that some stones have quite a marked expansion when wettened. This is normally taken up by the joints; but in exceptional circumstances as with large monolithic columns, the movement may be significant in its effects.

5.9 Remedying stone decay

Repairs to decayed stonework fall into two stages: firstly, the removal of harmful elements such as soot and deleterious salts, usually by careful washing; and secondly, the repair, piecing or renewal of missing and damaged stones themselves.

Washing stonework There can be no doubt that the streaks and smears of sooty deposits on stonework often make nonsense of architectural form. We have not in our climate the deep, cast shadows of sunnier countries; and a building must rely for its effect upon gentler variations of light and shade. Even when the sun is shining, the black patches

Natural washing by rainwater: soot encrustations have left pronounced dribble marks on this Portland stone

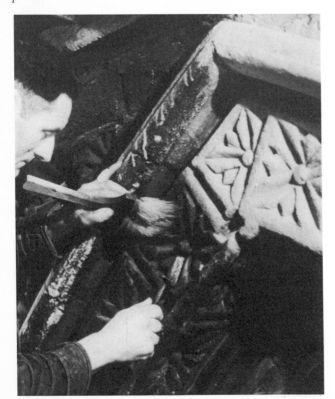

Stonework cleaning in Westminster Abbey: to avoid damage by excessive water, pumice dust was used

of urban soot deposits mask and obscure the true architectural effect. Neither from the point of view of structural health, nor that of appearance, is there any justification for sooty stonework.

For the guardian of historical buildings, the problem is complicated by sometimes unthinking public sentiment. Should St. Paul's Cathedral have been washed? The thick and patchy cloak of chemical deposits which it wore before cleaning could have been doing nothing but harm to the stonework. Wren must surely have conceived his masterpiece in white Portland stone, with reflected light in its shadows, and all its forms heightened by subtle graduations of light and shade. By the middle of this century there was only a matt and sooty black, streaked with white by the rain. Only the magnificent sculptural design of the Cathedral enabled it to stand up to such maltreatment and yet come recognisably through. Yet such was the tenacity of sentiment, and so associated in the minds of many people were St. Paul's and London grime, that the idea of cleaning provoked a vigorous correspondence in the *The Times*.

At Westminster Abbey equally, there can surely be no question that the recent cleaning of the interior stonework was right and necessary. The shining darker shafts of Purbeck marble, punctuating and outlining the design, had become almost indistinguishable from the remaining stonework, the whole interior merging into one formless dull black surface. After cleaning, the architectural idea grows clear and sharp; and once again the Abbey appears as it was meant to be seen. It is a sobering thought that despite improvements in atmospheric pollution, it may only be a few generations before the Abbey has again vanished in new layers of grime. Surely meanwhile, there is a case for air conditioning of any really important architectural interior such as this, in an atmosphere such as ours?

The first step in washing stonework is to protect the building from accidental damage by water. Especially where a building has thin stone walls and contains valuable decorations and furnishings, great care must be taken to prevent open moisture paths by which water can penetrate inside. A great deal of trouble was caused during the early days of washing some of the Georgian Crescents in

Bath, when it was found that the facing stones of the curved facades were not cut with proper radiating joints, but only butt-jointed with their corners touching on the face, and joints widening into cavities behind. Any open cracks and moisture paths should be grouted *before* intensive washing, and features such as window-openings carefully protected by tarpaulins and screens. Excessive water must also be deflected away from the foot of a building, where it might otherwise cause damage to foundations and cellars. In towns, additional shelter may have to be provided to protect passers-by.

Work will start at the top of the building, the scaffolding being removed by stages as the work descends. When cleaning is carried out from a suspended cradle, a set of nozzles may be slung below it, so that the wall is always prepared in advance of the descending masons. For the uppermost levels of the building, a pump may sometimes be needed to raise a sufficient head of water.

Whenever delicate details such as figure carvings in poor condition become accessible for repair, careful record photographs should next be taken before anything is touched. Subsequent treatment should be given extremely gently, under the personal direction of the architect, loose fragments of stone being removed only so far as this is vitally necessary to prevent increasing damage by rain and frost.

The most difficult and inefficient way to clean stonework is to advance upon it and to scrub, without preparation of any kind. So much of the labour, and of the risk of accidental damage, can be avoided by proper washing. The adhering grime must first be thoroughly loosened with a prolonged and direct fine water spray, after which brushing with bristle brushes will be the only further treatment needed. Thick encrustations of soot can be lifted away with a wooden scraper—metal tools are best avoided. Wire brushes are generally only suitable for cleaning metal-work, but may sometimes be used on really hard stones such as granites, in large, flat areas where there is no possibility of mischief. Bronze brushes are then best. Throughout the work, only pure, clean water should be used. Much unnecessary harm has been done to stone by washing it with caustic soda, soda-ash and similar preparations. While these may quickly bleach the surface into an

advertisement-like whiteness, they are actually very harmful to stone, and by leaving behind damaging salts, will rapidly bring about accelerated decay. Modern detergents mostly contain sodium sulphate, and are thus also chemically harmful, even part from the searching breakdown of water repellence which their use implies.

It has been said that diluted hydrofluoric acid may in expert hands be used for cleaning some sandstone, leaving no salts behind. It is also claimed that local stains can occasionally be removed by solvents, such as ammonia for copper stains. But extreme care must be taken to remove the residue by careful washing, and there is nothing to guarantee that salts are being washed out, and not in. These processes should surely therefore be regarded as a very last and very doubtful resort.

Cleaning stonework with water and a limited amount of wire brushing: there is no need to shift every trace of dirt

Safer remedies include the removal of oil stains by spirits such as carbon tetrachloride, white spirit or benzine. Another is a limewash 'poultice' applied to the surface, to draw the foreign element out of the stone and into itself, to be brushed away. Paint can be carefully removed with organic strippers, but the caustic type must never be allowed near stonework. It really is safer to exclude from the site all soaps, chemicals and preparations but water.

Where cleaning by water is for any reason impossible, a gentle abrasive such as pumice powder is sometimes used (as in the interior of Westminster Abbey); or alternatively, steam-cleaning may be adopted. The steam jet is a convenient means of reaching stonework in awkward positions or at great heights, and the warmth of the arriving steam does no harm to the stonework, while it may bring cheer to the mason. But the higher cost of maintaining the boiler and equipment normally makes steam cleaning more expensive than the simpler process of washing it with water. Whatever the method, the workmen should appreciate that the purpose of cleaning is always the health of stone, rather than any false newness of appearance. Only when this is clearly understood will there by no temptation, when everything is nearly clean, to do violence to the one tenacious dirty patch. In this connection as in so many others, a sympathetic and workmanly co-operation between architect and craftsman on the scaffolding is worth a hundred letters.

Stone 'preservatives' Apart from the various solutions designed to repel surface water by filling the pores or controlling surface-tension, modern experiments have produced materials designed to reinforce the actual physical binding medium of the decayed stone itself.

The first trials were made with sodium silicates; but these decompose under atmospheric conditions to form harmful sodium sulphate, and their use has largely been discontinued. Experiments were later carried out with silico-fluorides, the theory being that on contact with limestone these would deposit silica, rebinding the broken face of the stone. In practice, however, it has been found that this deposition can only take place when the natural calcite

Washing stonework by protracted spraying with clean water

content of the stonework has in turn been attacked and weakened.[1] Ethyl silicate is a useful and harmless binding material. An adhesive sometimes used for sticking loose pieces of stone in position is made by dissolving celluloid in an acetate solution.

When decorative stonework such as statuary is concerned, in which the chief aim is to save every vestige of a friable and flaking surface by constant attention, such devices as adhesives and bonding agents may be justified. But few 'preservatives' have been found really suitable for general use. There are dangers both in substances which can chemically attack any constituent, and equally in those which tamper with the physical surface structure of a natural material like stone. Either is as liable to cause active harm as to prevent it.

In the normal case, and for the ordinary maintenance of large areas of stonework, it cannot be too strongly stressed that the only treatment which can be readily recommended as being safe and almost always worth while is regular, careful washing with clean water.

Repairing damaged stonework For all troubles due to the

---

[1] A detailed description of the chemistry of the process was given in *Building Materials* of June, 1957, by a pioneer architect in this field Col. Bertram C. G. Shore, Hon. FIQS, LRIBA, FFAS.

internal expanding forces of frost and crystallising salts, the first remedy is the improved control of moisture movement.

Where stones have been destroyed by frost, it is essential to remedy the conditions which invited the damage. This can usually be done by means of additional cover-flashings and protection. Where damage has been caused by salts, their source must be traced. Often, earth will be found to have been piled above a damp-proof course. Another frequent source of trouble is the raising of roadways and pavements, especially where these are set in a bed of polluted clinker. If a pavement has been raised, it may be necessary to renew the facing stonework of the plinth in granite or other non-porous stone, to act as a vertical damp-proof barrier. It is often recommended that new stone inserted into old walling should be protected from any possible contamination, by backing it with bituminous paints; but there would seem to be many situations in which this artificial barrier can only accelerate damage to the older stone. If salts appear on the inside of thin features such as stone mullions, for example in seaside situations, the only remedy may be to experiment in waterproofing them by means of materials such as silicones.

The only way to remove harmful salts is by patiently and repeatedly washing them to the surface and brushing them off. Coats of limewash may help to 'draw' them from the wettened masonry, to be brushed away and discarded. Many repeated soakings may be necessary; but eventually it should be possible to bring the stonework to a reasonably clean and healthy state.

Once its cause is cured, to remedy the actual effect of stonework decay is usually straightforward, and will consist in piecing or renewing the worst-damaged stones. Paving and similar stones can sometimes be 'turned' to present their unworn lower face. In situations where a previously unanticipated extent of traffic must now be expected, it may be necessary to substitute a harder stone. The choice between repair and renewal is always a delicate one, and must be taken one stone at a time. If weather is being admitted to carved detail such as window tracery, for example by a missing section of hood-mould or string-course, the decision is clear. But every effort must always be made to maintain the identity of the building, and to prolong the life of original materials as far as reasonably possible.

Stone of the exact match, from the same quarry and bed as the original, can rarely be obtained. At Gloucester, an old quarry has recently been re-opened for the special supply of the Cathedral. It is extremely difficult to obtain up-to-date information about the smaller quarries except by direct enquiry, since they mostly lack the publicity and advice facilities of the larger combines. This is a pity, and a greater degree of co-ordination for these smaller firms would be of great service to those with the responsibility of maintaining old buildings. The British Stone Federation[1] now publishes a directory of quarries at present operating, which is extremely useful.

Wherever the original stone is no longer available, a replacement should be sought in which the geological type and structure, physical properties and appearance are as nearly as possible matched. The best guide to the behaviour of a given stone in building is undoubtedly local observation and experience. The Building Research Station are further always glad to carry out practical laboratory tests, and to advise on the suitability of selected samples for given situations. When a stone is removed, the problem arises as to whether it is to be dressed to its original face, in anticipation of further renewals on this 'correct' line, or whether the eroded face is now to be accepted as permanent. It is important to avoid a 'patchy' effect, for example in a wall of finely-dressed and uniform stones from a single quarry; and the situation may call for a good deal of common-sense and compromise. New facing stone must always be of adequate depth, so as to become a genuine part of the wall, and not a thin applied casing. Wherever possible, the original joint pattern should be continued, and replacements confined either to piecing or replacing individual stones.

Mortar for replacements should equally as nearly as possible match that of the original wall, being always softer than the stones, so as to 'chaperone' and protect them. A soft lime mix of the order of one part lime to six parts sand is typical; and a light gauging just before use with one part of Portland cement to some six parts of the remainder

1 37 Soho Square, London, W1.

Two methods of building up a reinforced base for plastic 'dentistry' repairs: tile and copper wire

of 19th century 'restorations' that the SPAB earned its nickname of the 'Anti-scrape'. Although the climate of opinion has changed since then, and with it the need for any exaggerated purism in such matters, it was by such ill-considered refacings and renewals that too much of mediaeval England perished under the Victorian chisel.

Plastic repair In recent years, a degree of success has been achieved by the plastic or 'dentistry' method of repairing stonework. As its name implies, this entails cutting out the damaged parts of a stone and replacing them by a filling material, reinforced and carefully keyed into it.

The damaged stone is first cut well back to a sound base, and drilled or cut to afford a good key, at sufficiently wide centres to avoid weakening the stone. Reinforcement, usually of copper wire, is next inserted and either hooked securely into the parent stone, or in exceptional circumstances run in with lead. The backing is lastly thoroughly brushed and slurried with white cement, and the new section built up, a layer at a time, and finished with a wooden float. The filling material consists of coarse sand or crushed stone-dust, bound either with Portland cement (sometimes white Portland cement) or with a zinc or magnesium oxychloride cement or organic binder. Silicon ester has also been used as a binder. Some firms specialising in this type of work send out their materials ready-mixed at a central depot, and in sealed waterproof containers; but this 'batching' system is really only appropriate where the whole of the stonework is from a uniform quarry and bed. The exact degree of moisture of the mix is of great importance in securing proper adhesion without subsequent cracking and crazing. Any mix incorporating Portland cement *must* be used while fresh, and within 45 minutes at the most, to avoid premature setting.

Another less expensive method of keying and reinforcing plastic repair is with tile insertions; and sometimes in unsophisticated stonework, tiles themselves may be visibly inserted as a kind of 'galleting', quite attractive in appearance.

The filling, particularly if it contains Portland cement, must be allowed to dry very slowly and protected from excessive sun and heat by wet sacks and tarpaulins. When almost dry, the unpleasant 'laitance' which even with a wooden float may appear on the surface, should be re-

is useful in ensuring a quick initial set. But the mix for every job must be decided individually after careful practical site experiment.

The suggestion may sometimes be received, when much of a wall surface has become scabbed and flaking, that the entire wall should now be cut back and redressed. Certainly there are a few cases in which this can be done without architectural violence. But generally the idea is a dangerous one, because walling is rarely so flat and featureless as to avoid difficulties at moulded openings, stringcourses and the like, and possibly the loss of original craftsmanship. It was by vigorously opposing this aspect

140

moved by brushing with a stiff, near-dry brush. Or the insertion can be oversized, and dressed back like stone with a chisel; but extreme care is then needed to avoid disturbing the bond between the insertion and its host.

Plastic repair should *always* be confined to the repair of individual stones, the original joint lines being carefully maintained and repointed in the normal way. As with rendering, it is best to carry the material to a straight or rectangular line like that of a stone joint. Infillings should never be less than 20mm in thickness, and delicate feather-edges and smoothings-into-line are always to be avoided. The special benefit of the method, apart from its economy, is the ability to repair small parts of single and otherwise undamaged stones, whose renewal would cause disturbance to the structure of the walling. No plastic material has, however, quite the same 'life' and variation as a piece of natural stone; and weathering increases rather than modifies the difference. Large areas of plastic repair will

in time develop the most depressing drabness of appearance, and projecting shoulders and details where natural stone would normally attract lichens may remain bright and assertive. The 'making-out' of all but the smallest details, like weather-holding defects in positions which cannot be pieced or where disturbance is undesirable, is to be avoided.

It is also imperative and difficult to ensure that plastic insertions do not commit the fault of dense pointing, by being less porous than the natural stone. The evaporation of moisture and deposition of salts are then concentrated at the junction between the filling and the stone, when it is the latter that will suffer.

As in so many other fields, since it is virtually impossible for site direction to be given on every detail by the architect, the only insurance that such details will be appreciated and looked after is the employment of a reliable firm of trained and experienced workmen.

Outline specification for stonework repairs to be carried out under architect's detailed site direction

1. PROTECTION AND SCAFFOLDING: Carefully erect shoring, protection and scaffolding, all as described in General Conditions, and as directed on site by the architect.

2. UNSAFE STONES: Carefully shore insecure sections of stonework and remove loose or dangerous stones and fragments, all as directed. Provide all necessary shores and supports, and cut out severely damaged stones where directed by the architect. These will include unsafe stones of cornice (e.g., one stone has already fallen from the . . . . angle of the . . . .) and the dangerously fractured masonry caused by additional load of columns added to the . . . . face.

3. REPLACEMENTS: Stones removed or missing are to be replaced as directed with new stones from quarry and bed to be agreed with the architect, and as similar as possible in bearing strength, porosity, permeability and appearance to the original.

4. CUTTING: All new stones are to be correctly bedded, with their natural bed at right-angles to loads or thrusts, except where otherwise instructed. The lines of all mouldings, curves, angles, etc., are to be worked out of the solid, as directed. No angle mitre-joints will be permitted; and, except where expressly otherwise instructed, no new stone shall be of less depth than 100mm from the face of the wall.

5. JOINTING: New mortar joints are to be of narrow width, exactly matching the existing, and equal to a sample to be approved by the architect.
Joint-lines are to be maintained exactly as at present, and repairs are to be regarded as being to individual stones rather than to walling.

6. MORTAR: Mortar is to be as nearly as possible a match to the original, as approved after careful experiment. A trial section of pointing is to be completed for the approval of the architect, in a mortar composed of . . . . parts fine crushed stone . . . . parts lime putty or hydrated lime, mixed with just sufficient water, and 1 part Portland cement added just before use. All stone is to be thoroughly wettened before jointing, and dense and impervious mortar is to be avoided.

7. BACKING: All stone facings to brickwork are to be backed with a slurry of 3 : 1 stone-dust and cement, to prevent staining.

8. CRAMPS: Harmful iron cramps and fixings are wherever possible to be removed and replaced as directed either by bronze, Delta bronze No. 4, copper, or other approved non-ferrous metal. Cut away for key, and insert slate or copper cramps where directed, to afford all necessary additional support (e.g., to cornice over . . . .). All cramps to be run with Portland cement.

9. CARVING: Detailed carving where required in new work is to be done either on the ground or in position, as directed, and by professional stone carvers. Old carved work is to be re-incorporated where possible, and soundly and properly keyed and cramped into new stone wherever required.

10. FLASHINGS: Cut chases 25mm deep where required by the architect, to take cover-flashings to cornices, etc., and to all water-holding projections such as window-heads, including positions where in several cases these have previously been omitted.
Attend upon and point up after specialist lead-work sub-contractor.

11. FALLEN MEDALLIONS, ETC.: Carefully re-fix fallen Coade stone decorative features wherever directed, securely cramped into walling as instructed on the site.

12. BALUSTRADE: Take down and re-assemble stonework of balustrade where directed; and point up the ends of steps where these are exposed by settlements, so as to exclude weather from the structure.

13. RE-POINTING: On completion of the required repairs, all loose and open joints throughout are to be carefully cleaned out, thoroughly wettened, grouted and pointed with mortar of mix as directed on site, filled solidly back as far as possible between stones

and finished very slightly recessed from face of stonework, in accordance with a sample section to be approved by the architect. On no account, is any joint to be widened to admit pointing: the re-pointing is intended purely as filling, to prevent the permeation of moisture between individual stones into the walling behind. Stronger cement mortar may be used only as directed in very exposed positions. The intention in general is that moisture should be drawn from stones to evaporate at joints rather than being trapped and driven to the face of stones along impervious joint lines. The mortar for pointing should therefore throughout be slightly softer than the adjoining stones.

14. WASHING AND BRUSHING: Very carefully protect all windows, openings and points at which moisture damage might be caused to the interior. Provide and hang tarpaulins so as to deflect water from the foot of the building and avoid damage to foundations.
As directed in detail by the architect, wash off all loose soot and grime only by protracted washing with direct fine water sprays and subsequent brushing with bristle brushes, equal to a sample to be approved. Tenacious grime, the removal of which might possibly damage the face of the stonework, is at all times to remain; and no soaps or chemicals whatever are to be employed. The intention is for only such cleaning to be carried out as is necessary to the health of the stonework.

15. RENDERING REPAIRS: Examine all rendering from scaffolding, and hack off where loose, as directed by the architect. In view of the difficulty of matching, no patching of surfaces is to be undertaken; and re-rendering will be confined to complete wall surfaces between straight lines and wherever possible between corners of buildings.
Carefully re-fix all loose and fallen sections of composition string-courses, securely cramped to wall as directed.
Wetten all walling very thoroughly before re-rendering, to ensure the best possible adhesion. The mix of the rendering is to be of the nearest possible match to the existing, as approved after careful experiment. All materials used are to be thoroughly sieved before mixing, so as to exclude lumps which might otherwise cause scratching and marking of the surface. The rendering is then to be very thoroughly mixed with a minimum of water and applied with a wooden float; and when practically dry, it is to be brushed down to expose the aggregate and marked out with joint lines to match the existing.

16. COMPLETION: On the architect's detailed approval of the completed repairs, carefully remove all scaffolding, plant and equipment, taking great care to ensure that no damage is caused to the completed works. Clear away all rubbish and tidy site generally, clean all windows inside and outside, and leave all clean and tidy and ready for return of occupants on completion.

Brickwork Mediaeval bricks were rough in texture and irregular in shape, and laid in shallow courses with thick joints of lime-mortar. From the 13th to the 17th centuries, bricks mostly imported from the Low Countries found ready use in East Anglia. In Tudor times, they were made locally in a wider variety of colours, and until 1600 or 1610, in courses of some 50mm only. In the late 17th century, brick sizes were standardised, and the rude mediaeval brick with its rough texture gave place to the smooth, crimson-coloured Georgian brick and pale, almost salmon-red 'rubbers' for decorative work, often laid on an extremely fine bed of lime mortar.

In repairing old brickwork, it is essential to appreciate the value, as in stonework, of keeping the mortar softer and more porous than the bricks themselves. More old brickwork has been ruined by repointing with hard and impervious cement mortars, and by the consequent efflorescence and frost damage, than by any other cause. As with stonework, vegetation and roots should first be cleared away; and if local rebuilding is necessary, the courses and bonding pattern must be carefully maintained. Old bricks from the inside of a wall may frequently be saved for re-use as facings, any newer bricks being used where they are invisible. In repointing brickwork, the joints should be raked out to a depth of at least 20mm, and the walling very thoroughly saturated with water before neatly repointing with a fairly dry mix. Nothing is more unsightly than pointing spread over on to the face of brickwork, and it is better to keep the surface slightly back than to risk allowing this to happen. The bricklayer must understand that the bricks, and not the joints, are the important element, and that the pointing is purely a protective filling between them.

Rendering and plasterwork Mediaeval walls were frequently intended to receive a thin coat of external plaster, or many thick layers of limewash. This was not a hard, thick sheathing like modern rendering, and the freestone dressings, used to obtained accurate corners and surrounds to openings, may be found with only the slightest setting forward. Any renewed rendering should therefore follow the irregularity of the walls, and 'die' against the quoin stones without steps and ledges. Another objectionable practice is the stripping of external plaster from timber-framed buildings, whose skeleton is thus unnecessarily bared to the world.

Rendering should always be thought of as a soft overcoat, and not an impervious casing to a wall. This overcoat absorbs moisture, and acts as a reservoir until it can dry out. A hard casing, once it has cracked, can on the other hand admit a stream of moisture which is then trapped behind it and cannot escape. In repairing old rendering, it is virtually impossible to 'patch' locally defective areas of a large surface. Even if the greatest care is taken to make the repairs a good match, they will always weather

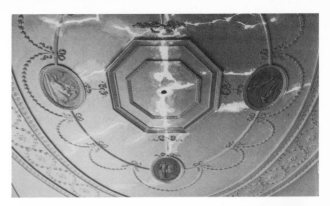

An Adam ceiling before, during and after repair

'Mathematical' tiling designed to resemble brickwork. This has failed through the rusting of iron nails driven into the walls

Header brickwork like this deserves a more careful repair than these assertive concrete 'arches'

'Roman cement' can sometimes be removed to expose earlier stonework of quality. This is impossible with modern portland cement rendering

to the surface, and will give a pleasant texture by exposing the surface aggregate.

Limewash is an excellent protection for walling, if renewed at frequent intervals: an admixture of tallow is traditional in some areas. Roman cement, often found in old rendering, can also still be matched. It does not obtain quite such a permanent 'grip' on brickwork, but has a much more pleasant colour and texture than modern Portland cement, and is less liable to cracking and crazing than its harder modern counterpart.

Internally, mediaeval walls were coated with many thick layers of limewash—the precursor of modern wall plaster. By the 16th century, thick hair plaster was in general use; and in the 19th century came the wooden

differently. It is far better to keep new work to a minimum, to be confined within definite lines such as corners, where changes in colour and texture will be masked by the angles of the building. Indeed, it is remarkable how great a variation is acceptable and unnoticeable on different planes: a similar effect is sometimes seen when the ceiling and walls of a room are redecorated with variants of the same colour, and when very often the intended contrast is disappointingly undistinguishable!

Walling to be re-rendered should first be thoroughly cleaned and consolidated, and then heavily and evenly saturated with water immediately before rendering is applied. The mix is best kept on the weak side, and on brickwork a proportion such as one part lime to three or four parts sand is suitable. Rendering may be lightly 'gauged' with Portland cement if desired, immediately before use. The inclusion of hair is a very sound practice. Only just sufficient water should be used to make the mix workable. In applying the rendering, a wooden float is useful; and care should be taken not to 'puddle' the surface, when it will craze and crack. A gentle brushing-down when the work is almost dry can help in removing any undesired 'laitance' which may have found its way

Rendering can almost never be successfully patched. When first applied this patching no doubt matched perfectly, but continuous weathering now exposes the difference

Wall-paintings at Charlwood, Surrey

battening and counterbattening of walls for lath-and-plaster, which provides such a tempting spreading-ground for dry rot.

The foundation for plasterwork in historical times was usually battening—for the most part of hazel or riven oak. Battens may have failed either through tannic acid attack upon their fixing nails, or through timber rot and pests. Sometimes, stout battening which served originally for centering, as in an elaborate plaster cove, may have become unnecessary once the plaster set. Where large flat surfaces have lost their battens, and it is desired to avoid disturbing ornate moulded plasterwork, it is usually possible to clean out the batten channels, and to cast into the 'key' thus given an entirely new plaster backing, reinforced by hessian or non-ferrous metal. Individual weak spots in plaster can be given extra support by brass cups and screws, countersunk into the work and plastered over, or by non-ferrous 'stitches' twisted around nails above. To avoid disturbance, screws may be used: when it is impracticable to drive these at the required angles, they may be set in the upper face of the joists, carrying long wire loops of copper or brass to support the plaster.

Not only mediaeval wall-paintings need be significant

145

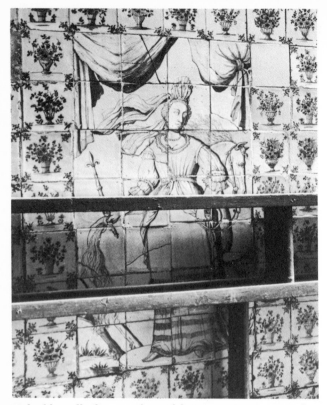

Valuable wall-tiling worth careful preservation: its irregularity is among its most endearing and characteristic aspects

Another frequent cause of failure is lack of adequate key. This may be caused by the fixing of battens direct on to flat surfaces such as beams, or very frequently merely by battens set at too close a spacing. On flat surfaces, large-headed galvanised nails will give improved key; and insufficiently spaced battens may sometimes be separated, basket-work fashion, by 'weaving' short lengths of batten under and over them. When renewing plasterwork, adjoining old work should be undercut to dovetailed, clean edges to afford maximum 'key'.

Conservation of wall-paintings Particular care should be taken before stripping any plaster from mediaeval walls to ensure that they carry no valuable wall-paintings, hidden under the coats of limewash. The exposing and repair of wall-paintings is an extremely delicate task, and should be entrusted only to experts. The names of recommended experts in this and other specialist crafts may always be obtained from bodies such as the SPAB, and the Council for Places of Worship.

The first step in preserving wall paintings is of course to dry out the wall. Limewash and other coverings will then be carefully removed by the expert; and it is sometimes found that successive wall-paintings of different dates have been applied on successive layers of limewash. In this case, each will be photographed as traces are discovered; but the original painting on the plaster is likely to be the best preserved. The expert will lastly 'fix' loose and flaking paint. A joint Committee of the SPAB and the Council for Places of Worship have compiled detailed recommendations as to the best techniques to be adopted. Any temptation to excessive retouching and restoration must be resisted. The effects of any kind of varnish or heavy wax 'sealing' of the surface may also well be disastrous. Where a wall painting has become seriously perished or is exposed to bright sunlight, it may be protected by screens, perhaps (as in Winchester Cathedral) carrying a careful conjectural restoration of the mural. A glass covering sometimes detracts by its reflections, and may endanger the painting by trapping atmospheric condensation.

The magnificent 'doom' paintings which occasionally still come to light in church buildings were only a part of a great decorative scheme, traces of which may be sought on other walls. A beautiful system of paintings has for example been discovered and restored at Kempley, in Gloucestershire. It is interesting to remember that individual pictures were often grouped to form a 'conversation piece', with figure talking to figure, the whole being conceived as a single polychromatic decorative scheme covering the entire interior. The practice encountered in some countries of lifting wall-paintings from their sites and transporting them to art-galleries is strongly to be deprecated. They are essentially part of an architectural interior, which without them loses half its meaning and is left an empty shell.

Special features: metalwork, rainwater furniture, glass, bells and fire precautions

5.10   Cleaning and repairing metalwork

Decorative wrought-ironwork is one of the most attractive, and at the same time one of the most vulnerable features of an old building. From time and neglect, it becomes either rusted and scaled, or else thickly encrusted and hidden by many layers of paint, which obscure its finer niceties and workmanship. The gates of the Victoria Tower of the Houses of Parliament, even in their short lifetime, have been found to have an entirely unsuspected degree of ornamental detail under their overcoat of paint.

Flaking paint may safely be removed by a suitable stripping agent; and the ironwork must then be thoroughly de-scaled and treated with a good rust remover. Missing and damaged sections can meanwhile be made good wherever needed, but remembering that it is better to eke out the life of old work than to renew it in too wholesale a fashion. Circlets and collars and similar details are frequently found to have burst, and will require repair by welding. It is occasionally useful to resort to the use of other metals, as in flaunching off water-holding hollows with lead; and there may be a case for local renewals in non-ferrous metal such as brass or copper, in situations where iron would quickly again perish. But generally, the repair of wrought-iron is a straightforward blacksmith's job, and will mostly consist of straightening bent work and welding and strengthening joints attacked by rust. As one expert has said to us 'We just heat it, then we hit it'—though we feel he did his skills less than justice in the description.

Before being refixed, ironwork should be thoroughly protected with one of the rust-inhibiting paints, preferably in grey or black and with such occasional re-gilding as is needed. Gilt paint is a vastly inferior substitute for gold leaf, and will quickly tarnish and look mean: if genuine re-gilding is financially impossible, it is better to omit it than to cheapen the effect in this way.

The ends of railings, saddle bars and similar features where these are built into stonework can often be tipped with bronze or sleeved with copper, to avoid any recurrence of rust damage.

Cast-iron front from a row-stall in Chester

Ankles of a lead statue whose armature has rusted

Elaborate iron hinge-plates proclaim the individuality of the blacksmith

Tennyson's house, Twickenham: a young tree grows in a hopperhead among external plumbing

Any impediment to the free movement of features like gates should be cleared away, and the hinge pins, fixings and furnishings made good. Mediaeval hinge- and key-plates are often of the greatest interest, and justify careful repair. If ornate wrought-iron hinges are no longer repairable as such, at least their decorative plates should be repaired and retained in position. The better Georgian door-furniture was sometimes beautifully executed in brass, and likewise deserves painstaking attention. Crude modern locks and handles substituted for the old—

especially the clumsy hasps and padlocks of the requisitioning military—are often very unsightly, demanding summary removal. It is not easy to find suitable replacements for missing door-furniture; but such details contribute much to the effect of a fine interior, and are worth much seeking.

5.11   Repairing rainwater furniture

The most neglected feature of all old buildings is undoubtedly rainwater furniture. If not constantly painted and properly maintained, cast-iron gutters and downpipes will quite rapidly rust; and the resultant outpouring of collected rainwater at concentrated points can easily do more harm than their absence altogether.

Wherever a roof can discharge harmlessly by means of widely projecting eaves or frequent spouts and gargoyles, it is sound policy to omit or even to remove eaves gutters entirely. Where rainwater collection does seem essential, both gutters and downpipes must be kept in the best possible repair. In old buildings they are usually either of lead or cast-iron.

Lead is very long-lasting if properly fixed in reasonable lengths, and with adequate provision for thermal movement. It must be *continuously* supported. Sloping lead branch pipes will almost certainly otherwise droop and sag; and vertical downpipes need frequent and generous fixing by means of projecting lead 'ears'. Original lead rainwater furniture is an important architectural feature, and should always where possible be retained and set in order. Ornate lead rainwater-heads are often a particularly beautiful feature, but are heavy and do need frequent attention, especially to their fixings. Damaged and dented pipes can be removed and re-dressed, and punctures and similar damage repaired by lead burning.

With cast-iron rainwater furniture, the chief enemy is rust, due to inadequate painting. Downpipes especially are often found to have been set so closely against walls that proper, regular repainting is quite impossible. They should always be refixed well clear of the wall by means of projecting lugs or 'holder-bats'. Repainting with bituminous and similar paints offers an added protection. Where renewals are needed, the question of future maintenance is important. Asbestos-cement and nowadays,

A delightful trompe l'œil feature from an English country house

plastic gutterings and downpipes sometimes a useful substitute, especially in positions where regular maintenance is impossible. Asbestos-cement is inconspicuous on stonework, but does offer risk of mechanical damage, for example by ladders. Plastic piping is available in useful rectangular sections, and if well fitted, is virtually maintenance-free. There is no need to paint the material— indeed, the habit of painting downpipes of all kinds in contrasting colours is more often objectionable than pleasing: except where they are a special feature, it is much better to use colours which will be 'lost' against the wall. Continental practice often employs light-gauge galvanised iron, replaced at frequent intervals: but there is always a danger that perishable materials may not be renewed until damage has been caused. All rainwater pipes of any material should always be fitted so as to allow sufficient 'slack' in the collars for expansion movements, and to permit the replacement of individual pipes when any are damaged.

Rainwater butts are a great nuisance, and a source of endless trouble. Where for some reason the soft-water storage they provide is specially required, they should still be seen as an intermediate reservoir *en route* for a proper soakaway, towards which a proper overflow and branch drain are provided.

Repairs to underground rainwater drains should be carried out in socketed pipes so as to maintain their alignment; and care must be taken to run them well clear of ground liable to excavation and settlements. The classical example is in the churchyard, where a position under the path is safest from disturbance.

5.12 Glass in old buildings

Early window glass was mostly thin, opaque and bubbly, and available only in small pieces, which had to be leaded together into larger sheets by means of thin lead 'cames'. Later crown glass, the most beautiful of all, was made by blowing and spinning a flat disc of glass. Squares were then cut from this for window glazing, the central part being discarded or relegated for use in outbuildings. The idea of employing this central 'bullion' of the glass in prominent positions is purely a Victorian affectation. The concentric circles and twinkling curves of crown glass give a wonderful 'life' and movement to a facade, which cannot easily be appreciated from photographs: it is the movement of the reflected pictures which lend the glass its unique attraction. New crown glass is at present unobtainable, but a very close imitation can be supplied by the manufacturers to special request, when the extent of the order permits.

Modern rolled sheet glass, by contrast, has irregular imperfections of no interest, and by contrast somehow just looks mean. Polished plate glass, especially in 19th century glazing, often owes much of its richness to bevelling of the edges, which should be carefully reproduced in any repairs. The etched glass of many a Victorian bar is already increasingly a rarity, and good examples may be a valuable as well as an attractive feature. All old

A stained glass window is re-assembled after careful cleaning and restoration

glass indeed is valuable, and merits the most careful protection from damage during building work of any kind. The richest of all is of course the stained-glass window, which as well as being ancient may be an important work of art.

Stained glass is an extremely vulnerable as well as a beautiful material. Its enemies range from polluted atmosphere to small boys. Once a stained-glass window has been removed from its position, the materials are a sorry-looking heap, and their value may not be realised. In stained-glass as in any other art, substitution is by no means the same thing as repair. Instances have occurred, especially in Victorian times, of an astonishing lack of appreciation of this fact, poorer coloured glass being inserted indiscriminately in the design, or even complete copies substituted for old windows. Since copies of damaged glass can only be a pale echo of the originals, it is essential for proper repairs to be carried out in good time.

In the case of really valuable glass, the first step is to photograph the window in position, and if possible in colour. This record is invaluable for reference in the subsequent work of restoration. The window is next removed and transported with the greatest care to the workshops, where further photographs may be taken, and a rubbing made of the leadwork pattern.

The glass can then be dismantled. Some pieces may be found to be seriously eroded, but the effect of different atmospheres upon the same glass is markedly different, and impossible to predict. If the erosion is not too serious, the surface may be bleached clear, or cleaned with acids or caustics, and repolished with wire wool or abrasives. Since much ancient glass will be found damaged or mis-repaired, it may well be desired to re-plan the layout and restore the original pattern of the window, making every effort to re-use all original glass to the best advantage. It may be necessary to fill in the gaps of the resulting jig-saw with small areas of new glass. These must be unostentatious and carefully matched; and any new artist's work which is unavoidable may be dated for identification. Old glass should be cut about as little as possible. Where a crack or break has occurred through an important detail such as a head, a join may be made by carefully nibbling away one edge and inserting a thin line of lead; or the damaged pieces may be sandwiched between two pieces of clear glass. In restoring stained-glass at Winchester College chapel, these were specially cast by the glazing contractors to match the irregularity of the ancient fragments, so as to avoid condensation spaces and uneven support. Similar plating may be necessary with coloured glass, to correct the tone or corroded original glazing which has been lightened by thining.

The lead 'cames' are meanwhile recast and rolled to the desired 'H' section, with milled inner surfaces, and cut and bent to fit the joints of the window. The joints are soldered on both sides, and copper tags added where support for the heavy glass can be obtained from saddle-bars. The window is finally made weatherproof by brushing in a cement consisting of linseed oil, red lead and whiting. Both sides are carefully cleaned down, and the window is ready for re-fixing.

Original 'ferramenta' should whenever possible be retained, but in many cases, old ironwork will be found to have rusted and split the mullions. Saddle-bars may then be 'tipped' with a non-ferrous metal such as delta-metal: they are usually allowed 6mm to 12mm bearing at each end. It is never desirable to run iron saddle-bars con-

Figures from a 14th-century Jesse window originally in the East Window of Winchester College Chapel, now restored and in Fromond's Chantry. The saddle-bar has been curved around the nimbus and the head of Wykeham (right) is a modern copy dated for identification

tinuously through a mullion; and vertical bars should stop short of the sill to avoid standing water and consequent trouble from rusting. Where saddle-bars would interrupt a delicate design, special ones may be made and bent to follow a main line of the pattern.

The repaired glass is at last painstakingly refixed in the window. After each section has been accurately centred with wooden wedges, the whole is fixed and pointed into place.

If it is at all possible to make arrangements for the regular, careful inspection and washing of the reinstated window in future, so reducing further repair and maintenance to a minimum, this is the time to do it. When the work has been well done, the effort of restoration will be found well worth while, as the original colours and design of the window can be seen to glow again from their traceried frame.

151

A bell-frame seen from above: window netting must be non-ferrous and well-maintained to exclude pigeons from a belfry

5.13 Maintaining church bells

A special problem in the care of churches is the repair of damage caused or aggravated by the ringing of bells.

Bells are heavy pieces of mechanism, and when rung on the 'English' pattern are swung in complete circles, so that the stresses set up are by no means negligible. In a sound and rigid frame, the swinging of a bell will set up a maximum vertical force of about four times and a horizontal force of some twice the weight of bell metal. The vertical load is of relatively little consequence, but its horizontal counterpart can be very significant. Should the bell-frame be in any way springy, or touching the walls of the tower, extra swaying and hammering forces are also set up. Further trouble may be caused when the rhythmic swing of heavy bells coincides by mischance with the natural 'period' of a slightly swaying tower, like that of soldiers crossing a bridge. The movements of the upper levels of a tower while the bell-metal is hurling in its circles are sometimes quite spectacular, and cannot be ignored.

Reductions in the structural forces set up by bell-ringing can be secured either by altering the position of the frame, or by re-setting individual bells. In general, the sideways forces set up by the bells will vary with the cube of their height above the floor. Very substantial reductions can therefore be obtained by lowering the position of the bell-frame. From a ringing point of view the rim of the upturned bell in its striking position should be at least two metres below the belfry window sills. The best outlet of all for sound is a roof lantern or spire: otherwise sound-control calls for good shutters of tongued-and-grooved boarding behind the belfry window louvres. The heaviest bells may also be arranged to swing in such a way as to cancel one another's movements and on the stronger axis of the tower. This is usually from east to west, along the line of the unperforated north and south walls. Bell frames are also best set on main beams at right angles to the swing of the heaviest bells; and the head of the frame should always be kept clear of the wall. Very occasionally too, the heaviest bells can be tamed by 'tucking them up'. This entails raising them in their mountings so as to reduce the radius of their rotation: but as the practice makes for sluggish ringing, it is not popular with campanologists. Adequate access is essential to any belfry whose bells are to be used. The bell-frame should be very stoutly constructed, and may be of wood or metal. Wooden frames need frequent inspection, to ensure that bolts and joints are tight and secure. Steel frames must be repainted periodically with a suitable rust-inhibiting paint. In all cases, the whole unit must be very securely and firmly fixed as a solid and integral part of the tower.

The bell-mountings and pivots equally require checking at frequent intervals and of course like any piece of moving machinery, they need adequate oiling. Ball bearings, however, should be lubricated only once in every 10–12 years, or damage may result. The bells themselves are subjected to heavy local wear by the beating of the clappers, and must therefore be periodically 'quarter-turned' to spread this evenly around the rim. The replacement of an ancient bell which has become damaged or cracked is always a ticklish problem: if it is decided to unhang the bell, it may often remain as an interesting display feature in the body of the church. In this case, security is important, to avoid loss by theft. It is sometimes a heavy responsibility for the architect to decide whether or not structural harm is being caused by ringing. Careful observation during and after trial, with periodical inspection and marking of structural movements by means of tell-tales, should however enable a firm decision to be taken. Where it is not possible to allow full-scale ringing, it may be necessary to restrict the use of the bells to chiming only, which can cause little harm to all but the most delicate and precarious of structures.

5.14   Fire precautions and lightning conductors

An important aspect of the care of buildings is lastly proper protection against fire. Adequate detection, warning and fire-fighting equipment must always be installed, and properly maintained in good condition. In general, the lighter and more portable hoses and extinguishers are the more likely to be useful in those urgent, early minutes of a fire when a building can quickly be saved or lost.

Chemical extinguishers are excellent; and the local Fire Officer is always glad to advise on their provision and positioning. Frequent checking and replacement is however an important item of maintenance, easily forgotten at future peril. If a property is not easily accessible to the fire brigade, or lacks a telephone or other means of warning, provision must be made for heavier fire equipment such as water tanks, hoses and pumps.

It has not infrequently been found, after a serious fire in an old building, that more damage was caused by the firemen's hoses than by fire. Superheated stonework may be quite sound and capable of re-use until played upon by cold water, which turns to steam with explosive force. If a burning building is throughout quite definitely well beyond saving on the arrival of the brigade, and is jeopardising no one else, it may be possible by exercising the greatest possible self-control to save the whole of the external walls—thus making extensive savings in rebuilding costs! Rose-tinted stonework is not necessarily harmed in any way, as many a wartime relic will testify. It is also necessary to take special precautions to dry out the structure after firemen's hoses have been at work: or dry rot may easily occur as soon as the moisture content is reduced to a suitable level. One fire is sufficient without a second insurance claim.

Pinnacle cramped together and supported by a lightning conductor on the West Tower of York Minster

A frequent cause of fire and sometimes of serious structural damage is lightning. Any building on high ground or in an exposed position must have a proper lightning conductor. A building standing in country opened up by the felling of trees may be particularly vulnerable. The lightning conductor is generally of copper tape, with riveted joints; and all bends must be of easy radius. It must of course be kept clear of thatch and other combustible materials, and is designed to link metal sheets and similar temptations into a continuous chain, terminating in an earth connection set well away from the building. The earthing rod, although unseen, is the most important link in the defence of the building, and must be carefully tested whenever the installation is checked.

153

Detail of a filled cavity in the timber framing

154

6. *Economising in repairs by using modern materials and techniques*

Blackmore Church
Essex

Blackmore Church is one of the most interesting and attractive churches in Essex. It stands a little apart from its village in unspoilt countryside, north of the main road from London to Chelmsford.

Whilst the main body of the church (dating from the 12th to 16th centuries) is of unusual quality, the building's most magnificent feature is the late 15th-century west bell-tower with its spire. Sir Nikolaus Pevsner (*Buildings of England—Essex*) describes this as 'one of the most impressive, if not the most impressive, of all timber towers of England'. It is most elaborately framed in massive oak and forms a superbly dominant feature in the landscape.

A programme of repair and improvement was financed by church funds, public appeals and grant aid from the Historic Churches Trust. The condition of the tower posed

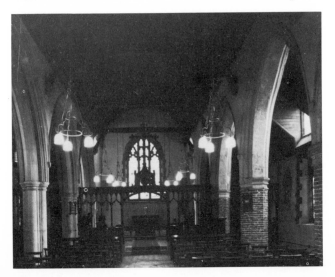

The nave before and after

especially difficult problems, as the massive timbers had been seriously weakened by beetle attack and wet rot, to the extent of threatening its entire stability.

The defects at the base were especially severe. Here the main oak plate supporting the entire structure was rotten on its underside through rising damp, and beetle attack had eaten away large internal cavities, especially at the vital joints. Past attempts had been made to prevent decay by covering the outside of the base storey in hard cement rendering, but these had been unsuccessful as well

155

A magnificent 14th-century church tower during and after restoration

difficult and expensive, owing to the large sizes of the oaks, the necessity of shoring up parts of the tower whilst timbers were renewed, and the need to retain the superb appearance of the original timber engineering unimpaired. An effective and economical answer was found by injecting compounds of synthetic resins and powdered slate into the decayed cavities through small drillings. This compound hardens into a material of great strength, which bonds securely to the oak and is itself damp-proof. By this means, strength was inconspicuously restored to the weakened joints and timbers, at the same time protecting them against damp. The unsightly external rendering was removed; and the timbers and their infilling beneath were also carefully repaired, reinstating the proper historical appearance of the Tower.

The total cost of the tower base repairs was approximately £4 300 (1970) representing a saving of several thousand pounds by comparison with conventional repair.

as unsightly, and tended rather to hold in the dampness than to exclude it.

Repair by conventional means would have been extremely

The Conservatory at Came in which the curved glass was successfully replaced with acrylic sheet

Came House
Dorchester

This conservatory is a most elegant and decorative building of circa 1840, constructed against the South facade of a handsome Palladian house. Although sympathetically faced with a classical stone screen and french windows, this is essentially a structure of iron and glass, of extreme intricacy and great technical quality.

When it was decided to repair the building in 1964 the conservatory, which had been left uncared for since the war, was in a sad state of decay. The damage caused by lack of maintenance, coupled with the ravages of the weather, made the work of reconstruction extremely difficult. Most of the curved glazing had been broken or

was missing. The weather had taken its toll of cast iron ribs and more particularly of certain sections of the work which were found to be of wrought iron and had rusted badly. The joinery was unpainted and had suffered; and the stonework of the front of the building had decayed. The gutters and downpipes were in a state of disintegration, and had caused much of the damage.

Although reconstruction seemed at first an almost impossible task, a start was made by finding a local blacksmith to descale and repair the iron tracery. Some of the members were so badly corroded that they had had to be renewed, and all were afterwards coated with a metal primer. The replacement of the glass presented a more difficult problem, as the original glazing had consisted of many hundreds of hand-cut pieces of curved glass, which fitted individually into the differing widths between the iron spars. It would have been exceedingly expensive to replace them in glass today. After considerable research and enquiry, acrylic sheet was adopted instead. Whilst giving an appearance similar to glass, this was much more manageable in cost. Each strip of sheet had to be specially cut to its own template by means of an electric saw. It was then bonded with adhesive to the very shallow rebates of the curved iron spars, and a continuous, protective sheathing of high-grade aluminium, backed by a bitumen-based adhesive, was lastly applied over the spars, over-lapping the edges of the acrylic sheet. An entire bay was repaired and reglazed in this way, and it was decided to test this for one winter, whose rigours it survived with such success that the remainder were completed in the spring.

Once the reconstruction of the roof and its problems had been solved, the rest of the repair was straightforward.

The lantern at the apex of the dome was given a new kerb, welded to the existing ribs. Inadequate and perished lead perimeter gutters were removed altogether, and replaced by glazed, half-rounded channels set and jointed in water-proofed cement. The cracked and defective stonework of the façade was repaired and repointed. Joinery, french windows and woodwork to the columns were all over-hauled, repaired and repainted. The tiled floor was replaced, together with the attractive iron grilles covering the heating system, which has now been connected to the heating system of the main house.

The work, together with the repair of Came House itself, was executed by local contractors with the aid of a Grant from the Historic Buildings Council for England.

Boston Manor: the entrance front after repair

7. Taking advantage of architectural, archaeological and decorative discoveries

Boston Manor
Brentford

Boston Manor was built by Lady Mary Reade in 1622, at that time just outside London. Her initials and the date appear on the ceiling of the main state room. In 1670, the Manor was sold to James Clitherow, in whose family it remained until, in its 17ha of Park and Garden, it was bought in 1924 by the Brentford Urban District Council. By 1960, war-time damage and prolonged neglect had brought the house to a distressed condition. A programme of repair, restoration and conversion was undertaken by the Brentford and Chiswick Borough Council, with financial assistance from the Historic Buildings Council, the Middlesex County Council and the Pilgrim Trust.

Straightforward repair aspects of the contract included the overhaul of the roofs and repair and reduction of the chimneys, the reinstatement of missing sash windows and the restoration of the external stone porch. Active outbursts of dry rot had to be eradicated, together with the depredations of death watch and furniture beetle. New

A ceiling detail: before and after repair and re-decoration

The principal stateroom: before and after

The ceiling is re-supported from above

electrical services and oil-fired heating installations were provided, and the building was completely redecorated and refurbished.

During this work, the splendid plasterwork ceilings of the interior received special attention. The magnificent ceiling of the main first floor state room dated from 1623 and was seriously cracked and propped from below. It was strengthened by the traditional method of overlaying stout hessian above, then grouting in new plaster between and over the ceiling joists. The ceilings were picked out in restrained background colours expressing their

Handblocked wallpaper discovered behind a later canvas covering

characteristic strap-work motif, withholding colour for the backgrounds of the very fascinating series of figure medallions set within its panels and representing the principal arts and sciences. In the state bedroom behind, the removal of 19th-century panelling revealed an original strapwork plaster frieze according with its ceiling; and this in its turn was carefully restored. Another fascinating feature was the stateroom fireplace with its central oval medallion of the sacrifice by Jacob of Isaac, his sword blade stayed by a stoutly modelled angel, watched by the ram caught in a thicket. Under the family motto of the Clitherow family was found the original inscription 'in the Movnt of the Lord it shal be seene'.

On the wide and generous main staircase was discovered behind later paintwork, a 'mirror-painted' panel reflecting the arcaded balustrade of its outer side. Above this on the upper staircase and behind a flapping Victorian paper on torn canvas was found a most beautiful 18th-century hand-blocked wall paper, now restored to view and carefully refixed.

The Manor House was carefully adapted as the Headquarters of the National Institute of Houseworkers Ltd, and after its restoration was re-opened by HM The Queen Mother. In this way another beautiful and historic building and its decorations were preserved for a further long spell of useful life.

St Nicholas Almshouse
King Street, Bristol

St Nicholas Almshouse, now in the centre of the city, was originally built in the year 1656, and was the first building beyond the Outer City Wall, whose ditch formed its cellars. The gabled front elevation was later extended as far as the present Eastern corner with Queen Charlotte Street: the extension was architecturally similar but with different detailing like the hood moulds over the ground floor windows.

The almshouse had front and back walls of local stone, with stoutly-framed oak partitions and roof timbers. An open external corridor and staircase tower gave access from the rear to each of the rooms.

During the second world war, much of the building was destroyed, including this rear corridor and the common room. There were no adequate kitchen, bathroom or lavatory facilities, and if the old house was to be brought back into use, it was essential that these should be provided, together with a Matron's flat and properly protected indoor staircase and corridors. It was required to incorporate this accommodation in self-contained units each containing a private bed-sitting room with its own kitchenette.

The problems were therefore both in planning and in repairing the structure at reasonable cost, within this derelict builing of great age and architectural value.

The job was tackled by first spending a small initial budget on opening up the structure, enabling a more accurate diagnosis of repair problems to be made. Local areas of plaster were removed, revealing a great deal of damage to structural timbers, especially where these had been wet over a prolonged period. Where it was dry, the oak of the original construction had aged and hardened to a remarkable degree, including the massive oak door frames to each room. It was found that some of the stone walls could be rocked by the hand and were unsafe, and that the floor joists passed through the thickness of the external walls, so that these had to be withdrawn and trimmed off, filling these pockets of weakness in the walls. Further weaknesses occurred where doorways had existed below the present ground level in the rear wall, and these were filled for additional strength.

It was decided to replan the accommodation in such a way that each alternate room would contain a pair of small kitchens, opening respectively from either side, and receiving daylight from the front and the rear. The grouping of the rooms permitted a matron's flat with an extra bedroom at the Eastern end; and with this were grouped the new bathrooms, spaciously planned and fitted for use by the disabled. A new rear access corridor was then planned along the entire courtyard elevation at the rear. This was designed in an architecturally contemporary manner, with panels of solid brickwork opposite the entrance doors to each unit, and of glazing opposite the inner kitchens at each of the two floors.

Before and after restoration and conversion

The central room at the upper floor, which was 'out-of-step' with this alternating arrangement of rooms and paired kitchens, also had a bold and interesting curved plaster ceiling, carrying bold relief ornament set with roundels of the four evangelists, and a cartouche with the ancient arms of the city of Bristol. It had evidently served as a chapel, and was set centrally over the entrance hall below. This part of the upper floor was therefore removed, exposing the fine ceiling as a feature of the entrance hall, and permitting the insertion of a light and open spiral staircase.

At a crucial stage of the work, an interesting and important archaeological discovery was made in the rear courtyard, which had been opened up and cleared of buildings to admit more light and air. At its western end, where the new common room was planned, it was decided to arrange a trial dig in association with the Director of the Bristol Museum to check the position of the old outer city wall, shown on the ordnance map by a broken line down the length of the Courtyard. Digging was commenced in a reserved manner, but great excitement was caused when a substantial curved bastion of the original Wall began to come into view. Funds were generously provided by an anonymous Bristol citizen for this excavation to be extended, and the Museum reported 'This section of the city wall, which runs from the Welsh Back

to the River Frome, was built after the expansion of the City in this direction in 1246, possibly about 1255, but certainly during the 13th century. The excavation was extraordinarily successful in locating one of the semi-circular wall bastions about 27m West of the site of the Back Street Gate. The bastion wall is revealed to a height of about 2·5m and to 1·8m thick. It is built substantially of millstone grit with a Dundry stone plinth. The external diameter is approximately 9m.

'The evidence indicates that the bastion and presumably the wall were disused by the end of the 16th century. About this time the bastion was cut into and used as a dwelling house and later as a coal store up to the time of building the almshouse.'

Many interesting finds were made of pottery and glass; and the wall had previously been identified in only two other locations.

Clearly, it was most desirable if at all possible that this important archaeological discovery should be retained and displayed for public enjoyment; but it occurred at a point where the new Common Room and bathroom block was planned. It was decided to span this clear over the excavation, diverting the drainage and carrying this instead internally through the cellars. A new concrete retaining wall, iron railings and step ladder were added.

In this way the original structure of the almshouse itself was respected and used, the extensions were contrived in a way not self-consciously period but answering to the needs of the present day, and these remarkable archaeological discoveries were accommodated and with the plaster work and features of the building, displayed for the maximum enjoyment.

The new staircase in the entrance hall and the light new rear screen wall.

8. *Simplifying buildings to restore them architecturally*

Penn House
Amersham, Bucks

This house, like so many great houses, and which originally dated from the 17th century, had been extensively and repeatedly enlarged, and suffered from long and straggling servants' wings, an out-of-date kitchen, and redundant staircases, which made it difficult and expensive to run. An important first floor room of the original 17th-century house was dilapidated and used as a lumber room. Other improvements to the house were required to make it more up-to-date and easy to run.

Furthermore, the house generally, and the roofs in particular, were in need of extensive repair and were incurring high costs in maintenance.

Accordingly, the owner decided to carry out a comprehensive programme of reductions, alterations and repairs. The principal items in this programme were:

Roof repairs
The roofs were first stripped, and their complex layout was greatly simplified. In particular, roofs now surrounded by internal valleys and gutters were replaced by simple, unbroken flats. The opportunity was at the same time taken of incorporating new skylights, for example to the main staircase below. The roof carpentry generally was extensively overhauled, and its layout and falls revised and improved, all timbers being meanwhile treated against further insect and fungal attack. Perished leadwork was recast and re-layed, and the roofs well insulated against future heat loss. All outer and visible slopes were then re-layed with salvaged and hand-made clay tiles on treated battens, replacement tiles being concentrated on inner and unseen slopes. Redundant chimney stacks were taken down and roofed over, and the guttering and rainwater downpipes throughout overhauled, so that the roof now forms an efficient and easily-maintained 'hat' for the entire building, with an enormous improvement both in comfort and in maintenance costs.

The roofs have been simplified by the removal of unwanted chimneys and inner roof slopes. A new staircase top-light has been added

Alterations

The whole of the redundant kitchen and scullery wing was demolished, and the house brought back to the original 17th-century North gable wall, which was refaced in new brick-work, a decorative original brick aedicule motif being carefully restored.

A new service entrance and strong room were provided. A new kitchen, stores and servants' sitting room now adjoin this entrance, looking on to a pleasant service yard. On the first floor, the existing lumber room known as the blue room was stripped, and the old walls repaired and strengthened; the original panelling was restored and missing sections replaced, restoring this as a charming bedroom. The existing bathrooms were adapted and improved, and a convenient additional bathroom provided within the retained main structure.

Finally, the existing heating and electrical installations were overhauled and adapted to suit the reduced area of the house.

Late eighteenth-century print of Asgill House showing its close proximity to the river

Asgill House
Richmond, Surrey

Asgill House was built by Sir Robert Taylor for a Lord Mayor of London, Sir Charles Asgill, in the early 1760's. It shared certain features in common with other late Palladian villas built by him for wealthy London merchants; handsome proportions, bold bays and deep eaves externally, ingenious planning, interesting-shaped rooms and dramatic effects internally.

Some time in the 1840's, what was originally only a weekend retreat became a later owner's family home, as which, within the standards of the day, it was then far too small. One alteration carried out in consequence of this was the removal of the half-pediments and the raising of the wings by one storey with flat roofs. A bulky wing had been built on, parallel to Old Palace Lane, to house additional bedrooms and bathrooms, together with a new vestibule and porch in the angle between it and the main building.

In 1968 the house had been untenanted for some years and was a prey to vandals, who had smashed a fine marble fire-place beyond repair, damaged others and stolen two

Asgill House showing the ugly nineteenth-century additions

of the paintings by Antonio Casali which decorated the octagonal saloon in the centre of the first floor. Fortunately, these last, were subsequently recovered by the police.

The architects' brief was to remove the 19th-century additions, so as to reduce the house to a size manageable with a limited domestic staff, and in the process to restore it to its original design, while incorporating modern comforts in the shape of central heating, sanitary accommodation and a ground floor kitchen.

Early in the present century, all the exposed Bath stone

facing had been renewed in Doulting—a very necessary repair, to judge by the decayed state of an untouched garden building. Further renewal was now required at the point where the 19th-century additions abutted against the original building; and as these were generally lower, the support to the original upper facings while the new 230mm skin was inserted below them presented problems of shoring, as did the renewal of a badly-built brick pier behind. Some dry-rot was discovered but this was not extensive as might have been expected from the general bad state of repair, and was summarily dealt with.

The upper courses of the flanking wings also required refacing, to follow the line of the restored half-pediments. These are as nearly as possible to the architect's original design, the slight difference in the level of the horizontal cornice compared with the illustration in *Vitruvius Britannicus* being dictated by the necessity of providing adequate headroom on the upper staircase. It would seem that both Sir Robert and his client must have been small men, judging by the height of many of the doors, while ironically enough the present architects' contemporary client was exceptionally tall.

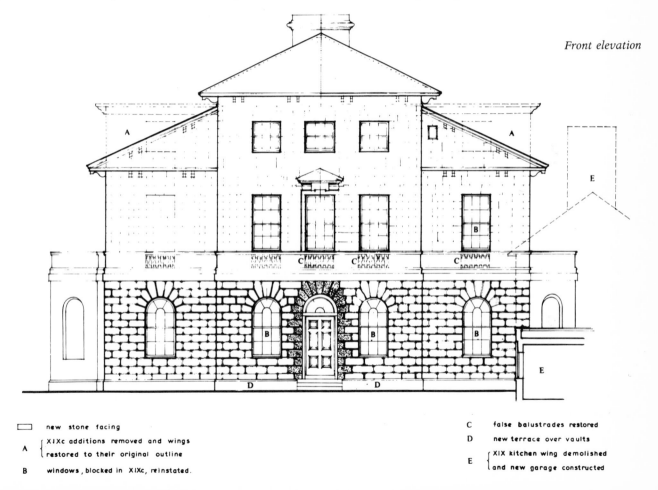

Front elevation

☐ new stone facing

A { XIXc additions removed and wings restored to their original outline

B windows, blocked in XIXc, reinstated.

C false balustrades restored

D new terrace over vaults

E { XIX kitchen wing demolished and new garage constructed

designed by Sir Robert Taylor c1760

restored by Donald. W. Insall & Associates 1970

The house after restoration was completed

Another addition to the original elevation was the formation of a terrace over a high 19th-century vaulted basement before the entrance front. Some of the walls in the 19th-century wing were utilised for the formation of a garage, kept low and simple in design, to replace the former stables now covered by the building known as Trumpeter's Lodge.

Within, the hall resumed its original function, with the

addition of a cloakroom. The drawing room on the east side retained its rather splendid 19th-century gilded cornice and here the notable Rococo fireplace needed only minor repair.

The dining room by contrast needed a new fireplace to replace the broken one, and this was obtained from a former dining room on the west side, which in turn now became a singularly spacious and well-equipped kitchen/breakfast room. The former kitchen in the basement was converted to a boiler room; and the rest of the low and dark chambers at this level, where generations of servants worked and slept, were abandoned.

One of the happiest of Sir Robert's pretty architectural staircases leads up in a singularly graceful curve to a first floor vestibule, which was vaulted and reduced in size to allow the formation of a principal bathroom. The main bedroom beyond, with its bed recess behind a delicate Ionic arcade, remains practically unaltered with the exception of a new French window on to a balcony. To cope with noise, caused by the proximity of the building to a railway line and to the air approach to London Airport, a simple and very inconspicuous system of double glazing was installed in the principal rooms.

The paintings in the saloon—the Casali room—were restored by experts, the florid surrounds being painted out and the whole room lightened in tone.

In the west wing, the guest bedroom was reduced so as to provide its own bathroom. Here as elsewhere arose the problem of providing modern sanitary facilities without tampering with the external appearance of the building or marring its internal decorative schemes. On the top floor were two charming double-apsidal bedrooms—another speciality of Sir Robert, with a powder closet between them. These are approached by a low arch, formed by the flues being gathered into a central stack—desirable architecturally perhaps but a climbing boy's nightmare. These attractive rooms were restored, and on the North side, a bedroom and bathroom were formed for a resident maid.

Now, for the first time for over a century, Asgill House can be seen as its architect intended it to be, enriched as well by its setting of matured trees, including a singularly fine copper beech. This work has been possible due to generous grants towards its cost (app. £50 000 (1971) from the Historic Buildings Council and the Greater London Council, who recognised its importance as one of the finest examples of a late Palladian Villa.

Marston St Lawrence
Northamptonshire

Village churches provide perhaps the richest store of architectural excellence in the English countryside, yet their conservation becomes an increasing problem as redundancies increase and repair costs soar.

Marston St Lawrence church, however, was very much alive spiritually even though the fabric was in a sorry state. Its recovery from dereliction is a salutory example of the way a carefully phased, economical yet thorough conservation project can be tackled. It was backed financially by an enthusiastic Vicar and PCC who explored every avenue of obtaining revenue as well as providing a stable income for the repairs by their planned stewardship scheme.

The south aisle has been shored up for 30 years by timber props which themselves were decaying. All roofs except that over the chancel were leaking, the tower roof was semi-derelict and the clerestorey walls were bulging outwards. Taken altogether, the task of repair seemed too great for this small village and it was perhaps not surprising that a scheme seriously considered at one stage would have included the demolition of both aisles and the clerestorey. But the church is a noteworthy example of mediaeval craftsmanship; and such a step would have forfeited any financial support from Trusts sympathetic towards church architecture, so that this scheme was rejected.

The Historic Churches Preservation Trust was prepared to give a grant towards the retention and repair of the south aisle, and with the aid of this backing, the PCC embarked on the first phase of the work—the stabilisation of the south aisle wall and repair of the roof.

Competitive tenders were obtained from several local contractors skilled in repair techniques. The small group of craftsmen engaged used materials with which they were familiar, and costs were carefully controlled by negotiated rates and kept to a minimum. The net cost of stabilising

The aisle stonework leaning and shored: before and after repair

the south aisle wall was approximately £2000 compared with estimates up to £8500 for alternative earlier schemes for repair or reconstruction.

The technique adopted was simply to insert reinforced

concrete columns and beams within the thickness of the mediaeval masonry, in effect girdling the aisle and stiffening it from within. The vertical columns were given long braced 'feet' under the floor and around the bases of the south arcade. The shattered east wall of the aisle which had been weakened by the later insertion of a roof stair,

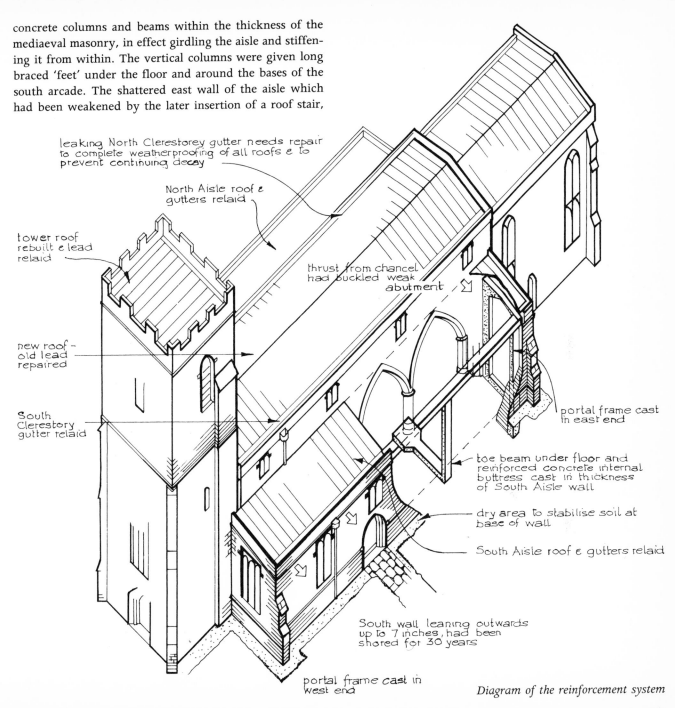

leaking North Clerestorey gutter needs repair to complete weatherproofing of all roofs & to prevent continuing decay

North Aisle roof & gutters relaid

tower roof rebuilt & lead relaid

thrust from chancel had buckled weak abutment

new roof – old lead repaired

South Clerestory gutter relaid

portal frame cast in east end

toe beam under floor and reinforced concrete internal buttress cast in thickness of South Aisle wall

dry area to stabilise soil at base of wall

South Aisle roof & gutters relaid

South wall leaning outwards up to 7 inches, had been shored for 30 years

portal frame cast in west end

Diagram of the reinforcement system

171

was stablised by an integral reinforced concrete portal frame to resist the thrust of the Chancel arch, and the west wall treated in the same manner.

Encouraged by this propitious start, the PCC took advantage of the saving by immediately authorising phase two of the repairs. This was carried out by the same contractors, whilst still on site, and included strengthening the south clerestorey wall, reslating the north aisle roof and recasting the lead gutter at a cost of £3200.

Having progressed so far with the repairs, it was felt worthwhile to make a final effort to complete work to all roofs and thus make the building really weatherproof. The Historic Churches Preservation Trust made a second contribution, matched by a generous local donation; and together with small amounts from many other sources in this country and in the USA, this made it possible to tackle phase 3 immediately after phase 2. The north clerestorey wall was stabilised and the nave gutters relaid at a cost of £1500.

Maintenance of an old building is a continuous process, and further work including conservation of stonework and repair of the floors is planned as funds permit. Yet by taking repair elements item by item and in order of priority, the conservation of this village church has been assured for many years.

Berrington Hall
Herefordshire

Berrington Hall was designed by Henry Holland in 1778 and is one of the finest examples of his work. The house stands pleasantly in its own park between Leominster and Ludlow, landscaped by Capability Brown, and is now owned by the National Trust. Following a comprehensive architect's report on the building, firstly an emergency repair and then a major conservation programme were placed in hand, the latter phased over a period of five years.

A disaster occurred shortly before the initial inspection. During a heavy winter and on account of inadequate heating, the plumbing had completely frozen and the house was evacuated. With the thaw, a basin in the attic

room overflowed, its tap having being left open, while an old waste outlet pipe direct to a roof gutter remained frozen. Water poured into the house through the first floor, and formed a lake on a highly decorative and most beautiful plasterwork ceiling to the Dining Room, which was already a good deal cracked and sagging. This was only just in time saved and was extensively propped, protected by cushioning stacks of straw.

It was found that this ceiling was already bowed eccentrically, with a maximum drop of 178mm. At this point concealed in a web partition in the bedroom above, an earlier tie-bar was found, suggesting the arrested failure of a main first floor beam. The tie-bar ran up to a system of steel beams partly concealed within the attic floor.

Gingerly, the nuts on the tie-bar were released, to see whether it might be tightened to lift and level the ground floor ceiling. Instead, the ceiling sprang up of its own accord. Apparently the upper steelwork bearings had settled, and so this complex structure had been loading the beam instead of helping it. The beam itself was of a compound form with paired outer members of pine, strengthened and in fact pre-stressed by an ingenious arrangement of raking hardwood struts between them,

The courtyard façade before and after the removal of the 19th-century bathroom tower. The pediment was reconstructed from the evidence of the stonework, which was later verified by old drawings

set between hardwood straps and a tightenable cast iron 'keystone'. A pair of steel channels was now threaded through the walls on either flank of this system, it being possible just sufficiently to accommodate their depth within the reduced 'bow' of the ceiling, and the whole was bolted together. The upper surface of the lath and plaster ceiling was found to have lost much of its key, and hessian reinforcement and plaster backing were added to carry it. Lastly, the first floor was re-boarded, the cracked ceiling was carefully cut out, filled and redecorated, and the shoring removed. At attic floor level incidentally, the offending pipes were soundly lagged against freezing.

The extent of this emergency programme was entirely unpredictable and could only be carried out as dayworks, the total cost being just under £3000.

The general inspection and report meanwhile revealed extensive and serious stonework decay, as well as several further outbreaks of dry rot due to leaking roofs. The badly laminating and locally quarried original stonework was a particular problem, and great care was taken, where renewal was necessary, to select a stone of similar character and colour as well as good weathering qualities. The condition of the exposed cornice and balustraded parapets was particularly poor and necessitated much renewal in new stone, the cornice being this time properly protected with lead dressings. At the base of the great columns of the south portico, the architectural unity of the damaged stonework was maintained by chiselling away their softened surface, then neatly setting around them 'collars' of stone, cut to fit from joint to joint.

Perished roof leadwork was next · wherever necessary re-cast, and the pretty hemispherical lantern over the staircase was at the same time repaired and re-glazed. One of the beams carrying this feature was extensively rotten and had to be plated with steel. The roof over the giant south portico was repaired and re-slated, the dormers

Staircase Hall: the restored ceiling and lantern

were re-leaded and virtually the entire parapet gutters re-laid to improved and regular falls.

Further leaks had wrought havoc in the wall-plates and truss-ends, many of which had to be plated to give a sound bearing. All existing and all new roof-timbers were comprehensively treated with a combined insecticide and fungicide. Disfiguring additions were removed and a number of important original features uncovered during the course of the work. An unsafe concrete balustrade surrounding the house at ground level was removed, revealing the rusticated basement. The perimeter dry area was in fact described by Holland in his 'Specification for Building Operations', which has survived and is exhibited in the house. Disfiguring external plumbing and wiring were removed from the elevations, but the most striking change was the removal of a gigantic and unsuitable bathroom-tower added in the early years of this century. This had carried the water-tanks and was heavily attacked by dry-rot. In renewing it, fragments were found of a former pediment; and this has been reinstated, regaining the classical symmetry and grace of a previously 'Ugly Duckling' courtyard elevation.

Lastly, services and decorations were overhauled. The heating system was improved, obviating the necessity of using portable and dangerous electric fires which had caused much earlier trouble, as well as the disastrous damage by frozen and burst plumbing. Damp-marked internal decorations were renewed, and in the Staircase Hall much of the decorative plasterwork was restored, while three oval medallions painted on paper (probably by Angelica Kaufmann) were expertly cleaned and a fourth repainted. In the Dining Room, it was particularly essential in selecting wall colours to complement the Nelson family's seascape pictures, as well as the delicate original ceiling. In both the handsome Holland library and the south entrance-hall, the original colours were traced under many layers of later paint and were restored.

A similar programme of repairs was carried out to the attractive domestic wings and the quadrants, linking them with the house to form its attractive entrance courtyard.

Financial control was carefully maintained over a long period by close supervision and co-operation between architects, quantity surveyors and good local contractors. Notwithstanding steeply rising costs over the later years of the programme, final costs of the main repairs were kept to within 6% of the budget estimate of £80 000 given five years before. Additional works to other buildings like the arched lodge gate were undertaken within a final total of £94 000, the work being financed almost wholly by Historic Buildings Council grants under the Historic Buildings and Ancient Monuments Act of 1953; each phase of the programme in turn was agreed with the specialist architects of the Department of the Environment. From the nature of the work, Bills of Quantities were impracticable in this instance, and rates were negotiated with main and sub-contractors. The building contract was then negotiated under the RIBA form, allowing a decreasing percentage of profit as costs increased. Scaffolding was purchased outright at commencement and credited on completion of the repairs.

In this way, aided by one of the largest Historic Buildings Council grants, an outstanding Henry Holland house has been saved. The National Trust have been provided with a detailed maintenance check list, together with a clear indication of future liabilities, in the continuing process of conservation.

Damaged ball finials

10. Buildings as one with their contents

The Library, Trinity College
Cambridge

The library of Trinity College, built between 1676 and 1699, is one of the finest secular buildings designed by Sir Christopher Wren. He conceived it for his friend Isaac Barrow, Master of Trinity, and the library was built by many of Wren's favourite craftsmen; notably Robert Grumbold, master mason.

The site chosen for the library was a difficult one. It stands next to the river Cam and was traversed by a loop of it, which although filled, continued to carry water below the building. Superbly engineered foundations were designed for these wet and unstable conditions, consisting of great inverted brick arches resting on a thick layer of clunch (see diagram).

The architectural design of the library equally presented major problems. It was built to complete an embryo quadrangle called Nevile's Court whose three already existing sides comprised early 17th-century buildings. Those on the north and south sides were extended to join with the new library, and presented a domestic scale and strongly Jacobean character with a continuous arched cloister. Wren's building was to be not only large in size and magnificent in character, but also decisively in his mature Renaissance style.

The difficult transition was achieved with consummate skill by the architectural treatment of the cloister beneath the library and its façade to Nevile's Court. Although the building is long and high, it is harmonious with its setting; and the richly modelled classicism of its Ketton stone exteriors produces a human scale. Internally, the building is of great richness and beauty. The entrance stair hall is reached from the cloister and has lovely staircase ironwork and a superbly decorated plasterwork ceiling. The library itself is a single, huge room occupying the whole of the

The interior after the remaking of the double glazing, the treatment of timberwork and re-whitening

Beautiful carved works like this Grinling Gibbons limewood decoration at the Wren Library, Trinity College, demands extreme care

upper storey. Its floor is of black and white marble, the oak bookcases are embellished with magnificent limewood carvings mainly by Grinling Gibbons; and the upper articulation of great arched windows, intervening pilasters and crowning cornice forms a marvellously cool contrast with the richness below.

The library had always remained substantially in its original architectural state, except for the coffered ceiling of 1851. Gradually however, the interior furnishings had been augmented by all manner of extraneous objects, such as a collection of antiquities in the entrance hall, and a series of island book-cases set in 1850 along the middle of the library itself. Obscured inner glazing had been added to the windows, robbing the building of much of its elegance. Thus insidiously, and aided by the natural grime of the centuries, the architectural spirit of the building had become obscured and de-valued. Trinity

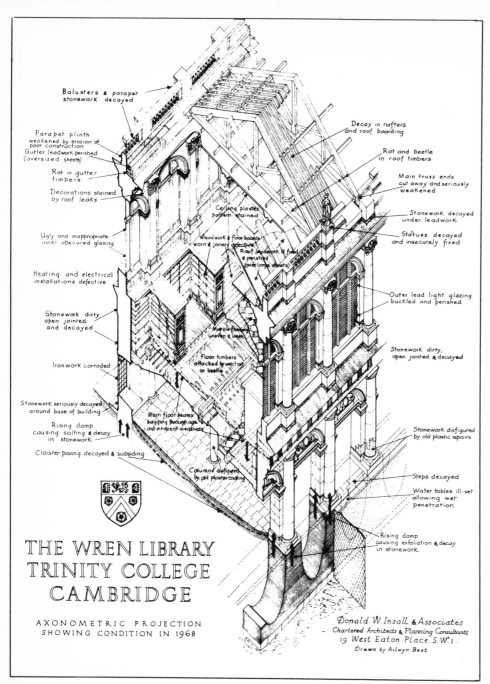

Balusters & parapet stonework decayed

Parapet plinth weakened by erosion of poor construction

Gutter leadwork perished (oversized sheets)

Rot in gutter timbers

Decorations stained by roof leaks

Ugly and inappropriate inner obscured glazing

Heating and electrical installations defective

Stonework dirty, open jointed and decayed

Ironwork corroded

Stonework seriously decayed around base of building

Rising damp causing salting & decay in stonework

Cloister paving decayed & subsiding

Decay in rafters and roof boarding

Rot and beetle in roof timbers

Main truss ends cut away and seriously weakened

Stonework decayed under leadwork

Statues decayed and insecurely fixed

Outer lead light glazing buckled and perished

Stonework dirty, open jointed & decayed

Ceiling plaster pattern stained

Woodwork & floor boards worn & joinery defective

Roof leadwork ill fixed & perished (over large sheets)

Marble flooring uneven & loose

Floor timbers attacked by wet rot or beetle

Main floor beams sagging through age and inherent weakness

Columns disfigured by old plaster coating

Stonework disfigured by old plastic repairs

Steps decayed

Water tables ill-set allowing wet penetration

Rising damp causing exfoliation & decay in stonework

THE WREN LIBRARY TRINITY COLLEGE CAMBRIDGE

AXONOMETRIC PROJECTION SHOWING CONDITION IN 1968

Donald W. Insall & Associates
Chartered Architects & Planning Consultants
19 West Eaton Place, S.W.1.
Drawn by Ailwyn Best

Axonometric projection showing the building's condition in 1968

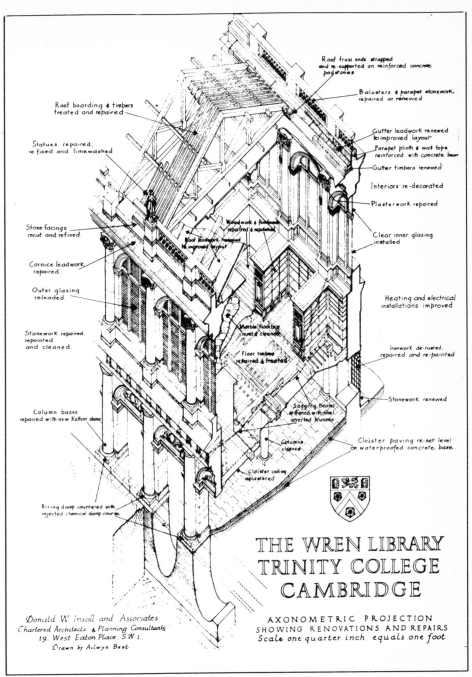

Roof truss ends strapped
and re-supported on reinforced concrete
padstones

Balusters & parapet stonework
repaired or renewed

Gutter leadwork renewed
to improved layout

Parapet plinth & wall tops
reinforced with concrete beam

Gutter timbers renewed

Interiors re-decorated

Plasterwork repaired

Clear inner glazing
installed

Heating and electrical
installations improved

Ironwork de-rusted,
repaired and re-painted

Stonework renewed

Cloister paving re-set level
on waterproofed concrete base

Roof boarding & timbers
treated and repaired

Statues repaired,
re-fixed and limewashed

Woodwork & floorboards
repaired & replaced

Stone facings
recut and refixed

Roof leadwork renewed
to improved layout

Cornice leadwork
repaired.

Outer glazing
releaded

Marble flooring
reset & cleaned

Floor timbers
repaired & treated

Stonework repaired,
repointed
and cleaned.

Sagging beams
stiffened with steel
inverted trusses

Column bases
repaired with new Ketton stone

Columns
cleaned

Cloister ceiling
replastered

Rising damp countered with
injected chemical damp course

Donald W Insall and Associates
Chartered Architects & Planning Consultants
19. West Eaton Place, SW 1.
Drawn by Ailwyn Best.

THE WREN LIBRARY
TRINITY COLLEGE
CAMBRIDGE

AXONOMETRIC PROJECTION
SHOWING RENOVATIONS AND REPAIRS
Scale one quarter inch equals one foot

Axonometric projection showing renovations and repairs

A floor sagging under the load of bookcases, seen from the ceiling of the cloister below

College became increasingly concerned at this, and at the structural condition of the library. Leaks in the lead roof were causing severe damage to the interiors; and the library floor was becoming unstable. The external stone-work was decaying and these and other signs of serious deterioration prompted the College to reassess the situation, and to prepare a balanced preservation plan.
After a thorough survey and detailed report, a programme of comprehensive renovation was placed in hand over

2 years. It was a College requirement that the library should remain in operation throughout the works. Accordingly a scheme was devised for carrying out the programme half-by-half. The library was bisected with a substantial screen, and all the books were moved into one end at a time, the floor having been propped to support the double load. The counterpart half of the library was then repaired under a temporary cover roof, integral with the external scaffolding. At half time the process was reversed and the renovation programme was repeated for the other half of the building. All contractors

Hangers added to reinforce the beams

huts and storage were grouped within the cloister itself, to avoid disturbance.
The first major problem to be tackled was the severe rising damp all around the base of the building, bringing damaging earth salts, whose capillary attraction had encouraged stone decay. The damp was countered by a transfused silicone damp proof course which reduced the wall moisture content from 10% to a little over 3% in only 6 months. At the same time the cloister paving which had sunk into the wet ground between the foundation piers, was taken up complete and relaid upon a concrete slab, incorporating a continuous plastic damp-proof membrane. The whole base of the building was thus protected against further rising damp.

Marble floor slabs displaced by settlement

The first removal of damaged walling stones revealed that the masonry was in fact little more than a thin veneer, facing a rough rubble core of brick and lime. The re-dressing of scabbed stones was first tried but this proved unsightly. Accordingly, decayed stones were replaced with new Ketton stone, finely jointed in lime mortar to match the original. This treatment was finally extended to the replacement of sections previously patched with plastic stone, the irregular shapes and inconsistent weathering of which had disfigured the meticulously careful original jointing. Particular skill was shown by the Cambridge masons when the great external column bases were reinstated by cutting accurate chases over the previously patched areas, then fashioning circular sleeves of stone, 100mm thick and fitting exactly into them. In this way the loading pattern was maintained undisturbed, and the integrity of the jointing and delicate weathering patterns were respected and restored.

The repair of the library floor was executed entirely from below. Removal of the cloister ceiling plaster revealed that the excessive bounce in the floor had been caused by progressive failure of the cross beams of long span, deflecting under the heavy loads of marble flooring and bookcases above. Even early in the history of the building, the weight of the bookcases had proved troublesome, flat diagonal tie bars being built into the classes to carry their weight from the walling. In some cases the paired beams had now become split horizontally through the divisive effect of raking struts inserted in their sides during the original construction. The weakness throughout was aggravated by beetle and wet rot attack. The structural engineers devised an ingenious and simple form of repair. Inverted mild-steel trussed stirrups were coach-screwed to the sides of the beams, and oak wedges inserted under their centres, the whole construction being afterwards housed within renewed plaster beam casings.

The beams were thus adequately and inconspicuously stiffened against further sag or bounce; and the timbers throughout were then given comprehensive chemical treatment before reinstatement of the cloister ceiling.

The upper walls of the library needed comparatively little repair. Major movement cracks were found to be completely expended, and indeed probably occurred when

The patched lead roof before recasting

the library was first built. They were solidly pointed to prevent wet penetration and minor stone decay was repaired. But the whole of the outside stonework needed sympathetic cleaning, since it was heavily stained with disfiguring and potentially damaging soot deposits. No attempt was made to restore the stonework to a pristine state, but loose surface deposits were carefully brushed away and more stubborn encrustations removed with blunt wooden chisels.

The balustraded parapet was found to be in extremely poor condition due to its severe exposure. The balusters especially were heavily decayed, and the parapet plinth and wall tops were found to be of weak rubble construction. Accordingly the parapet was dismantled complete,

Damaged stonework of a roof parapet balustrade

and its plinth reinstated as a reinforced concrete ring beam. This in turn was faced with the original stones, re-cut and re-used. Each baluster was inspected and repaired individually; and while some needed total renewal, many were given new caps or bases, bronze dowelled to the sound shafts.

The leadwork of the roof and parapet gutters, although cast and of good heavy weight, had been laid in overlarge sheets, and not surprisingly had failed through inadequate head fixings and excessive thermal movement. It was accordingly removed complete, re-cast to smaller sheet sizes and ultimately relaid to an improved layout with hollow rolls and deepened drips. The bearing ends of the king-post trusses, thus exposed, were found to be seriously defective. Most of their strength had been cut away when the parapet gutters were lowered in the last century, no doubt because of water penetration through the plinth of the balustrades. Many were supported upon only a few inches of doubtful walling.

Accordingly, reinforced concrete padstones were now carefully inserted below them, half by half. Many of the lower truss joints were also found to have been split by the type of jointing adopted and these were reinforced on each side with mild steel plates. Beetle and wet rot attack was also treated after de-frassing the timbers, and improved natural ventilation was introduced into the roof space through neat louvres in the leadwork, so as to discourage any future attack.

Although the remedy of these structural defects was the main cause of concern, Trinity College rightly placed great importance also upon matters prejudicial to the proper appearance and enjoyment of the library. Thus, the painted glass in its end windows, which had been obscured and damaged by wartime antiblast paper, was carefully repaired by specialists. The obscured inner glazing and its frames were removed entirely and replaced with clear glass neatly mounted and restoring to the building both inside and out, an entirely forgotten lightness and elegance. The handsome wrought ironwork screens were removed and repaired and shot blasted, rust-proofed and re-painted. It is interesting to note that these had horizontal saddlebars built into the stonework, but vertical bars stopped short of the sills. Internal woodwork was repaired and cleaned, and following the installation of inconspicuous new heating and lighting installations, the interiors were cleaned down and re-decorated in coats of ceiling-white. The marble floor slabs were re-levelled and re-set, and the previous intrusive centre bookcases and other impedimenta were removed. Appropriate new fittings were designed in oak items like the card-index catalogues. The handsome vista of the interior was thus restricted to its proper proportions and distinction. Missing tables from the book-bays were made up to match the original Wren design.

In this way the library has been set in structurally secure condition for the future, and at the same time architecturally restored to its essence as Wren conceived it. The contract was negotiated with nominated contractors, on the basis of bills of quantities for fixed-price items and negotiated rates for stipulated dayworks. Damp-proofing, glazing, cast leadwork heating and electrical work were sub-contracted to specialists, the remainder of the work including stone-masonry being carried by locally-based and well organised main contractors. The cost of the work and its duration were both maintained within the given estimate of £128 350 over a period of 2 years.

The Vyne
Basingstoke, Hants

The Vyne is a handsome brick and tile house dating from the early 16th century, and was built by William Sandys, Knight of the Garter, and confidant of King Henry VIII. For over a century the house remained in the family, who then sold it to a barrister of the Middle Temple. It was this barrister's grandson, John Chute, who as an eminent amateur architect (he had once designed a house for Hugh Walpole's sister) contrived the spectacular central staircase which James Lees-Milne has described as 'as triumph of art over circumstance'. It is perhaps as well that several schemes for Gothicising the exterior were never carried out: but the Chapel is a determined exercise in this style. On the death of Sir Charles Chute in 1956, the house came to the National Trust, together with its contents. The house was at that time in poor order and called for extensive repair and renovation.

In accordance with early Tudor custom, the site of the Vyne is a secluded one. The house is U-shaped in plan, with a shallow two-storey porch on the South front and an impressive portico on the north. The portico, said to have been designed by John Webb, was added in the mid-17th century.

Externally, lead roofing, rainwater pipes, brickwork and masonry were repaired, and damaged roof tiles were replaced. Inside, dry rot, woodworm and beetle were eradicated; the house was rewired floors were relaid; and most of the principal rooms were redecorated. In addition certain changes were made to the plan of the house to provide for the tenant, a two-storey flat that would not interfere with public access to the remainder of the house. There is also a smaller flat for the custodian, part of which (eg the print room) is open to the public.

Apart from the theatrical staircase and hall, with its carved timber columns and balustrades and coffered plaster ceilings and soffites, the most interesting feature of the house is the long gallery. There is, according to James Lees-Milne, 'no other gallery of comparable size that preserves panelling of such early date or of such sophisticated carving'. The walls of the gallery comprise four tiers of linenfold carving incorporating at the top and bottom of each panel a unique device—badge, crest, goblet or monogram. This had been marred by layers of brown paint, which it is hoped one day to remove. Meanwhile, 29 panels severely attacked by beetle were painstakingly repaired with the aid of plaster-casts taken from the originals.

Another interesting feature is the print room. This is a small sitting room on the South front incorporating a fashionable device of Regency times, almost the entire wall area being covered with prints of various subjects. These had been heavily varnished, and were now removed carefully from the walls and professionally cleaned, before being remounted. Their edges were protected by specially-printed border strips, and they were treated with non-staining varnish.

The grandiose and decorative classical staircase, with branched upper flights, dates from 1765. Its fluted wooden columns are delicately curved; and the mouldings of the coffered plaster ceilings are finely detailed. But the whole composition was spoiled and degraded by its uniform colouring of margarine. After repairs, it was decided to bring out its design in a delicate scheme of pale grey-green backgrounds and white detail. This aspect of the work in particular called for special skill and also for speed, as a date for the reopening had already been fixed. A firm was found who retained a high-class decorating department with some 30 highly-skilled painters, whose conduct on site may fairly be said to be governed more by their integrity as craftsmen as by the strict letter of a specification. In fact not only was the great deal of 'picking out' work executed with great skill and neatness, but the background colour itself varied under the personal direction of a skilled foreman, to equalise some of the effects of unequal lighting. An additional problem was that of evenly decorating walls and surfaces where, because of extensive repairs, areas of old and new plaster alternated. An oil sealer was used, to give equality of suction and to prevent patchiness. The paintwork was given a stipple finish while still tacky, so as to eliminate brush-marks and give an attractive, faintly-textured surface. The tips of the acanthus leaves of the capitals were picked out in gold.

The renovation of furniture and furnishings was entrusted

The Staircase Hall as first acquired by the National Trust and after re-decoration. Its margarine colouring was changed to a soft green and white and the balustrade dies have since been finished with two urns

mainly to the Council for Small Industries in Rural Areas. Two mid-18th century tables in rococo taste on the first floor landing had for example grey marble tops on softwood frames, gesso gilt: to reveal their gilding, dark brown paint was removed. Elsewhere, a set of Queen Anne chairs and settee, all in walnut with parcel gilding, were found riddled with furniture beetle and covered with a drab modern fabric. The frames were baked and treated with insecticide, re-upholstered and covered with grey-blue raw silk.

Although small in comparison with some country houses, the Vyne is pleasant to view. There are no guides or attendants, and the house is furnished as if lived throughout. Books are left lying on the tables; there is music in the music stands, flowers are in the vases, and in the print room stands even a bowl of fruit.

The cost of the building work had to be restricted within an initial budget of £15 000 and was £14 844. This was met with the aid of a grant from the Historic Buildings Council. The work being of a type difficult to price fairly by competitive tender was carried out under three degrees of priority, to which each specified item was allocated. When placed in hand, the top priority items were carried out first and second priority next, leaving only a small proportion of the least important items undone. Local contractors were selected, so as to be able to give continuity of future maintenance: plasterwork and woodcarving were placed in the hands of a specialist firm and an individual master craftsman.

11. Capitalising the assets of an estate and repair within a controlled budget

Knebworth House and country park
Hertfordshire

Knebworth House stands on high ground in the centre of an imposing park and was originally completed in 1540. The house was substantially altered in the early 19th century, when it was given its present romantically battlemented, pinnacled and gargoyled façades. To cover the cost of maintaining and indeed saving Knebworth, the family decided to follow the example of other owners of large properties, and to increase dramatically the number of visitors to the house (which has itself been open to the public for the last twenty years) and to its park. To conserve this historic building, an extensive programme of repair work has been undertaken.

In conjunction with the Hertfordshire County Council and the Countryside Commission, Knebworth Park was meanwhile declared a country park under the terms of the Countryside Act, 1968; at present its area is 101ha.

A major condition of approval by the County was that access to the Park should be independent of existing local roads, which would be heavily overloaded, and directly from a nearby roundabout on the motorway. This entailed building a 7·6m high embankment down from the roundabout to the Park. Including entirely new drives and a remade old one within the Park, approximately 3·5km of new road has been built; this cost about £55 000 and was the first major expenditure on the Country Park. Mainly to assist with its construction, a grant of £25 000 was made by the Countryside Commission. Without this aid the scheme could not have been viable, and Knebworth House would probably itself have been lost.

Park atractions

Within the park, new attractions include picnicking (specific picnic areas have been provided where cars may be taken), an adventure playground and a 610mm narrow gauge steam railway. A 9km deer fence has been constructed around the Park, to which deer will now be introduced. Already the cricket and archery clubs are flourishing and ponies and horses can be hired from the new Knebworth stables. A pony trail in the Park is linked with the 'round Stevenage bridleway' in preparation by the Stevenage Development Corporation and Stevenage Urban District Council. The park will be made available for shows, rallies and gymkhanas. A garden centre and gift shop are established and a pets corner is proposed. Within the formal gardens there are free-flying budgerigars. The 100-year old maze is slowly regaining its lost excitement after drastic pruning to curb rampant overgrowth.

The attractions within the Park will now be continuously developed to give pleasure to an increasing number of visitors. Just over 120 000 people visited the Park in the first year of the programme, compared with only 8000 the previous year. The target is 200 000 visitors per year. On any one day for a special event the Park is expected to be capable of receiving without difficulty, 5000 cars.

Knebworth barns

The decision to declare Knebworth Park a country park, greatly increasing the number of its visitors, called for more accessible and expanded catering and lavatory facilities.

At the point where the new drive layout delivers visitors from the park to the formal garden, provisions for refreshments and lavatories were needed. Any building on this site, within easy view of the house and standing in an open and prominent position, demands a sensitive and careful treatment.

A traditional building was quickly agreed as being most suitable and the use of salvaged materials from the estate, like timber and old clay tiles, was considered. At this stage, attention was drawn to two early 17th century barns already on the estate. After careful investigation of prob-

timber buildings have thus been conserved and their useful life extended; at the same time fulfilling a national need to widen the recreational facilities of the countryside.

The seasonal use of the barns

The Barns have been designed for both summer season and winter use. During the summer, Lodge Barn is a self-service cafeteria and Manor Barn a waitress-service restaurant, for luncheons and home-made teas. During the winter when the Park is closed, the Barns will be let for weddings, banquets, receptions and dances, at which 350–400 people can be accommodated. The catering has been sub-let, and a license obtained to sell liquor. The barns can be used individually or simultaneously and are heated accordingly.

Two barns: one successfully towed to a new site and the other re-erected

lems and costs, Manor Barn was raised on wheels and moved bodily 1km to its new site. A second barn called 'Lodge Barn' was too far away to move bodily and was then unpegged, taken apart and reconstructed alongside Manor Barn. Old and new buildings both have their walls clad in horizontal weatherboarding, and their roofs tiled in old red clay tiles. The two barns, united by new buildings including kitchen, staff rooms and visitors' lavatories, now serve as a restaurant for visitors to Knebworth House and country park. Two magnificent

Finance: investment and return

The care of a house like Knebworth is a relentless process, and a country park slowly develops and adapts itself to demand. The capital investment in such a project is large, though as attendance grows, so will the returns. Investment in the country park will continue, and the returns can only be considered within its whole context. The figures for initial *investment* were:

Roads	£55 000
Barns	60 000
Deer fence	4 500
Works to house, garden and park	7 500
	127 000
Less Countryside Commission grant	25 000
	£102 000

A net *return* of 20–25% p.a. before tax is required on this investment if the finance is to be serviced and repaid, producing an adequate surplus to achieve the main object—the restoration and maintenance of Knebworth House and estate. A net return of £20 000 represents 10p per head on 200 000 visitors. Allowing for overheads and running expenses, difficult to predict in a seasonal, weather-affected and labour-intensive industry, the achievement of this objective probably requires a gross spending of 40p to 50p per head.

Woburn Abbey
Bedfordshire

Woburn Abbey stands in 1200ha of magnificent parkland; and a major programme of conservation undertaken by the trustees of the Bedford Settled Estates and the Duke and Duchess of Bedford set out to maintain, largely for public enjoyment, this complex of historic buildings and its surroundings. A noteworthy feature of this project was the rehabilitation of many different buildings of high architectural value to serve new functions, thus keeping them in beneficial use in the light of present day requirements.

Close control over costs was maintained, firstly by preparing a Programme with each phase costed by quantity surveyors, secondly by utilising detailed bills of quantities wherever possible, and thirdly by obtaining competitive tenders from main contractors and sub-contractors all skilled in conservation work. Successive and separate main contracts for each stage of the programme after the third phase were negotiated by mutual agreement, although it would always have been possible to seek competitive tenders if in any year negotiation had proved unsatisfactory.

The sculpture gallery and south stable block

The sculpture gallery in this group of Grade I listed buildings was designed by Henry Holland in 1790. It was built as an orangery and set on the south side of the south stable block which together with the north stable block had been designed by Henry Flitcroft thirty years earlier. This orangery had been converted into a sculpture gallery by Wyatville in 1818, and so it remained until a few years ago.

A comprehensive survey and report prepared on the condition of 18 historic structures in the park revealed the poor condition of the gallery. Dry rot was rampant throughout the roof spaces and several parts of the ceiling had collapsed. The gallery, consisting of two larger rooms and a central domed space, all with a fine southerly prospect over the Abbey gardens and park, potentially offered unrivalled accommodation for large-scale gatherings in this part of England.

Repair work put in hand as a matter of urgency included comprehensive Dry Rot eradication, conservation of moulded plaster ceilings by strengthening from above, reconstruction of a large coved ceiling on new stainless steel supports, reslating the roofs and recasting the lead gutters. All this work had to be carried out during public occupation of the building under a carefully organised timetable, and was completed at a cost of £20 000 in the 8 months' contract period.

Many of the sculptural exhibits were redistributed around the Abbey, and the interior of the Gallery was redecorated and furnished with fine large Mortlake tapestries (woven for the Abbey in the 17th century and now taken out of store and conserved on new backings) to provide a series of rooms for private hire as reception, banqueting and ballrooms. Since it was re-opened, the gallery has proved an extremely successful enterprise all through the year, and shows how an historic building can take on a new

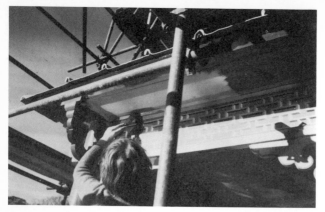

Restoring the Chinese Dairy

The final effect

lease of life adapted to functions entirely appropriate to their surroundings.

Old stabling and grooms' accommodation in the remainder of the south stable block was converted under the personal supervision of the Duke and Duchess into galleries for the display and sale of antiques.

The Chinese dairy

This Grade I group of buildings, which includes a game larder and game store over an ice well, was designed about 1790 by Henry Holland around one of a series of lakes in the Abbey park. It is a fragile structure enlivened with chinoiserie decoration, painted and stained glass, and canvas wall panels lined with bamboo. Water penetration through worn roof coverings was threatening the timber framework of the buildings, and several outbreaks of dry and wet rot were evident. As frequently happens, the atmosphere of disrepair was provoking vandalism, with a rash of graffiti, and some of the delicate and valuable painted glass was broken.

Repairs included conservation of the glass, reconstruction of decayed parts of the roof structure, reslating, recasting leadwork to roofs, regilding decorative dolphins on the lantern, and cleaning and retouching decayed sections on the 'Chinese' decorations.

The game store and larder were now redundant as such, making it important that new uses should be found for these buildings. The former is therefore now flourishing as a craft shop, with the adjoining circular larder now serving as a Gallery for the display of small paintings and engravings. In both cases the original floors, wall tiles, counters and shelving were retained. This contract was put out to competitive tender and completed after eight months' work at a cost of £18 000. The quantity surveyor's estimate for budget purposes had been £20 000.

The abbey treasure vaults

This project illustrates one solution to twin problems facing many country houses, namely security for family heirlooms and a use for the quarters at one time occupied by numerous living-in staff. At Woburn, typically, the staff kitchens and servants' hall were at basement level, and these stone vaulted rooms were converted to provide

The Chinese Dairy, Woburn: delicately painted glass before and after repair

for the more secure display of the Bedford family silver and porcelain. At the same time the Post Office required a new telephone exchange room for the Abbey. To avoid constructing a new small building in the Abbey grounds, an additional basement room was excavated, and in doing so, some of the original mediaeval Abbey walls were encountered. In-situ conservation and display of the masonry was undertaken as part of the Contract, loose pieces of door and window moulding recovered from the rubble being exhibited nearby. The contract for both the conservation and rehabilitation of the basement was negotiated on bills of quantities, and carried out at a cost of £34 500.

Laundry and north stable block

Stabling and domestic requirements of a large country house in the 18th century were extensive. Additions to Woburn Abbey by Henry Flitcroft about 1760 were planned in the grand manner and included the two quadrangular stable blocks, each some 50m by 40m set symmetrically in the park on rising ground to the east of the Abbey. The so-called North Stable Block in fact comprised coach houses and coachman's accommodation

The silver vaults: before and after

and a large Laundry building stands on the north side of the courtyard.

Unfortunately, a fire many years ago destroyed much of the east range, and most of the remainder became disused. Indeed, water pouring through the roof of the west range made this part uninhabitable; and dry rot had so badly infected nearly all the timber in the laundry block that demolition of this building had been contemplated. It was under these conditions that nearly half of the Abbey itself had been demolished in the early 1950s but since then the climate of opinion for conservation, backed by the 1953, 1962 and 1968 Planning Acts has changed. The north stable block is statutorily listed as Grade I—of the highest architectural value—and the survival of this historic building depended in large measure upon a viable use being found for all the accommodation it provided.

Concurrent with conservation of the fabric, therefore, improvements were carried out to provide at first floor level 6 one- and two-bedroomed staff flats (extendable later to 10 or 12 flats), and the laundry block was converted into a pottery workshop with display space, and an exhibition gallery above. The stable courtyard is on a main public route through the Abbey grounds, and the large ground-floor rooms were converted to display articles of good modern design complementing the antique market in the south stable block.

The work was carried out over two years and in two separate phases. The first contract was tendered for competitively, and the second phase negotiated with the same contractors. Bills of quantities were used throughout. Repair included renewal of much of the roof structure, with new floors throughout. Decaying bonding timbers had produced excessive stresses in brickwork below the western cupola, and intricate and extensive reinforced concrete strengthening was necessary to regain the stability of this structure. Stonework repair was a major task. The total cost for both phases was £140 000.

No grants were available for any of the repair work, but full discretionary grants have been obtained towards the cost of providing the 6 new flats.

Kelmscott Manor
Oxford

Kelmscott Manor is a particularly lovely stone house, set amongst the quiet water meadows alongside the upper Oxfordshire Thames. Stylistically, the building is typical of the Cotswold domestic vernacular of the 16th and 17th centuries. The main part is a simple yeoman farmer's house of circa 1570, but substantial additions were made a century later in a slightly grander vein, betraying the first tentative Classical detail. The result is a highly picturesque architectural group, clustered under steeply gabled roofs of Cotswold stone.

The house has achieved its greatest fame through a quarter of a century of associations with William Morris, the founder of the Society for the Protection of Ancient Buildings. Morris leased Kelmscott in 1871 and used it as his country retreat until his death in 1896. His widow purchased the House, and it remained in the ownership of the Morris family until 1937. Throughout these years, much of the finest art and craft work of the Morris circle was collected together at Kelmscott, but was informally distributed throughout the domestic rooms as family possessions, and only occasionally shown to visitors. The building had also fallen into a bad state of repair, paradoxically in part because of the family's understandable resistance to any change which might affect for them, its direct evocation of William Morris.

When in 1960, the house passed to its present owners, the Society of Antiquaries of London, its state thus posed some special problems of arrangement and use. On the one hand, increasing public interest in William Morris could be expected to bring many more visitors to Kelmscott than hitherto. On the other, it was decided that the Manor must remain primarily as a living house; not as a museum. But the dual functions for visitors and tenants were hopelessly muddled; neither was satisfactorily fulfilled, and the building's future use and security were problematical. It was decided that some reorganisation and re-fitting of the

The kitchen: before and after

interiors was vital, and this formed an important element of the total repair and renovation programme which ran from April 1965 to October 1967.

Kelmscott Manor: the garden exterior, including the new public entrance

A simple answer was found by re-planning Kelmscott so as to separate the 'Morris' rooms from the private living quarters. A former secondary entrance was reinstated for visitors, giving direct access to the rooms to be shown to them. This was provided externally with a new porch and cloakroom. Internally the existing staircase was extended up to the attics so that these could be visited without passing through the private living rooms. The Morris rooms can in this way be used as a self-contained unit, whilst still serving as integral living-rooms for the occupants whenever the house is not open to visitors.

The private part of the house was also re-ordered. No home can survive without a good engine-room; and a well-equipped new kitchen was provided, together with three good bathrooms. Complete new services, including central heating were installed, and great care was taken to contrive these as inconspicuously as possible. The opportunity was taken of remedying some ill-considered previous alterations. A fine oak 17th century screen was discovered cut up and patched, serving to partition a bedroom: it was repaired and restored to its proper place in the ground floor entrance hall. The 16th-century 'screens passage' had been blocked off by a later lavatory addition, which was removed. Previously re-shuffled external door and window openings were mostly reinstated, except where (as for example in the Morris family rooms) certain alterations were felt to have acquired their own special validity in Kelmscott's historical evolution.

Although the internal re-ordering of the house was a comparatively simple matter, the repair of the structure as a whole was an extremely complicated operation. Neglect and natural deterioration had reacted upon poor and vulnerable construction to produce conditions of near collapse at several points. Rain was leaking through roofs, and

The roofspace after repair: the rafters are new semi-seasoned oak and the flooring wherever possible is elm

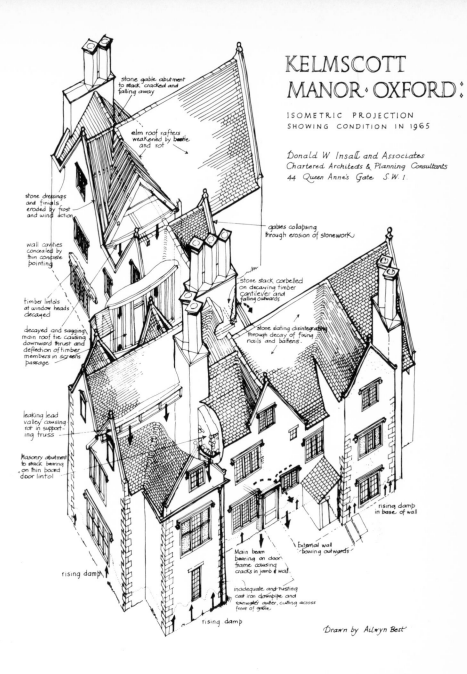

KELMSCOTT
MANOR · OXFORD :

ISOMETRIC PROJECTION
SHOWING CONDITION IN 1965

Donald W Insall and Associates
Chartered Architects & Planning Consultants
44 Queen Anne's Gate S.W.1.

stone gable abutment
to stack cracked and
falling away

elm roof rafters
weakened by beetle
and rot

stone dressings
and finials
eroded by frost
and wind action

gables collapsing
through erosion of stonework

wall cavities
concealed by
thin concrete
pointing

Stone stack corbelled
on decaying timber
cantilever and
falling outwards

timber lintols
at window heads
decayed

stone slating disintegrating
through decay of fixing
nails and battens

decayed and sagging
main roof tie causing
downward thrust and
deflection of timber
members in screens
passage

leaking lead
valley causing
rot in support-
ing truss

Masonry abutment
to stack bearing
on thin board
door lintol

rising damp
in base of wall

External wall
bowing outwards

Main beam
bearing on door
frame causing
cracks in jamb & wall

rising damp

Inadequate and rusting
cast iron downpipe and
rainwater gutter, cutting across
front of gable

rising damp

Drawn by Ailwyn Best

rising damp had penetrated the floors and lower walls, causing extensive damage to structure and finishes. Beetle and wet-rot were rife in the floor and roof timbers; and the stonework of gables, parapets and window-surrounds was badly decayed. Perhaps most serious of all was the instability of parts of the main stone structure of the building. The exterior walls appeared to be sturdy but proved upon opening-up to be constructed of thin inner and outer skins of rubble, unbonded and cored between with river mud. For a riverside site, this method of construction had in fact possessed advantages, allowing the building to settle freely on unstable ground. But damp penetration and thoughtless past alterations had seriously weakened this construction, relying as it did upon mass rather than strength. On the North side, weakened by the past insertion of additional doors and windows, the entire upper wall, gable and roof loads were resting on two slender stone piers, which were progressively failing under these untoward and concentrated loads. Inside the house, a great central stone chimney was found to be cantilevered on timbers now completely rotten. In Morris's own bedroom, a single wooden plank over the door, sagging dangerously, was found to be supporting a great mass of masonry above, on which in turn rested part of the roof. Reinforced concrete was carefully inserted, length by length, to support and re-distribute the loads. Decayed timber lintels over windows were similarly replaced in concrete, with which the tottering gables were reinforced from behind. Decayed stonework dressings were individually repaired with plastic stone, or renewed with natural stone where otherwise beyond repair. The removal of earlier hard cement pointing often revealed large cavities in the walling, and these were grouted before re-pointing in lime mortar.

Rising damp was combated by the creation of a drained 'dry area' around part of the house and by means of continuous damp-proof membranes under a new solid ground floor. Old gutters had failed to catch the water from the irregular stone eaves; and new ones were provided discharging clear of the building from spout ends.

The repair of the roof was a lengthy job calling for total stripping, section by section. The old slating pegs, nails and battens had failed; and the elm roof timbers were seriously degraded by wet rot and furniture beetle. Nine out of every ten needed renewal, in which semi-seasoned oak was found to be ideal: indoors and where exposed, this was simply limewashed. The oak trusses were mostly in better condition, though one of them was so badly decayed not only at both ends but centrally as well, that the great weight of the roof above was being shouldered by suffering and bowed internal partitions, instead of by the outside walls. The main tie was taken out and replaced by a new oak beam. Elsewhere once decay had been cut away, new ends were scarfed on or beams plated with steel.

Following the repair of the roof timbers, the roofs were felted for insulation, provided with new pre-treated battens and rehung with their diminishing courses of stone slate, using alloy nails throughout for fixing.

In the first floor, decay of inbuilt beam and joist-ends necessitated some replacement, but most were found capable of repair by simple steel straps and cleats. All structural timbers were treated against continuing insect and fungal attack; and the decayed floor boards were renewed with some particularly well-seasoned and beautifully figured elm, fixing by screwing to allow for any subsequent movement. The spiral wooden stair at the south end of the house had to be entirely rebuilt. It was discovered that it had been built over two former staircases, both decayed, and in turn supported on nothing more than a pile of rubble.

It was in fact characteristic of Kelmscott that conditions invariably proved worse on opening up than surface indications had suggested. This does sometimes happen with an old building, but here occurred to a quite unusual degree. The work was entrusted to local contractors with a natural appreciation of the problems arising from traditional construction and of the capabilities of its building materials, and they carried it out admirably. Supervision was necessarily detailed and 75 site visits were made, an especially flexible approach being required to cope with individual site problems as these developed and changed from week to week.

Bibliography

GENERAL

BUCHANAN, COLIN & PARTNERS *Bath: A Study in Conservation* London 1968 HMSO £3.50

BURROW, G. S. *Chichester: A Study in Conservation.* London 1968 HMSO £7

CANTACUZINO, SHERBAN. (ed) 'New Uses For Old Buildings.' *The Architectural Review.* London May 1972 Volume CLI Number 903

CESCHI, CARLO *Teoria e storia del restauro* Rome 1972 Mario Editore £3

CLIFTON-TAYLOR, ALEC *The Pattern of English Building* London 1972 Faber and Faber Ltd. £10 hardback £5 softback

'Conservation Areas: Preserving the architectural and historic scene.' Civic Trust Survey. *The Architects' Journal* January 18, 1967

CROSSLEY, F. H. *Timber Building in England.* London 1951 B. T. Batsford Ltd. Out of print

Department of the Environment. *New Life for Old Buildings* London 1971 HMSO 50p

ESHER, VISCOUNT *York: A Study in Conservation* London 1968 HMSO £7

GODFREY, W. H. *Our Building Inheritance* London 1944 Faber and Faber Ltd. Out of print

HARGREAVES, JUNE M. *Historic Buildings: Problems of their Preservation* York 1964 York Civic Trust

HARVEY, JOHN *Conservation of Old Buildings. A Select Bibliography* London 1969 Reprinted from the Transactions of the Ancient Monuments Society, New Series 16, 1969 Ancient Monuments Society 3p

HARVEY, JOHN *Old Buildings—Problem and Challenge* Macclesfield 1954 Reprinted from the Transactions of the Ancient Monuments Society New Series II 1954 pp35–43 Macclesfield Press Out of print

HARVEY, JOHN *Conservation of Buildings* London 1972 Adam and Charles Black £4.75

INNOCENT, C. F. *The Development of English Building Construction* London 1916 Cambridge University Press Out of Print.

INSALL, DONALD W. & ASSOCIATES *Chester: A Study in Conservation* London 1968 HMSO £7

INSALL, DONALD *Lavenham: past-present-future. A Report for the County of West Suffolk and the Rural District of Cosford.* West Suffolk County Council: 1961

INSALL, DONALD W. & ASSOCIATES *Thaxted: an Historical and Architectural Survey for the County Council of Essex* London: 1966

KENNET, WAYLAND *Preservation* London 1972 Temple Smith £2.40

MINISTRY OF WORKS, Ancient Monuments Branch (now DOE) *Preservation of Historic Buildings: Exhibition Catalogue* London 1955. Ministry of Works

MONUMENTUM An occasional periodical which gives valuable in-depth technical studies in a parallel English/French text. Louvain, Belgium International Council of Monuments and Sites. Annual subscription: ICOMOS members $8.00 U.S. Non-members $12.00 U.S.

PEERS, SIR CHARLES R. 'The Treatment of Old Buildings' RIBA *Journal* 21 March 1931 pp 311–320 London 1931 Royal Institute of British Architects

PLENDERLEITH, H. J. and WERNER, A. E. A. *The Conservation of Antiques and Works of Art* London 1972 Oxford University Press 2nd edition £6.50

POWYS, A. R. *Repair of Ancient Buildings* London 1929 Dent Out of print

S.P.A.B. Technical Leaflets 1: *Outward leaning walls* 30p Information on other technical leaflets at present in preparation is available from the Society

SPAB *The Treatment of Ancient Buildings Damaged in Wartime.* London SPAB 3p

WARD, PAMELA. (ed) *Conservation and Development in Historic Towns and Cities* Newcastle-upon-Tyne, 1968 Oriel Press Ltd. £3.75

WORSKETT, ROY. *The Character of Towns* London 1969 The Architectural Press £4.00

LEGAL AND ADMINISTRATIVE

Memorandum on The Ancient Monuments Acts London 1953 Council for British Archaeology 2p

Protection by Law of National Monuments and National Buildings London 1948 The Georgian Group Out of print

HEAP, DESMOND *An Outline of Planning Law* London 1969 Sweet and Maxwell. 5th edition £2.75 Paperback edition £1.75

Ancient Monuments Acts 1913 and 1931 HMSO

Historic Buildings and Ancient Monuments Act 1953 HMSO

Housing Act, 1969 HMSO

Housing Repairs and Rents Acts 1954   HMSO
Town and Country Planning Acts, 1947, 1954, 1962, 1968 and 1971 and Explanatory Memoranda   HMSO
Civic Amenities Act 1967   HMSO
Redundant Churches and Other Religious Buildings Act 1969   HMSO

CHURCHES

CAROE, A. D. R.   *Old Churches and Modern Craftsmanship* Oxford 1949   Oxford University Press   Out of print
A Handbook on the Installation, Preservation and Repair of Bells, Bellframes and Fittings   Cheltenham 1954   Central Council of Church Bell Ringers   15p
Council for the Care of Churches   *Annual Reports*   London Church Information Office.
GODDARD, HENRY G.   *Heating your Church*   London   1970 Church Information Office   40p
Council for the Care of Churches   *How to look after your Church* London 1970   Church Information Office   25p
Council for the Care of Churches   *Lighting and Wiring of Churches: Recommendations and Conditions*   London 1970   Church Information Office   35p
Council for the Care of Churches   *Church Roof Coverings*   London 1952   Church Information Office. Out of print but under revision.
Council for the Care of Churches   *The moving and re-erection of Churches*   London 1956   Church Information Office   7½p
Council for the Care of Churches and the Ecclesiastical Architect's and Surveyors Association   *Church Inspection and Repair* London 1970   RIBA Publications Ltd.   £1.00
Church of England: National Assembly   *Inspection of Churches Measure*   London 1955   HMSO   4p
FROST, ALAN (ed)   *Towers and Belfries*   Central Council of Church Bell Ringers   Expected publication date: late 1972   75p
SYMONS, VIVIAN   *Church Maintenance*   London 1968   Marshall, Morgan and Scott   £1.75

TECHNIQUES: GENERAL

Building Research Establishment (formerly BRS)
Building Research Bulletins)
National Building Studies) Bulletins, Special Reports, Technical Papers, Current Papers etc.
BRS   *Digests*
Post-War Building Studies
Notes on the Repair of Damaged Buildings.   London   HMSO
The Georgian Group
Georgian Pamphlets Series
Georgian Leaflets Series

TIMBER STRUCTURES, FUNGI AND PESTS

British Wood Preserving Association   Records of Annual Con-
ventions   London   BWPA
Council for the Care of Churches   *Church Timberwork, Books and Fabrics: Damage and Repair*   London 1957   Out of print
Department of the Environment   *Dry Rot and Wet Rot*   Advisory Leaflet 10.   London 1971   HMSO   4p
Ministry of technology: Forest Products Research (now DOE)
BLETCHLEY, J. D.   *Insect and Marine Borer Damage to Timber and Woodwork: Recognition, Prevention and Eradication*   London 1967   HMSO   Out of print
Princes Risborough Laboratory (Part of Building Research Establishment and formerly The Forest Products Research Laboratory)
Bulletins and Leaflets   London   HMSO
RICHARDSON, STANLEY A.   *Biological Deterioration of Ancient Buildings*   Winchester 1970   Richardson and Starling Ltd.
Timber Pests and their Control   High Wycombe, Bucks. 1964 Timber Research and Development Association   75p
Timber Research and Development Association   Information Bulletins, Research Reports etc.

WALLING, STONEWORK, RENDERING ETC.

ARKELL, W. J.   *Oxford Stone*   London 1946   Faber and Faber Ltd.   Out of print
Building Research Establishment (formerly BRS)   *The Weathering, Preservation and Maintenance of Natural Stone Masonry*   London 1952   HMSO   Out of print
MARTIN, D. G.   *Maintenance and Repair of Stone Buildings* London 1970   Council for the Care of Churches   Church Information Office   25p
Council for the Care of Churches   *Wall Paintings: Questions and Answers*   London 1970   Church Information Office.
Council of Small Industries in Rural Areas   *Wrought Ironwork* London 1968   COSIRA 5th Edition   90p
LLOYD, NATHANIEL   *A History of English Brickwork*   Montgomery 1925   Out of print
O'NEILL, HUGH   *Stone for Building*   British Stone Federation Publication   London 1965   Heinemann   £1.35
PURCELL, DONOVAN   *Cambridge Stone*   London 1967   Faber and Faber Ltd.   Out of print.
SCHAFFER, R. J.   'Stone in Architecture'   *Royal Society of Arts Journal*   October 1955   London   RSA
SHORE, B. C. G.   *The Stones of Britain*   London 1957   Leonard Hill   £3.75
SHORE, B. C. G.   'Silicon and the Preservation of Stones in Buildings'   *Building Materials*   June, 1957   Kent   A4 Publications Ltd.
Stone Industries   *Natural Stone Directory*   London 1972   Park Lane Publications Ltd.   £1.50
WARNES, A. R.   *Building Stones*   London 1926   Benn   Out of print
WIGHT, JANE A.   *Brick Building in England from the Middle Ages*

to 1550   London 1972   John Baker Ltd.   £7.50
WILLIAMS-ELLIS, C.   *Cottage Building in Cob, Pise, Chalk and Clay*
London 1920   Country Life   2nd edition.   Out of print.
WITHERS, MARGARET   'Natural Stone. Product Selection for
Architects'
RIBA *Journal*   November 1971   London   The Royal Institute of
British Architects

FIRE PROTECTION

Fire Precautions Act 1971 Chapter 40   London   HMSO   35p
British Standards Institution   *The Protection of Structures against
Lightning*   BS CP 326: 1965   London   The Institution   £1.25

British Standards Institution   *Fire Fighting Installations and
Equipment*   BS CP 402. 3 Parts, 1952 and 1964   London   The
Institution Parts 1 and 2   85p, Part 3   70p
Fire Protection Association   *Fire Prevention and Fire Fighting in
Churches*   London 1957   FPA   Out of print
Fire Protection Association   *Fire Protection in Cathedrals*
London 1956   FPA   Out of print
Fire Protection Association   *Fire Protection of Country Houses*
London 1958   FPA   Out of print
Fire Protection Association   *Thatch*   Technical Information
Sheet No 1012   London 1966   FPA   Single copies free

Illustration acknowledgements